ROBOTS, REASONING, AND REIFICATION

ROBOTS, REASONING, AND REIFICATION

"Where is my Robot?"

L.F. Gunderson
Gamma Two, Inc.
Denver, Colorado, USA

J.P. Gunderson
Gamma Two, Inc.
Denver, Colorado, USA

 Springer

Authors

L.F. Gunderson
Gamma Two, Inc.
209 Kalamath Street
Unit 13
Denver, CO
80223, USA
lgunders@gamma-two.com

J.P. Gunderson
Gamma Two, Inc.
209 Kalamath Street
Unit 13
Denver, CO
80223, USA
jgunders@gamma-two.com

ISBN: 978-1-4419-4680-5   e-ISBN: 978-0-387-87488-3

DOI: 10.1007/978-0-387-84816-7

Printed on acid-free paper

springer.com

While in principle everything may be under strict control within the machine, the remote space-time surroundings are in the general case known to the system by extrapolation only, that is predicted with some uncertainty. As psychological functionalism, when actually carried out, has thus been found to be forced into probabilism, a cybernetics with ecological involvement must contain probabilistic elements. – Egon Brunswik, 1950

Preface

This work was created from the statement "But, all you have to do is make the robot recognize its surroundings. Salamanders do it, and how complex are they?" Little did we know what a long path was started with those simple words. This book is a small step on that path, which we hope leads to robots that can serve as true and useful assistants to humans. At the least, we hope for some help with the tasks that are described by the 3 d**** words (dull, dirty, or dangerous).

Fair warning, this work is a synthesis of ideas from many disciplines. As such, we have depended on the work of many other researchers and philosophers. The heart of this work, the lens model, comes from the work of Egon Brunswik. Even though he died in the 1950's, his ideas are still strong enough to resonate into the 2000's and into our robot. Another researcher who's work has greatly influenced this work is Walter Freeman, Professor Emeritus of Neurobiology at the University of California, Berkeley. We have relied heavily on his work on preafference and attention to guide the development of our robot. In addition, we have used research from a myriad of different fields. Our huge thanks to all the researchers who's work we used to synthesize this new theory.

Denver, CO
July 2008

Louise F. Gunderson
James P. Gunderson

Acknowledgements

This book would not have come into being without the support of a number of people. Much of what we are presenting here is the outgrowth of discussions with some really intelligent people at conferences and workshops, around the world. High on that list are the people who put together and orchestrate the Performance Metrics for Intelligent Systems (PerMIS) workshop, sponsored by the National Institutes of Standards and Technology. This includes an enormous amount of work by Elena Messina, Raj Madhava, Jim Albus, and Alex Meystel. We particularly want to thank Alex, whose encouragement has meant the world to both of us.

Many thanks to Christian Brown and Randi Himelgrin. Without your support, this book would never have happened. Chris put in untold hours of hard work, soldering circuit boards, chasing robots, and above all participating in endless design meetings, and asking the hard questions. Much of what we have developed in testing methodology was a direct result of long discussions with Randi about the state of testing in the real world.

Jim

Much of the chapter on surviving in a dynamic world resulted from a seemingly innocent question posed by my thesis advisor at the University of Virginia: Worthy Martin. He asked "What do you mean it can deal with the unexpected?" Thanks, Boss!

Louise

Thanks to Ellen Bass for introducing me to the work of Egon Brunswik and to Don Brown for being patient while I worked out the details of judgment analysis in my dissertation.

Contents

1 Introduction 1
   1.1 Bridging the Gap 2
        1.1.1 Bidirectional Mapping 3
   1.2 Reification and Preafference in Biological Entities 4
   1.3 More Advanced Brains 5
   1.4 What This Book Is and What It Is Not 6
   1.5 Structure of the Book 7
   1.6 A Note on Typefaces and Terminology 7
        1.6.1 Anthropomorphization 8

2 Some background material on probability and biology 9
   2.1 Layout 9
   2.2 Probability in the Real World 10
   2.3 Why a Biologically Principled Argument? 11
        2.3.1 Biological Principles 13
   2.4 What Is a Biologically Principled Argument? 14
        2.4.1 Biology Is an Observational Science 14
        2.4.2 Life Has Structure 16
        2.4.3 The Theory of Evolution Explains the Observed Diversity
               of Life 17
   2.5 So Why Is Our Model Biologically Principled? 18
        2.5.1 Why Not Just Use Expected Value? 19

3 Using Cognition and Physiology to Build a Cognitive Model 21
   3.1 Reification in Biological Entities 21
        3.1.1 Recognition 22
        3.1.2 Preafference 23
   3.2 Biological Storage 26
        3.2.1 Explicit Memory 27
   3.3 Emotion 29
        3.3.1 Emotion as mediator 29

4   Representation 31
    4.1   Representing Features of the World 33
    4.2   Representing Goals 34
    4.3   Representing Actions in the World 35
          4.3.1   Enabling Conditions 35
          4.3.2   Outcomes 35
          4.3.3   Representing Likelihoods 36
    4.4   Exogenous Events 37

5   Perception/Action System 39
    5.1   Robot as Perception/Action System 40
          5.1.1   Robot as Body 41
          5.1.2   Robot as Sensor 42
          5.1.3   Robot as Agent of Change 43
          5.1.4   Low Level Control Loop - Procedural Memory 45
          5.1.5   System Safety and Routine Actions 47
    5.2   Examples of Perception/Action Systems 47
          5.2.1   Fred - a simple test robot 47
          5.2.2   Basil 51
    5.3   Summary of Perception/Action Systems 54

6   Design of a Reification Engine 57
    6.1   Model Selection Criteria 57
    6.2   Judgment Analysis 59
    6.3   Designing the `Reification Engine` 62

7   Bridging the Sensor to Symbol Gap 65
    7.1   Supporting Bidirectional Mapping 66
          7.1.1   A Third Approach 68
    7.2   Reification Architecture 68
    7.3   `PerCepts` and Reification 71
          7.3.1   `PerCept` Data 73
          7.3.2   `PerCept` Function 76
    7.4   `Mental Model` 77
    7.5   Current World State 79
    7.6   Reification functionality 80
          7.6.1   Initialization 80
          7.6.2   Mapping the World onto its Model - Recognition 81
          7.6.3   Projecting the Model onto the World - Preafference . 82
          7.6.4   Updating the Current World State 84
    7.7   Wrapping Up Reification 84

8   Working Memory and the Construction of Personal Experiences 87
  8.1   Transient Memory 88
          8.1.1   Working Memory and the Current World State 89
          8.1.2   Internal State 92
  8.2   Episodic Memory 92
          8.2.1   Emotive Tags 96
  8.3   Memory Services.. 97
  8.4   Providing Memory Services to the Reification Process........... 98
  8.5   Memory, What Was That Again?............................... 98

9   Semantic Memory and the Personal Rough Ontology 101
  9.1   Semantic Memory 101
          9.1.1   What is a Personal Rough Ontology?................... 102
  9.2   Building Semantic Memory 104
          9.2.1   Structure of the Ontology 106
          9.2.2   The nodes in the multi-graph 107
          9.2.3   Relationships, the Edges of the Graph 112
          9.2.4   A Note on Representing Probabilities 114
  9.3   Persistent Storage in the Personal Rough Ontology 115
  9.4   Transient versus Persistent Knowledge 115
  9.5   Extracting Problems for the Deliberative System 117
  9.6   Focusing Attention by Finding Sub-Ontologies 117
          9.6.1   Weighted Transitivity 118

10   Deliberative System 121
  10.1   Deliberation 122
  10.2   Reasoning About the Present 124
          10.2.1   Sense-Symbols from the `Reification Engine` 125
          10.2.2   Symbols from the Ontology 125
          10.2.3   Internal State 126
          10.2.4   Reasoning with `WorldSets` 126
  10.3   Choosing the Future 128
          10.3.1   Planning as Search 129
          10.3.2   Adapting to Failure 134
  10.4   Plan Evaluation and Selection 135
          10.4.1   Acquiring Distributions 135
          10.4.2   Simulator Fidelity 136
  10.5   Summary 137

11   Putting it All Together 139
  11.1   How it Fits Together 139
  11.2   Goals and Environment 141
  11.3   Knowledge Sources... 143
          11.3.1   Ontological Knowledge 144
          11.3.2   Reification Knowledge............................. 148

        11.3.3 Perception/Action Knowledge 148
    11.4 The process 149
        11.4.1 Perception/Action..............................149
        11.4.2 Reification....................................149
        11.4.3 Execution 149
        11.4.4 Deliberation 150
        11.4.5 Execution, Reification and Action 151
        11.4.6 Perception/Action - Reflex 152
        11.4.7 Execution Failure 152
        11.4.8 Back Up to Deliberation 152
        11.4.9 Procedural Memory and Localization 153
    11.5 A Few Notes About the General Flow 154

12 Testing 157
    12.1 Testing the Robot, or How Does One Test an Embedded System? ..157
    12.2 eXtreme Programming 158
    12.3 Methodology for Testing Embodied Systems............159
        12.3.1 Benefits of Partitioning the Tests 161
    12.4 General Testing Guidelines 162
        12.4.1 General Partitioning Guidelines 162
    12.5 Testing in the lab 163
        12.5.1 Hardware 163
        12.5.2 Static Tests 164
        12.5.3 Dynamic tests 167
    12.6 Formal System Tests - Testing In The Real World......169
        12.6.1 Testing Recognition 169
        12.6.2 Testing Preafference..........................174
        12.6.3 Testing Self-Localization 179
    12.7 Summary 181

13 Where do we go from here 183
    13.1 A Stopping Point 183
    13.2 Next Steps 185
        13.2.1 Adding Learning to the Model 185
        13.2.2 Adding Additional Data Sources 185
        13.2.3 Porting the Brain into New Bodies 186

Glossary 187
    References 190

Index 199

Acronyms

List of abbreviations, symbols, and acronyms

ATV	All Terrain Vehicle
CNS	Central Nervous System
CWS	Current World State
DARPA	Defense Advanced Research Projects Agency
EET	Estimated Execution Time
fMRI	functional magnetic resonance imaging
GPS	Global Positioning System
I/O	Input / Output
IR	Infra-Red, typically referring to sensors
LIDAR	Light Detection and Ranging
MCMC	Markov Chain Monte Carlo [simulation]
MRM	MultiResolution Modeling
NASA	National Aeronautics and Space Administration
OODA	Observe - Orient - Decide - Act [loop]
POC	Probability of Occurrence
ProPlan	Probability–Aware Planning and Execution System
PWM	Pulse Width Modulation
RAM	Random Access Memory
RDF	Resource Description Framework
ROF	Retry On Failure
SAM	Surface to Air Missile
UART	Universal Asynchronous Transmitter Receiver
UAV	Unmanned Aerial Vehicle
UML	Unified Modeling Language
XML	eXtensible Markup Language
XP	eXtreme Programming

Chapter 1
Introduction

Where is my robot?

You know - the one that acts like the ones in the movies; the one that I just tell what to do, and it goes out and does it. If it has problems, it overcomes them; if something in the world changes, it deals with the changes. The robot that we can trust to do the dirty, dangerous jobs out in the real world - where is that robot? What is preventing us from building and deploying robots like this? While there are a number of non-trivial and necessary hardware issues, the critical problem does not seem to be hardware related. We have many examples of small, simple systems that will (more or less) vacuum a floor, or mow a lawn, or pick up discarded soda cans in an office. But these systems have a hard time dealing with new situations, like a t-shirt tossed on the floor, or the neighbor's cat sunning itself in the yard. We also have lots of teleoperated systems, from Predator aircraft, to deep sea submersibles, to bomb disposal robots, to remote controlled inspection systems. These systems can deal with changes to the world and significant obstacles provided that one or more humans are in the loop to tell the robot what to do.

So, what happens when a person takes over the joystick, and looks through the low-resolution, narrow field of view camera of a perimeter-patrol security robot? Suddenly, where the robot was confounded by simple obstacles and easy to fix situations, the teleoperated system is able to achieve its goals and complete its mission. This is despite the fact that in place of a tight sensor-effector loop, we now have a long delay between taking an action and seeing the results (very long in the case of NASA's Mars rovers). We have the same sensor data, we have the same effector capabilities, we have added a massive delay yet the system performs better. Of course, it is easy to say that the human is just more intelligent (whatever that means), but that does not really answer the question. What is it that the human operator brings to the system?

We believe that a major component of the answer is the ability to reify: the ability to turn sensory data into symbolic information, which can be used to reason about the situation, and then to turn a symbolic solution back into sensor/effector actions that achieve a goal. This bridging process from sensor to symbol and back is the focus of this book. Since it is the addition of a human to the system that seems to enable success, we draw heavily from current research into what biological systems (primarily vertebrates) do to succeed the world, and how they do what they do. We look at some research into cognition on a symbolic level, and research into the physiology of biological entities on a physical (sensor/effector) level. From these investigations we derive a computational model of reification, and an infrastructure to support the mechanism. Finally, we detail the architecture that we have developed to add a reification to existing robotic systems.

1.1 Bridging the Gap

There has long been a gulf between artificial intelligence researchers who focus on deliberative symbol manipulation and those who focus on embedding control systems into robots. Much of this gulf has been ascribed to the different approaches, working from the symbolic down versus working from the control system up. The general consensus has been that as the two ends work toward the middle, the gulf will narrow and narrow until it disappears. Underlying both these beliefs is the assumption that once the core research is addressed, it will just be a matter of pushing the research frontier toward the opposing viewpoint until they meet. If one continues the bottom up (or top down) approach long enough, eventually one gets to the top (or bottom) and the complete problem is solved. However, recent research has suggested that the gulf may not be bridgeable by work from either side, rather it may require a specific research approach that is different from either the sensor-based or the symbolic domains.

From the viewpoint of the embedded systems approach, the critical task is the recognition of physical and perceptual cues, while mapping those cues onto a symbol system is outside the scope of the research. From the point of view of the deliberative approach, a symbol manipulation system is developed, and it is outside the scope of the symbol system to recognize the physical and perceptual characteristics that define the thing referred to by the symbol. A purely deliberative system might be manipulating abstract strings such as 'block' and 'red'. These abstract symbols have no meaning other than the allowed manipulations in the symbol system. However, if these symbols are meant to refer to real-world objects or characteristics (e.g., if the things referred to have concrete or material existence) then the symbols must correspond to objects in the real world to be effectively used. In recent research the terms *symbol grounding* and *symbol anchoring* have been used to describe the process as well.

In a recent paper by Coradeschi and Saffiotti[38], the argument is made that the Symbol Grounding problem, as presented by Harnad[93], has features in common with Pattern Recognition. Coradeschi and Saffiotti argue that these two problems have an area of overlap (See Figure 1.1A), which also overlapped with the anchoring problem. However, it is more likely that there is in fact no such area of overlap, and that the process of anchoring or reification spans the gap between these two domains, as in Figure 1.1B.

The term reification is taken from philosophy and is defined[134] as "the process of regarding or treating an abstraction or idea as if it had concrete or material existence." Reification is a two way process, because there are two primary information flows that must be maintained to effectively connect symbols to objects: one is the flow from objects in the physical world onto the symbols, the second is from the symbols onto the objects. This problem is compounded by the fact that a symbol system typically does not have direct access to the objects in the physical world except via the mediation of the perceptual system.

1.1.1 Bidirectional Mapping

To be effective the reification bridge must be capable of answering two fundamental questions:

1. How will symbols appear in the my sensors; and
2. How will this sensor pattern correspond to a symbol?

These correspond to the two functions that a reification system must provide (See Figure 1.2). If the deliberative system has a reachable goal to achieve and a collection of operators that it can apply to modify the world, it can (with sufficient time and computational resources) find a sequence of actions or set of behaviors to achieve that goal. This has been a solved problem since the earliest days of artifi-

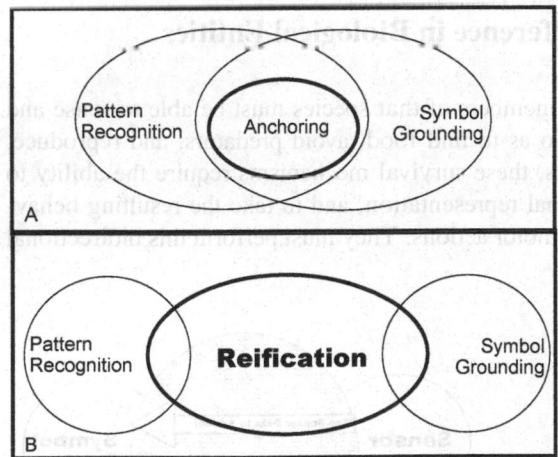

Fig. 1.1 Possible relationships of pattern recognition, symbol grounding, and reification. In A, the problem of anchoring symbols to sensor/action patterns should be approachable by either top-down or bottom-up improvements. However, in B the problem cannot be solved by either top-down or bottom-up approaches, since there is no area of overlap. Rather, a third approach is required, one that solves the reification problem first, which then provides the bridge between symbol and sensors.

cial intelligence research. However, to achieve this goal in the real world the system must be capable of finding the things in the real world needed to achieve each of the actions. It is one thing to produce the step "Pick up the red block from on top of the blue table," it is quite another know what the sensor pattern that corresponds to the symbols will appear like to its sensors; to find the red block in the real world and grasp it. To be effective, the system needs the ability to build a sensor map that corresponds to the expected state of the things in the real world. This map must correspond to the symbols in the internal model. This is the process of determining how symbols will appear in sensor data, and is one necessary function. The biologic equivalent of this ability is preafference which will be discussed in detail in Chapter 3.1.2.

The second necessary function is the ability to create symbols out of the sensor data. If one has a robot tasked to deliver mail around the office, it needs to be capable of noticing the stairs as stairs, not as a series of parallel lines on a level floor. Failure to correctly put the sensor data into a semantic context can result in the robot tumbling down the stairs, when it thought it was simply crossing a decoration on the floor. Without this ability, it is not possible for the perceptual system to recognize exogenous changes to the world, which must be recognized to either take opportunistic advantage of conditions or to avoid problems which crop up after the plan has been put into effect. This is the symbol grounding problem, which we call recognition, and will also be discussed in more detail later. These two basic functions seem to be features common to almost all vertebrate brains. So it seems reasonable to begin by looking at the research into primitive vertebrate cognition.

1.2 Reification and Preafference in Biological Entities

For any species to survive, the members of that species must be able to sense and manipulate their environment so as to find food, avoid predators, and reproduce. In the case of vertebrate species, these survival mechanisms require the ability to map sensory data onto a neuronal representation, and to take the resulting behavior choices and map those onto motor actions. They must perform this bidirectional

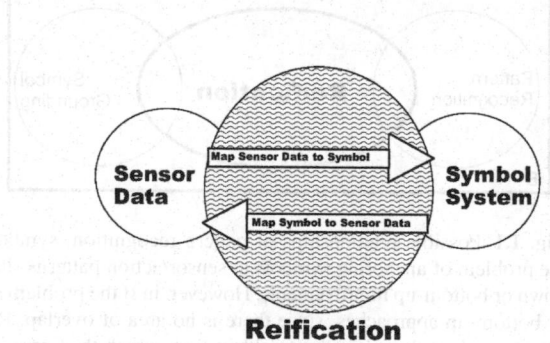

Fig. 1.2 Reification provides a bidirectional mapping between the symbol system used by the deliberative system and the sensor based system.

mapping between the sensory-motor systems and the (potentially primitive) deliberative system. Discussing only the problem of finding food, they must be able to discover how their perceptions of the environment relate to the presence of food. For extremely simple, non-vertebrate species (e.g., amoebas) this might be a purely reactive mapping between chemical sensors on the surface and a gradient ascent behavior. However, for more complex (e.g., vertebrate) species, there is a mapping between the perception of sensory information, and some neuronal representation that is manipulated to assure survival. This is the process of recognition. Conversely, this vertebrate organism must be able, after sensing hunger, to know what features of the environment to use in the search for food. Current research indicates that this is done by priming the sensory cortex with the sensations to expect after taking goal directed action. This is the process of preafference. The combiniation of these two processes is called *reification*. Both of these processes are discussed in more detail later.

While it is clear that humans can reify, it has been argued that more primitive biological entities are simply "hardwired" reactive systems - they simply respond to a stimulus without any cognition. However, it can be postulated that, in a changing environment, an organism that relies only on an inherited reactive system will be at a disadvantage to one that can reify. If this is true, one would expect to see reification in very primitive organisms. This leads to the question "How complex does a brain have to be before it can reify?"

Salamanders have been used for decades by scientists researching brain function. While the nervous systems of all vertebrates have a common structural plan, the salamanders and their allied species have preserved a type of brain structure which closely resembles that of the most primitive amphibians[97]. These brains have most of the critical functional areas that are shared by all vertebrates, yet their brains are simple enough to allow clear research results. For example, amphibians do have specialized, hardwired prey recognition cells, which allow for the recognition of an object as potential prey[172]. This would suggest that they have the structure of a hardwired reactive system. However, at least one amphibian, the tiger salamander, can be trained to recognize a new scent, which implies that they are capable of reification of new sensory input[51]. Reification occurs at a very low level in the vertebrate brain. The reification methodology described in this book is guided by the example of these very primitive brains. It will be described in more detail in Chapter 3.

1.3 More Advanced Brains

Of course, it might be claimed that these simple creatures use this primitive process, but we humans are more sophisticated and rely on a more advanced mechanism to do the same thing. One of the reasons that the tiger salamander brain was chosen as a model, is that the core functions of all mammalian brains (including ours) have the same structural components as this primitive brain. It is clear that humans have some sort of a reification mechanism. Artists have long known that we interpret visual images into familiar (if distorted) representations. One practice to overcome this mapping from the distal image to a distorted proximal image is to inverting the images, and then draw the upside down image. This allows the artist to duplicate what is actually there, rather than the interpreted image. Psychologists and philosophers have addressed this non-conscious automatic mechanism for much longer than artificial intelligence has been a discipline:

> We do not see patches of color, but trees and houses; we hear, not indescribable sound, but voices and violins[119].

It is clear that, in humans, the conscious mind deals not with low-level sensor data, but with symbols. It is also clear that when we look for things in the environment we do not look for "three orthogonal rectilinear surfaces of similar dimension, with a reflective electromagnetic signal with a wavelength of approximately 650 nanometers." Instead we look for the red block, and some non-conscious mechanism translates this into the sensory/perceptual indicators that can be used to recognize the block when we see it.

1.4 What This Book Is and What It Is Not

In this book, we construct a framework that can be used for the construction of a biologically principled cybernetic brain. We use a mathematical model from cognitive science to construct the `Reification Engine`. Freeman, among others, has proposed that only a true working neuronal model of a brain can extract semantics from sensory information[70]. While such a neuronally based model might be necessary to build a human level intelligence, we believe that for simpler intelligences, this level of fidelity is not required. Therefore, this book does not contain an attempt to build a working neuronal model. Readers who are interested in that type of work should look at work by Kosma[117] or Edelman[61], among others.

However, we do not believe that it is sufficient to simply describe an architecture or a framework that might achieve a gain in intelligence. There is an enormous gulf between the design and the reality, and the discipline of engineering is based on bridging that gulf. Except where we specifically call out otherwise, all of the theories and designs we present have been encoded and tested on an actual robot. We have found that the practice of embodying the architecture has exposed problems that can cause the design to fail. Among the aspects of the design that we have not yet implemented is the learning side of the overall loop.

In addition, in order to be able to proceed with confidence and make claims about the ability of the system, it is necessary to have complete confidence in the underlying system. During the development of the software and hardware we have made extensive use of automated testing. In addition we have done testing in the robot's ecosystem. If the test case requires the robot to travel across the room, and return, we must wait, patiently (or not), for the robot to trundle there and back again.

We feel that this level of testing is required to demonstrate that reification gives a robot enough semantic intelligence to reason effectively and achieve goals in the real world.

1.5 Structure of the Book

The first two chapters examine the clues provided by the brain structure of living systems. In Chapter 2, we discuss some background material in biology and probability that is needed for the next chapter, in which we discuss the brain structure of land vertebrates. Chapters 4 – 5 describe the computational framework needed to support the Reification Engine and look at the embodiment of sample robots. A cognitively based mathematical model, taken from the work of Egon Brunswik, is described in Chapter 6. This is used to produce the design of the Reification Engine which will be used to bridge the gap from the 'world-as-perceived' to the 'world-as-modeled'. We merger current research by cognitive scientists, neurophysiologists, and researchers into artificial intelligence with this model in Chapter 7 to complete the design for the Reification Engine. In Chapters 8 – 10, the remaining cognitive structures required for a cybernetic brain (memory and a deliberative system) are discussed. In Chapter 11, the construction of the cybernetic brain from its constituent parts is discussed. In Chapter 12, we discuss the unit testing used in the construction of the brain and the specific robotic testing done to validate the claims of this book. Finally, in Chapter 13, we draw conclusions and discuss future work. This future work includes the need for the robotic system to be able to learn from and adapt to changes in the world, including the ability to add new types of knowledge to its model of the world, and to be able to recognize and reason about new objects, tasks, and goals.

1.6 A Note on Typefaces and Terminology

The construction of the reification system draws on research from many different disciplines, and each of these has its own terminology. Regardless of the background of the reader, there will almost certainly be terms of art used in this book that are unfamiliar. We have tried to compile a glossary of the less well known terms, and when a term of art is introduced, we have generally called it out by using *emphasis*. If the term is unfamiliar, please take a quick look at the glossary (located just before the reference section), to make sure that we are using it in the way you expect.

1.6.1 Anthropomorphization

Anthropomorphization is defined as "The attribution of human motivation, characteristics, or behavior to nonhuman organisms or inanimate objects." As you read
this you will see that we often refer to the robots as 'he' or 'she.' This is due to a
number of things, but high on the list is the fact that humans ascribe human characteristics to many of the inanimate objects in their environments. If we treat our cars
as human-like, how much more should we anthropomorphize the human-like robots
that we are attempting to create. This process has one significant effect: it defines
our expectations of the object. Since we are designing an intelligent, autonomous
robot, we have similar expectations of the behavior of the robot and the behavior of
a servant. We will try to keep it to a minimum, but I am sure we will miss a few
references.

Trying to keep track of the many aspects of the biologically inspired design, the
implementation, and the concepts can be difficult. This is especially true when we
may be referring to a term from neuroanatomy, one from psychology, and a similar
one from the actual software that we built to embody the mechanism, all in the same
sentence. We have tried to be consistent with the use of different typefaces to call
out the various aspects. In general:

- Normal text is used for the body of the work, and for most psychological or
  neuroanatomical terms, once they have been introduced;
- *Italics* are used to introduce a new term, or to set off the *concept* from the thing;
- `Typewriter face` is used when we are referring to a software component;
  and finally,
- 'single quotes' are used to indicate a conceptual entity as opposed to the physical
  thing it refers to, and to set off one term from another, when the context is so
  complex that we need an additional mechanism (we have tried to keep this to a
  minimum, really).

Chapter 2
Some background material on probability and biology

In this book, we build a cognitive model that can deal with an uncertain and constantly changing universe. We have ample evidence that living organisms have this ability, and rely on it for daily survival. Rather than reinventing biology whenever possible, we use living creatures, such as salamanders or other primitive land vertebrates, to act as the design guide for the cognitive modules that must be present to create a successful autonomous robot. However, in order to take advantage of these biological examples, some of the basic assumptions that underly biology must also be discussed. The focus of this chapter is summarized by the following questions:

- How do living systems deal with a probabilistic universe?
- How can we discuss these models in a principled way?
- If we are going to use living systems as our guide, why use salamanders and rats instead of humans?

2.1 Layout

The general layout of this chapter is this: In Section 2.2, the features of the real world that make a probability-aware system important are discussed. Since all natural organisms live in this probabilistic environment, it makes sense to look at how these systems achieve the kind of performance that we desire in our robots. However, if we are going to derive our design from these biological entities, we need to explore the concept of a biologically principled argument, rather than the engineering approach of a mathematically principled argument. The need for a biologically principled argument is discussed in Section 2.3. The way in which an argument can be constructed to make it biologically principled is presented in Section 2.4. Finally, The reasons that we believe our model to be biologically principled are discussed. This section also includes a discussion of the conservation of the traits that are important to the success of a species in a dynamic and uncertain environment, and we will take a brief look at why we have chosen a biologically principled path, rather than using a mathematically principled mechanism..

2.2 Probability in the Real World

The use of simplifying assumptions is almost a history of science. From the earliest beginnings of scientific exploration the goal has been to turn a world perceived as chaotic and unpredictable into a world that has order and determinism. To meet this goal, time after time, the choice was made to simplify the model by eliminating the aspects that were unruly. The exemplar of this tendency is the science of physics, which began the process of solving problems with assumptions like "In the absence of air resistance," and "Given a frictionless plane." As long as what was simplified away was not an essential characteristic of the phenomenon being studied, this process was very effective. The underlying conviction was that the world was fundamentally a deterministic place, one which ran like clockwork, except for this nagging unpleasantness associated with the fact the cannon ball did not always hit the target, the pendulum began to slow down, and the boilers kept exploding. But, if one could just measure everything a little more accurately, and calculate with a few more digits, this pesky error term would continue to get smaller and smaller, and in the limit, vanish. Or so it was believed until it became apparent that some systems would never behave, some things could not be measured without changing their values, and, finally, that the basic building blocks of the universe were fundamentally probabilistic[125]. The world was perceived as a chaotic and unpredictable place because it is one; and nothing can be done about it.

In parallel with the developments in physics, the same progression occurred in the area of machine intelligence. First, the simplifying assumption was made, that intelligence is deterministic. Then, if one could just measure a little more accurately, calculate with a few more digits, increase the computational power just a few more orders of magnitude, the problems associated with deploying intelligent systems into the real world would get smaller and smaller, and in the limit, vanish. More and more current research is suggesting that this approach to autonomous robotics will also fail, and that what is needed is to make the basic building blocks of intelligent systems probabilistic[115, 151, 194].

Intelligent systems must model the world as uncertain, reason about observed variability, and simply assume that nothing is certain. However, to be deployed into the 'real world' and function effectively, the intelligent system must also be responsive - having a robot that must stop for even a minute to re-compute a plan can be inconvenient if the robot is blocking a doorway when it stops, or dangerous if it is crossing a street. So a balance between the complexity of the representation and the effectiveness of the results must be achieved.

Fortunately, we have around us living systems that have evolved to live (and thrive) in a probabilistic world. For all living systems, their perception and their mapping of symbols onto objects is necessarily probabilistic[162]. We know that eyes, ears, and other biological sensors are just as prone to error as any electro-mechanical sensor, and, as anyone who has knocked over a coffee cup, or missed an easy shot on a pool table will attest, our ability to execute actions in the real world has only a probability of success, not a guarantee. Living creatures succeed in a complex, uncertain world, and do so by evaluating the probability of success of their plans. Even non-verbal animals make decisions which depend on an assessment of probabilities[60], and their survival depends on making the correct assessment.

While the argument has been made that, in non-human species, these behaviors are hardwired, ample research has been done to demonstrate that just as the world is a dynamic place, many of the cognitive models used by living creatures are also dynamic, and are changing in response to the experiences of the creature. In natural systems the state of the surrounding environment can and does change unpredictably. In particular, new prey and predator species appear and old prey and predator species disappear. This means that the successful species must be able to learn about new environments, rather that strictly being hardwired. One demonstration that a stimulus response is not hardwired is the ability of the species to be trained to recognize a new stimulus. In Section 3.1 we describe the Pavlovian training of salamanders as an example of their ability to learn new stimulus.

Living systems can both adapt and learn from their experiences. These living systems express many of the characteristics that we desire in our intelligent, autonomous robots. For living creatures to succeed and achieve their goals, they use their abilities to function in an uncertain world. This means that, for a robust intelligent system (biological or cybernetic) to succeed in the real world, it must be aware of the probabilistic nature of the world and capable of adapting to new environments. However, learning from an existing system is not a trivial task. If we are going to derive our design from biological systems, it is not sufficient to simply grab a term and redefine it to suit ourselves, we must make sure that the principles we extract are valid, and that we are applying them correctly.

2.3 Why a Biologically Principled Argument?

It is common in mathematical and computer science discussions to hear that an argument is (or is not) mathematically principled. In this context, it is understood that a mathematically principled argument is one in which first, the underlying assumptions are valid, and second that any transforms that are applied are applied correctly. Think about learning how to do proofs in a mathematics or logic class. There is a complex and formal process that one must follow to extend our knowledge into new terrain.

John von Neumann presented a lecture at Yale in 1956 in which he laid the groundwork for the research path that would be followed for the next fifty years. This path focused on modeling the brain as a digital, mathematical system. However, he added the note:

> It therefore justifies the original assertion, that the nervous system has a *prima facia* digital character. Let me add a few words regarding the qualifying 'prima facia.' The above description contains some idealizations and simplifications, which will be discussed subsequently. Once these are taken into account, the digital character no longer stands out so clearly and unequivocally.[138]

This viewpoint of abstracting away the details that 'get in the way' of a clean mathematical model is still prevalent. As a result almost all of the research into artificial intelligence has been driven from the mathematical perspective, so that in the foreword to the 2000 edition of von Neumann's lecture, Paul and Patricia Churchland lamented:

> Curiously, however, these two kindred sciences – one focused on *artificial* cognitive processes and the other on *natural* cognitive processes – pursued their parallel concerns in substantial isolation from each other, from the 1950s right through to the present. The people who earned advanced degrees in computer science typically learned little or (more often) nothing about the biological brain ... Equally, the people who earned advanced degrees in neuroscience typically learned little or nothing about computational theory...[34]

The field of artificial intelligence evolved from the study of logic and mathematics, and so much of the underlying culture is mathematical. It is common to analyze new approaches by confirming that the appropriate mathematical and logical tools have been applied. However, when talking about biologically based artificial intelligence, one does not generally hear an argument about the way that this model of intelligence fits into the general pattern of biological intelligences. One term that is used to describe the correspondence of a model with a biological model or system is biologically inspired. In fact a biologically inspired argument can be closely modeled on a biological system as is some biomimetic work on lobsters[5] and salamanders[100]. However, some work that claims to be biologically inspired, such as much of the work in the area of cellular autonomy, does not bear a close resemblance to any known biological systems. Another term that is used in this arena is the term biologically defensible. A biologically defensible argument is one that, while it may copy the specific details of a biologic structure or process, does not violate basic biological principles [48].

The authors feel that this term does not go far enough. In this work, we will use the term biologically principled. By biologically principled, we mean an argument that starts by using basic principles of biology and builds a model from those principles. As in a mathematically principled argument, in which each piece of the argument can be derived from the relevant mathematical principles, each piece of a biologically principled argument should have a basis in the relevant area of biology.

The next logical question is, why is it not enough that a study is mathematically principled? The problem with any mathematical solution is that it can be coherent (i.e. cohere to basic principles) without corresponding to the probabilistic real world. Let us look at the problem of solving the question "What equation gives us the answer 2". While there are an infinite number of correct solutions to this equation, most humans will use a very small number, and most will probably start with "1+1". In the same way, there are an infinite number of solutions to the problem of building an artificial intelligence, that are mathematically coherent.

This falls out of the nature of computers as implementations of Turing Machines[132]. If any one program solves a specific problem (e.g., for an input it

---

[1] A Turing machine is a conceptual model of computation which can shown to be capable of computing anything computable.

produces the desired output), there are numerous variations on that same program which will produce the same output. In the trivial case, the replacement of flow-control structures with functionally equivalent structures produces a different program with the same results. Finally, the introduction of non-effective instructions like assigning a variable value to itself, can be added *ad infinitum* to produce new programs that solve the same problem. So, if we can find one solution, we can generate infinite variations which are functionally equivalent, but different in structure.

Natural intelligences, however, come in a finite variety, and can be classified into a small number of types. As we discuss in more detail later, all land vertebrate brains use the same basic structures, from salamanders on up. So rather than giving us an infinite number of possible brain types, we have a finite number, which makes experimentation and design a bit easier. But in order to use this finite number, we need to understand the underlying biological principles that make one biologic solution to the problem of intelligence different from another.

2.3.1 Biological Principles

So, for an argument to be biologically principled, it must conform to the general principles of biological systems. All natural intelligences are biological and so obeying basic principles would seem to be at least useful. Yet we often see robots that clearly violate one or more basic biological principles. For example, even one of the simplest of all organisms, bacteria, has memory[116]. Certainly, amphibians have memory. This means that attempts to build memory-free processes are not biologically principled. However, the pursuit of memory-free and model-free implementations of intelligent systems has been an active research area in robotics since the 1950's. This research area has been strongly driven by mathematical principles, at the expense of biological principles. The driving emphasis is that there are significant mathematical complexities associated with maintaining a detailed, consistent, and accurate model of the outside world - complexities which have often exceeded that capabilities of available hardware. The work on reactive systems, brought to the fore by Rodney Brooks[20, 21, 22] has inspired many researchers to explore mathematically principled designs that violate biological principles.

So why don't we see the use of biological principles? One problem is that biology is an observational science. Rather than learning from first principles, as in mathematics, the student learns by observation and builds a sense of what is biologically plausible over time. So, to use the previous example, a biologist would know that, at the very least, all animals have some form of memory, therefore they would reject the use of a memory free model. This brings us to the second problem. In an observational science, theories must change when they are disproved. This means that a biologically principled model may have to change, if the theory that it is based on changes. This is a very different proposition than a mathematically principled model, since mathematical theories rarely change, they just become superseded. The basic principles of biology are based in observations and this might suggest that the biologically principled foundation is too shaky to be relied upon. While the theories do change, they change very slowly.

2.4 What Is a Biologically Principled Argument?

In this section we propose a definition of some basic biological principles. It should be noted that, if there are 10 biologists in the room, there are probably 11 lists of the essential biological principles, so this list is neither exhaustive nor final. It is, however, a starting point for discussion.

- Biology is an observational science.
- Biological organisms have a hierarchy of structural levels.
- The theory of evolution explains the observed diversity of life.

  - Individuals of a species or population vary from one another.
  - These variations can be inherited.
  - Biological organisms compete for resources such as food and mates.
  - Traits which contribute to reproduction and survival in organisms are conserved across generations.

The basis for this abbreviated set of principles can be found in any good basic biology text such as Campbell and Reece's Biology, which is now in its Eighth Edition [32].

2.4.1 Biology Is an Observational Science

First, and most important, biology is an observational science, like chemistry and physics. As such it relies on both hypothesis and observation. As all scientists know, an observation can not validate a hypothesis, but it can disprove it.

> Hypothesis therefore plays a necessary role, which no one has ever contested. Only, it should always be as soon as possible submitted to verification. It goes without saying that, if it can not stand this test, it must be abandoned without any hesitation. This is, indeed, what is generally done; but sometimes with a certain impatience. Ah well! this impatience is not justified. The physicist who has just given up one of his hypotheses should, on the contrary, rejoice, for he has found an unexpected opportunity of discovery. (H. Poincaré [159], Page 150).

Chemistry and physics are also experimental sciences, much of the progress is made by performing carefully design experiments. In the biological sciences, because of the complexity of studying natural systems, careful observation must sometimes take the place of experimentation. In some cases it is physically impossible to run experiments. There can be several different reasons for this, including the observation of events in interstellar space such as supernovas, colliding galaxies, and the evolution of stars. While some recent experimental work has been done on interstellar impacts, such as the NASA *Deep Impact* project, in general, we can't set up an experiment to slam a comet into a planetary mass to confirm or disprove a hypothesis. This set of domains also includes the observation of evolutionary change in the fossil record, research into volcanic eruptions, research into earthquakes, and so on. Some experimentation may be possible, but in general, one has to observe the events that naturally occur.

In other cases it is simple to set up a potential experiment, but impossible to do so without changing the outcomes. This is especially true in the domains of living systems, such as biology, ecology, and behavioral sciences. Since living systems are adaptive, and are capable of learning from their environments, any change to the environment can alter the behavior that is being measured. An example of this is the observation of stereotyped feeding behavior in amphibians. For many years, most amphibians feeding behavior was reported as having limited variation of timing or extent of motion. This limited range of repetitive or ritualistic movement is called *stereotypy*. Later work showed that this observed stereotypy was caused by the researchers feeding the animals a single prey type, presented in a uniform manner. In a more natural environment, this apparent stereotypy vanished. The observations, while correct, were an artifact of the feeding conditions in the laboratory [47].

Until recently, in the domains of chemistry and physics, it was generally considered that measuring the results of an experiment had no effect on the outcomes. However, this also changes when the measured quantities become so small that quantum effects must be considered. In those cases, the uncertainty principle developed by Heisenberg[96] must be used. It states that locating a particle in a small region of space makes the velocity of the particle uncertain; and conversely, that measuring the velocity of a particle precisely makes the position uncertain. In the domain of biology and ecology, this principle was so well internalized that no one ever needed to formalize it. It is well known that, for the observation of animal behavior in intact ecosystems, the changes in the ecosystem required for the experiment would change the observations.

Finally, some experiments can not be run for ethical reasons, such as some types of human behavior studies. Before the advent of non-invasive scanning techniques, the study of neurophysiology depended on the chance occurrence of traumatic damage to the brain, and the observation of any resulting behavioral changes. While animal studies could rely on damaging specific areas of the brain and observing the deficits caused by that damage, ablating human brain tissue to see what happens is not an option. Even now, some types of damage are so rare in humans that only single case studies are available. Work on animals has provided significant gains to our understanding of the structure of the brain, but at extreme cost to the animals being studied.

In these cases, and in others, observational sciences cannot do traditional laboratory experiments, where they would make a single, specific, targeted change to one variable (while holding the others constant) and precisely measure the results. Rather, the support for the hypothesis must be derived from a long series of repeated observations, analyzed statistically, and with luck, demonstrating a conclusive result. This is a far cry from the techniques of an experimental science like chemistry or physics. Yet the methodologies behind the observational sciences are both strict and well principled.

In all observations and experiments, it is important to demonstrate statistical validity, but in observation it is of the utmost importance. Creating models from observed data poses some significant hazards. It has been shown that when there are a number of explanatory variables in a model (more than 50) many variable selection methods will provide regression equations with high correlation values for independent variables[69]. This means that the features used in a model must be chosen with great care and thought. This also suggests that, in the absence of other factors, a more parsimonious model should be favored [2]. For an excellent study of model selection in biological system see [30]. It also should go without saying that there must be enough experiments or observations to yield statistically significant answers. So, for any experimental or observational study, in order to conform to general scientific principles, we must have a hypothesis to be tested, a reasoned argument for the features to be analyzed, and enough data to support a statistically significant result. So, this set of requirement is part of the necessary conditions for a biologically principled study.

2.4.2 Life Has Structure

Biology is based on structural levels. In this hierarchical structure, each level is built from the level below it. To give one example, the atoms carbon, hydrogen, oxygen, nitrogen, and sulfur are the building blocks of the 20 amino acids. These 20 amino acids are the building blocks of all proteins. These proteins are the building blocks of the components of cells. Cells are the building blocks of all life. This type of analysis can be repeated in a number of different ways.

There are two important principles at work here, 1) that life is ordered hierarchically and 2) that life has structure. Even apparently simple organisms, such as bacteria, have internal structure. A bacteria has a cell wall to separate it from the outside. It has a nucleoid, that contains most of its DNA. It has ribosomes, that translate RNA into proteins. It does not have a uniform internal texture [32]. Brains also have structure. To look at a specific primitive brain, take the example of the hagfish. Hagfish are a group of marine, eel-shaped, jawless fishes, that have been found in the fossil record from approximately 330 million years ago and are still found in modern oceans [7]. Their ancestors are considered to have evolved before the evolution of jawed vertebrates. These very primitive vertebrates, have separate brain areas for different functions[192]. Brains are not like pudding. This means, that for a cybernetic model of a brain to be biologically principled, the model must support the structured forms seen in animal brains.

---

[2] Occam's razor strikes again

2.4.3 The Theory of Evolution Explains the Observed Diversity of Life.

This subsection contains a brief and relatively simple overview of evolution. If you are familiar with evolutionary theory, you might want to skip this section. If you want to learn more about evolutionary theory, more detailed information can be found in Futuyma's book on the subject[73].

The theory of evolution is the unifying principle in modern biology. It was initially developed by Charles Darwin and published in the Origin of Species in 1859. In this work, Darwin called the initial theory, *the theory of natural selection*. The principles of natural selection are built on the following premises.

First premise - Individuals of a species or population vary from one another. Darwin based this premise on the observation of both wild and domesticated species. In all of these observed species, individuals, even siblings, differ from each other. In addition, the observation of an individual only discloses the phenotype of the individual. The phenotype is the qualities of an organism that can be observed, such as size, color, development and behavior. These qualities are the result of interactions between the genotype of the organism and its environment [106]. Following Darwin, biologists were able to discover the reasons for the changes in genotype between even very closely related individuals. There are two basic reasons for variation. In sexually reproducing species, the offspring inherit half of their genetic material from each parent. This recombination of genetic material creates some of variation in phenotypes. Another cause is a natural rate of genetic mutation. All species, both sexually and asexually reproducing, have a natural mutation rate, which forms the basis for all new genes.

Second premise - These variations can be inherited. Again, Darwin based this premise on the careful observation of both wild and domesticated species, much of which is memorialized in *The Variation of Animals and Plants Under Domestication*[44]. One of his great interests was the breeding of domestic pigeons.

> Believing that it is always best to study some special group, I have, after deliberation, taken up domestic pigeons.[43].

Now, we have the ability to analyze the genes responsible for the inheritance of variation. This information validated Darwin's careful observation.

Third premise - Biological organisms compete for resources such as food and mates. Darwin observed that all organisms produce more offspring than could possibly survive. He was clearly influenced by Malthus, who in 1821, wrote the influential book *Principles of Political Economy Considered with a View to Their Practical Application* in which he concluded that much human suffering was a consequence of human overpopulation [124]. Darwin further observed that organisms with a reproductive advantage would tend to be better represented in the next generation. The essential argument of natural selection is that, over time, the sum total of small favorable mutations will result in major changes. Darwin called this *descent with modification*. The canonical example of this is the beaks of finches in the Galapagos islands. It is now estimated that 14 different species of finch found in the Galapagos descended from one ancestral finch species over the last 5 million years (or less). These species differ from each other in size and bill shape. It is hypothesized that the evolutionary process was driven by differing food sources on the different islands [164].

Mutations which contribute to reproduction and survival in organisms are conserved across generations. As we mentioned above, mutations of the genotype are random. The mutations of the genotype, in conjunction with the environment, will cause a difference in the features of the resulting phenotype. There are three possible outcomes for the phenotype. The feature caused by the mutation may have no effect on the fitness of the organism, in which case the variation is neutral. The feature caused by the mutation may decrease the fitness of the organism, in which case the variation will not be conserved. The feature caused by the mutation may increase the fitness of the organism, in which case the variation will be conserved. So, when a particular feature is seen to be constant in many related organisms, it can generally be concluded that the effect of the underlying mutation is either favorable or neutral. More strongly, because natural selection will not favor a neutral variation, if the feature occurs over a large number of generations, it probably increases fitness.

Because these mutations are happening in all species over time, it is not possible to directly examine the original individuals and look for changes in its descendants. Sometimes it is possible to detect changes in bones and structure from the fossil record, but for brains this is generally not possible. The construction of the relationships of (invisible) ancestral relationships between living organisms is called cladistic analysis. This analysis allows for the inference of the place in the evolutionary sequence that a specific variation arose. More information on this subject can be found in [169]. By the above argument, if a specific variation occurred early in the evolutionary sequence, and occurs in all of the current descendants of that organism, it must increase fitness. Cladistic analysis also allows the researcher to detect when the same feature occurred independently in multiple species. Both conservation and independent evolution are strong arguments for the importance of that feature.

2.5 So Why Is Our Model Biologically Principled?

First, the model we present here is tested in a scientific manner. We have not only constructed a theory, we have also written the software, and built the body to house it. By placing this theory into practice, we have allowed it to be tested. Our hypothesis is: *This brain (with reification) will perform better than this brain without reification.*

Second, this brain is built in a structured and layered fashion. The components in this brain are taken, in general, from components in the vertebrate brain. These will be discussed in more detail in the next chapter.

Third, this model uses as its basis the conservation of important traits. As mentioned above, it's a harsh world out there. All animals are simultaneously searching for food and trying not to become someone else's meal. In order to cope with this fact, all species have a similar basic strategy, mutate your genes (genotype), and see how well the mutated organism does in the world (phenotype). This simple strategy has a few interesting implications. The first of these is the fact that if a mutation is of advantage to the species' phenotype, the mutation will be conserved. So what does that say about brain evolution? Very few major new structures have appeared in the vertebrate brain [141][192] in the last few million years. Now this should not be taken to mean that brains have not been evolving over time. While major reorganizations are rare, minor changes in neuronal pathways are constantly occurring [141]. As was discussed in the previous section, the fact that the basic structures of a human brain are similar to the basic structures of a salamander brain implies that something about that structure is important to the survival of both species.

Since we have demonstrated that something about the structure of vertebrate brains is important, why not just study humans? There are three reasons for this. First, and possibly most important, making a human level brain has some tricky moral and ethical implications. If the brain is conscious, is turning it off murder? Can one control a human level intelligence? Second, for most of the tasks for which an autonomous intelligence would be used, a human level intelligence is overkill and it can be demonstrated that too much intelligence is as dangerous as not enough [85]. Finally, if the relevant data can be obtained, amphibians are simpler to model. In the words of C. Judson Herrick, a noted neurologist:

> From the dawn of interest in the minute structure of the human brain, it was recognized that the simpler brains of the lower vertebrates present the fundamental features of the human brain without the numberless complications which obscure these fundamentals in higher animals[97].

In fact, it has been shown that larval salamanders can have their brain anatomy surgically altered in drastic ways without major behavioral changes.[156] So, simpler brains will be used as exemplars when possible. In some cases, such as much of the memory research and some of the neurotransmitter research, it simply is not possible to obtain the information from non-human subjects. In these cases we will use what studies are available. When possible, we will draw from studies of more than one organism.

2.5.1 Why Not Just Use Expected Value?

So, why are we going to all this trouble in the first place? One of the most mathematically principled approaches to dealing with an uncertain and dynamic environment is the use of probability theory and the expected value calculation. Literally hundreds of artificial intelligence programs have been written which are based on calculating the likelihoods of possible outcomes, and ranking their relative costs and benefits to decide on a course of action (See the summary by Tate[193], for an overview of Artificial Intelligence software). And these work extremely well, in the correct circumstances. Unfortunately, one of the necessary conditions for many of these systems is a complete, accurate, and exhaustive analysis of the exact likelihoods of every possible action and outcome. In the real world, this is simply not achievable.

So, in order to try and make a better brain, let us look at how vertebrates have successfully addressed this type of problem. By human standards, most other vertebrates are computationally challenged. Many vertebrates, such as birds, rats, monkeys, apes, and lions, can learn to identify numbers[81] Alex, a gray parrot, and Ai, a chimpanzee, learned to use the concept of zero[152][12]. Ayuma, a chimpanzee, can outperform humans in numeric memory tests[101]. However, there is no evidence of more complex math, such as an expected value calculation, being used even by chimpanzees. Even humans, who in general could do the calculations, use heuristics rather than expected value calculations. This is explored in detail by Gerd Gigerenzer[75]. These non-expected value approaches seem to work in the real world.

But, robots are not mathematically handicapped like people. They are capable of calculating expected values for even very complex situations. So why not use an expected value calculation? For many of the routine operations of the robot, an expected value calculation will be used. An expected value calculation has, at its core, an assumption that all of the outcomes are known and that all of the probabilities can be computed. But, for many of the conditions that our robots face, these conditions are not met and so these calculations are not feasible. So, in the next chapter, we will construct a biologically principled model for a cybernetic brain.

Chapter 3
Using Cognition and Physiology to Build a Cognitive Model

So why don't I have my robot yet? What is different about natural systems and the ones that we construct? What do living systems have that our autonomous robots lack? What is it that a living brain brings to the table that enables them to function and succeed in a complex, uncertain, and dynamic world? In order to answer that, we will start by considering amphibians. For any species to survive, the members of that species must be able to sense and manipulate their environment so as to find food, avoid predators, and reproduce. They must be able to perceive the things in their world, and they must be able to respond appropriately to the circumstances that they recognize.

3.1 Reification in Biological Entities

Many robotic systems have sensors and effectors that are on par with living systems, so what makes the difference in a living system such as a salamander? Is it the ability to plan, the ability to envision the possible outcomes of future actions? In order to be able to hunt their prey, amphibians have and utilize a very primitive planning system. It may be nothing more than the ability to predict the future position of a bug flying by, but it is a primitive model of the future. In this chapter, we will show that in addition to these abilities, amphibians have the ability to map perceptions onto symbols and symbols back onto perception. Mapping perceptions onto symbols allows them to learn the perception patterns that represent new food or threat sources. Mapping symbols onto perceptions allows them to predict the outcome of their behaviors. Both of these abilities are necessary for survival in the wild. At this point it is useful to define a few terms: *Recognition*, *Deliberation*, and *Preafference*.

Recognition is the process of mapping sensory input onto a symbolic representation that can be reasoned about. Philosophers have long argued, and some cognitive scientists believe, that we (as living systems) do not live in the 'real world,' rather we live in a symbolic representation of the real world [72] that is formed from our perceptions. This symbolic model is strongly grounded in the real world, but it is more like a simplified virtual reality model. It is built by mapping the sensory input into a neuronal representation. We will define this complex mapping of sensory input into a collection of neuronal representations as recognition. Once a brain has these neuronal representations, they can be manipulated as symbols.

The process of manipulating these symbols is defined as **deliberation**. The manipulation of these symbols depends on a complex structure of relationships between symbols. For example, given that we have recognized a 'door', our understanding of door includes attributes: a door can be opened or closed, a door leads from one space to another space. There are actions that we can take: we know how to open the door by twisting the handle, and swinging the door on its hinges, etc. These complex associations are used by the deliberative system to make choices between actions that might achieve goals.

The second term, **preafference**, is a little more complex. There is a common saying that "You see what you expect to see." Cognitive scientists have long known that this is literally true for humans. As we move through our days, we are constantly building and updating a complex model of how we expect the world to look, feel, and sound in the next few moments. Research by Walter Freeman has shown that vertebrate brains prime their sensory systems with a rough template of what to expect, and this template is used to reduce the incredible complexity of the world. His term for this process is preafference: the mapping of the expected state of the world onto to the expectation of sensory data [72]. Preafference in organisms is discussed in this chapter, some mechanisms for solving it in cybernetic systems will be discussed further in Chapter 6.

This two-way mapping of sensor information onto a symbolic representation, and the mapping of expected states onto an expectation of the sensor information, we call **reification**. It appears that this is the key thing that living systems bring to the table. It allows them to function successfully in the world, and it is a key deficit in many robots. In order to get an insight into the biological mechanisms of reification we will examine research on brains of salamanders as a starting position, then we will move to higher mammals.

3.1.1 Recognition

Starting with recognition, it is clear that any living system must be able to find food. For sexual species, they must also be able to find mates. These needs require, at a minimum, the ability to recognize food objects and members of the same species. The next logical question is, "How much of this recognition is hardwired?". Put another way, how much of the behavior is coded in the genotype and then expressed in the phenotype. The answer can be found in the biological literature. If a response to stimulus across a wide variety of individuals is always the same, then we can hypothesize that the behavior is regulated by the genotype. Starting with salamanders, some behaviors, such as sexual responses are always the same. The fact that male salamanders of the species *Ambystoma mexicanum* always increased their activity when exposed to the scent of females of their species suggests that this behavior is determined by the genotype[147]. It makes sense that mate identification would be controlled by the genotype. However, for feeding behavior, another basic need, most amphibians show varied feeding behavior, with diverse types of movements used in feeding[47]. In effect, feeding behavior appears to be driven by deliberate choices that are influenced by environmental cues.

But the argument might be made that these behaviors, while varied, are simply fixed responses to known stimulus. If we can show that new behaviors can be learned, particularly to novel stimulus, then there is a reasonable argument that there is some mechanism for recognition of new stimuli. There are some interesting demonstrations that salamanders are in fact capable of learning to recognize new stimuli. One of these is the recognition, by red backed salamanders (*plethodon cinereus*), of the holders of adjacent territories. It was shown that red backed salamanders were significantly less likely to attack a salamander with whose scent they were familiar. They showed more aggression to unfamiliar salamanders. While it is feasible that a salamander could be genetically programmed to recognize a species-specific stimulus (like the scent of a male), it is infeasible that such programming could be used to pre-program the identities of all possible fellow salamanders. This *Dear Enemy* phenomenon shows that a salamander is capable of recognizing a number of others of its species and classifying them as either known or unknown[103]. However, the argument could be made that, recognizing conspecific individuals is a natural thing, and somehow could be preprogrammed.

So let us go to a completely synthetic experiment. Salamanders can be trained to learn new odors in a classical conditioning experiment. In experiments done in the 1990's, salamanders learned to associate the odor of various synthetic chemicals with an electric shock[51]. This suggests that novel sensory inputs can also be classified, since associating the smell of buytl acetate with an electric shock is not something that would be selected for in a natural environment. The classification of novel input is evidence for a flexible mechanism of recognition that allows the organism to recognize and classify objects that it has not previously encountered. Higher animals, such as mice, dogs, and primates are also capable of learning to recognize new stimulus.

3.1.2 Preafference

Now we turn to preafference. Preafference is defined by W. H. Freeman as:

> The preafference precedes feedback by proprioception and interoception loops from the sensory receptors in the muscles and joints to the spinal column, cerebellum, thalamus, and somatosensory cortex. The corollary discharges convey information about what is to be sought by looking, listening, and sniffing, and the returning afferent discharges convey the current state of the search. When an expected stimulus is present, we experience it. When not, we imagine it. [72]

The brains of rats clearly show a preafferent signal when they are expecting a learned odor. This signal is used to prepare the sensory processors for the results of an action or, in the case of a learned behavior, for an expected stimulus [110]. Moving to primates, monkeys have been shown to have an modification of neuronal responses in the visual cortex when a visual stimulus was presented in an expected location. This modulation was not seen when the stimulus was presented in random locations[183]. They also have been shown to reach for an object where they saw it last, even if they can no longer see it[79]. This implies that they have a strong expectation of what they would see (if they could). Humans also reach for the expected position of occluded objects, implying that they have a model of the expected world state. This ability to prepare the brain for an expected stimulus is clearly important for an organism in a constantly changing world.

Now that we have made a colorable argument for the two directions of reification, recognition and preafference, we can turn to building a cognitive model of the process. Reification consists of:

- A recognition mechanism that translates the sensor data into symbols; and
- A preafference mechanism that translates the symbols into the expected sensor data.

It should be noted that reification does not exist in a vacuum. In order to have some data to utilize, there must be a a source of sensory data. This is supplied by the robot's sensors represented by the perception/action system in Figure 3.1.

Fig. 3.1 The core reification loop supports the bidirectional mapping of sensory data onto symbols and the reverse mapping of expected world state onto what the sensors are expected to detect. These two tasks (recognition and preafference) are critical functions that all living systems depend on to survive in the world.

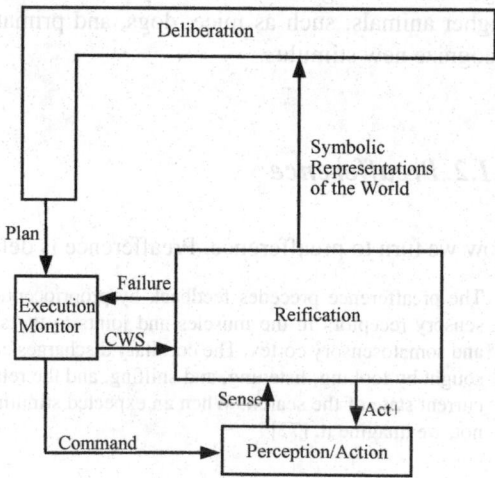

This system will sense the world, so that the recognition mechanism has something to work with. In addition, in order for the preafference mechanism to model the effects of actions, there need to be actions to work with. This requires a deliberative system, which takes the symbolic representations of the world and makes a plan. The execution monitor feeds the actions in the plan to the reification system, which uses preafference to predict what the sensors will report. So, in order to model what we know about reification, the model must have the following components:

- A perception/action system that can affect and perceive the world (Chapter 5);
- A recognition mechanism that translates the sensor data into symbols (Chapter 7);
- A deliberative system that can manipulate the symbols (Chapter 10);
- An execution monitor that can sequence the actions coming out of the Deliberation module; and,
- A preafference mechanism that translates the outcomes of the actions into the expected sensor data (Chapter 7).

Note that the recognition and the preafference mechanisms are two complementary functions of reification.

In order to discuss its use, we will introduce a hypothetical unnamed robot. Our hypothetical robot is humanoid, that is to say bipedal, upright, with dextrous grasping members at the ends of two arms. The robot has human quality vision, hearing, agility, and strength. We will assume voice input and human level natural language processing - in short, it is one of the robots we see in the movies. This robot has been told to pick up a red block. It first creates a plan (details on the deliberation module can be found in Chapter 10). Then the entire plan (Plan) is passed to the Execution Monitor, which processes each step in the plan, in sequence. Let us suppose that the first action is to sense the actual location of the block. This preafference mechanism, in the reification system, takes the expected symbolic state for the world after the first action in the plan is taken, for example the red block is on the table, and creates a matching expected sensor state. It then passes the expected state and the action (Act+) to the Perception/Action module. The action is taken, and the resulting world state is sensed. An analysis is made of the difference between the expected state and the observed state, which is added to the sensor data and is passed to the recognition mechanism, in the reification system. If the difference between the observed and the expected state is small enough (the block is approximately where it is expected to be), the next action of the plan is taken from the execution monitor and given to the preafference mechanism. However, if the plan has been completed or the difference between the observed and the expected state is too large (the block on the table is blue), the sensor data is turned into symbolic data by the recognition mechanism, which passes this symbolic data back to the deliberation mechanism. In Chapter 6, we discuss the method that we used to construct a model of reification, based on a model created by Brunswik.

3.2 Biological Storage

As you have probably noticed, so far there is no memory in this model. Clearly, for this model to be biologically principled, there must be at least one memory structure, if only to store the symbols that correspond to the model of the external world. This leads us to the observation of biological memory structures. Research on memory is generally done by studying memory deficits. In animal studies this is generally done by damaging a part of the brain and experimentally determining what the animal can, or can not, remember. Since most animals can not explicitly tell the researcher about their memories, this requires very clever experiments. In human studies, rather than damaging the subjects, researchers wait for damage to occur and then test the subjects on their specific memory deficits. Obviously, having a subject that can explain his/her experience is a major advantage. Therefore, for memory studies, we will jump straight to human research. Most of the memory research concerns forms of amnesia (a failure of memory) and the type of damage that may have caused it. Amnesia comes in two basic flavors. The first, retrograde amnesia, describes a difficulty in remembering things that happened before a trauma or illness. The second, anterograde amnesia, describes a difficulty in acquiring new information after a trauma or illness [149].

Before we continue, it should be noted here that memory researchers do not agree on all of the following concepts. We have picked what appears, right now, to be relatively well accepted work, but this could change. If the underlying concepts change radically, then we will change the model to fit the data. Because this book is not about a brain based device, as discussed above, we are not attempting to model the actual engram formation and memory recovery. For more details on those processes, you should read Daniel Schacter's very entertaining work on memory[178].

One major distinction in memory research is between short and long term memory (or short and long term storage). In this distinction, short term memory is memory that is transient, perhaps 20 seconds long. It can only hold a few objects, most famously 7 ± 2 [130]. Short term memory was described in 1968 by Akinson and Shiffrin[4], but as with most memory research, the existence of the long term/short term memory distinction is debated [149]. Recent work has suggested that short term memory and long term memory may have different properties [45]. We have created a `Working Memory` module to model the short term memory for our robot.

Another major distinction is between implicit and explicit memory. Implicit memory is memory that can be used without conscious recollection of previous experience. One form of implicit memory is procedural memory. This is the memory of how things are done or rules for doing things. An example of this is a patient, described by Schacter, with profound amnesia who could still play golf. This patient could not remember playing any specific game or even recall the specific details of the current game, however, his memory for the rules, terminology, and physical demands of golf was unimpaired [176]. This type of observation is often used to support the existence of a specific procedural memory system, but this conclusion not universally held. Some arguments suggest a set of implicit learning systems that are operating outside of the cognitive learning system [149]. In our model, procedural memory is included as part of the perception/action system.

Implicit memory can also prime recognition tasks, even in people with amnesia[177]. A famous example was described by the physician Clapardéde. He hid a pin in his hand and then shook the hand of a woman with profoundly anterograde amnesia, pricking her. Later, she refused to shake his hand, even though she was not able to explicitly remember the incident. Rather, she made general excuses for not wishing to shake hands [35]. Even though she was unable to use explicit memory to recall the incident, her implicit memory caused her to avoid a potentially painful incident. This implies that the implicit memory can be used by humans and that memory structures may be significantly more fluid than the division between explicit and implicit implies. In fact, a patient with both retrograde and anterograde amnesia was able to use this priming mechanism to learn how to enter data from company records into a computer[31]. However, at this point a cybernetic memory can have no implicit part (or it is all implicit, depending on your viewpoint) so, while it is clearly important, we are not addressing priming as a link between explicit memory and implicit memory.

3.2.1 Explicit Memory

Explicit memory can be divided into several types, although again, the exact divisions are still being debated. We will use Tulving's division of explicit memory into semantic memory and episodic memory[201]. These are described in more detail below.

3.2.1.1 Episodic Memory

Episodic memory is defined as the storage of events or episodes and the temporal or spatial relationships between these episodes. The remembering of episodic memory takes place in the first person[200]. An example of episodic memory would be "I remember when I first tasted spiced coffee. My friend Ron showed me how to make it, in the kitchen of the house that I grew up in." Episodic memory can be thought of as a log file, in which both the remembered event and the features of the event are stored. These features may include the basic emotions discussed in 3.3. However, in humans, episodic memory is somewhat fluid. It can be altered by being verbally described. It has been demonstrated that after seeing a face, being asked to verbally describe that face significantly decreases the ability of the subject to subsequently recognize the face[180]. This decrease in recognition ability is called verbal over-shadowing. Expertise in an area, such as the identification of the odors of wine, can decrease the importance of this verbal over-shadowing[150]. It should be noted that episodic memory can be altered by other processes. Damage to certain regions of the brain can cause amnesia, such that the person can not recall events from their past, even though they retain more general knowledge[149]. This is the canonical form of amnesia where the person loses memory of their personal experiences, while retaining memory of what a chair is, and how to drive a car. While we should keep in mind these subtleties for future research, in this model, episodic memory is stored as a separate memory module.

3.2.1.2 Semantic Memory

Semantic memory is the memory of the relationships between objects [200]. It may have emotive or perceptual tags, but these are not required. An example of semantic memory might be "Spiced coffee uses cinnamon, nutmeg, and allspice. Coffee contains caffeine. Spiced coffee reminds me of my friend Ron. I like Ron (emotive tag)." Notice that this does not have the first person narrative quality of the Episodic memory. Semantic memory can be modeled as an ontology, but with a few significant differences from the way in which ontologies are generally designed. First, it is clearly possible for humans to hold inconsistent ideas in their semantic memories. This ability is described in detail in Kahneman and Tversky's Prospect Theory, which describes the differences in the way that people judge losses and gains[109][108]. This implies that a model of a semantic memory should not be subjected to rigid truth maintenance. Second, each human holds a unique semantic memory. While we all should have learned a selection of the same basic facts in grade school, the vicissitudes of an adult life will have left us with a significantly different store of relationships in our semantic memories as adults. Because of these two facts, we are calling our ontologic model of the semantic memory a personal rough ontology, to distinguish it from the global truth-maintained ontologies that are generally used.

Clearly episodic and semantic memory are related. Episodic memory can be considered as the way in which memory is first encoded. These memories are then translated and encoded as semantic memory. This ability can be demonstrated not just in humans, but also in rats[62]. It is clear that sleep enhances this transfer, but the precise mechanisms are not yet understood[55, 191]. While it is very important to model this transfer mechanism, it is beyond the scope of this book.

Given the previous discussion, the memory model that we have chosen to used has four basic modules. These are:

- Semantic memory, which we will call the `Personal Rough Ontology`. This is described in Chapter 9.
- Episodic memory, which is described in Chapter 8.
- Short term memory, which is also described in Chapter 8.

After adding in a mechanism to track the internal state of the robot, this results in the model shown in figure 3.2.

3.3 Emotion

So far, we have talked about emotive tags in the Episodic and Semantic memory sections, but the nature of these tags has not been defined. This begs the question, why would a cybernetic brain need emotion? Starting with the biologically principled argument, all mammal brains have the same set of *basic emotions*, driven by the same neurotransmitters in the brain[146]. In fact, all of the basic neurotransmitters are conserved across all vertebrates [192].

3.3.1 Emotion as mediator

So what is the point of all this machinery? The brain acts as a mediator between the inside world of the organism and the outside world in which the organism lives. Observations of the world trigger emotions and those emotions prepare the body for the appropriate response [189]. The simplest of these emotions are the basic emotions FEAR, SEEKING, PANIC, and RAGE [146]

As an example, consider a mouse in the presence of a cat. The scent of the cat triggers the emotion of fear in the mouse. The fear prepares the physiology of the mouse to first freeze and then flee. In laboratory experiments designed to explore the role of fear, mice have been genetically engineered to have no ability to smell

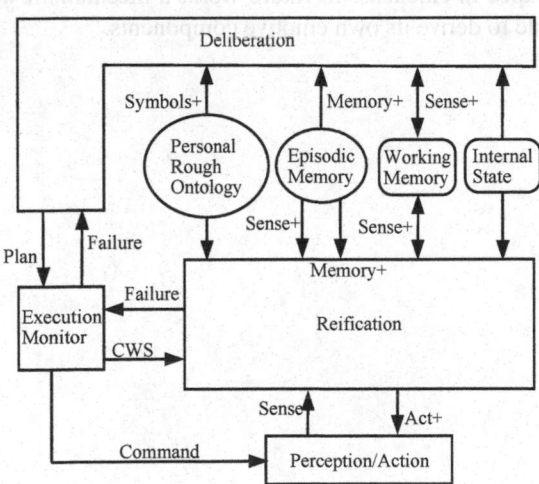

Fig. 3.2 The four memory systems added onto the robotic cognition loop.

a cat [113] or no ability to learn fear [185]. In both cases they act in a fearless way in the presence of cats, running up to them and smelling them. Needless to say, in a natural setting, a mouse with no fear of cats would not last long enough to reproduce. Humans also have difficulty functioning without these emotions. Damasio describes the social difficulties of a patient who was lacking fear. In this case, the absence of fear made her too trusting of other people [41].

The same argument about the need for emotions, which in turn trigger behavioral and physiologic changes, also applies to robotic systems. Let us take the case of a robot given the task to get on a plank at one end, travel to the other end, and then get off of the plank. In one case the plank is lying on the ground. In another case the plank is suspended high enough that the robot will be damaged if it falls. The robot has the capability to select the speed at which it moves, and the amount of time it spends sensing its position. Its model includes information about how accurately it can navigate, and how far it will drift off its planned course. Without some sense of fear or danger, the robot will travel the plank as fast in the one case as in the other. However, this is not a desirable behavior, since the consequences of a fall are significantly more severe in the second case. If the robot is allowed to "feel" the emotion of fear at the prospect of a fall from a height, then it will exhibit the behavior of proceeding more cautiously over the suspended plank. The FEAR component has clear advantages for a robotic system

The SEEKING component would be useful in cases where the robot is tasked to find objects or to obtain its own energy. The use of PANIC is less clear, but it could have important survival characteristics. For example, in an emergency situation, the robot might need to take a chance on damaging itself in order to avoid a dangerous situation. The use of RAGE is not obvious, but it may be of use in military or security applications.

In our model, the emotive component will be given to the robot, both in the storage of episodic memory and semantic memory. This is equivalent to certain types of inherent fears, such as the fear of cat smell in mice and the fear of hawk shapes in chickens. In future work, a mechanism will devised for the robot to be able to derive its own emotive components.

Chapter 4
Representation

One of the distinguishing characteristics of a deliberative system is that it maintains a representation of the world. Unlike a reactive system[22], which uses the world as its own model, the deliberative process requires the ability to represent the world as it currently exists, and also possible future states of the world. The word 'deliberation' is defined as discussing or considering all sides or outcomes. These possible states are necessary to be able to compare alternatives, If our robot is going to be able to ask "What would happen if I did this?" our deliberative system needs the ability to maintain models of the current world state, and possible changes to that world. To consider what might happen, our deliberative system must have some knowledge of what might go wrong when it attempts to make changes to the world. In addition, to act intelligently, there must be some consideration of what other events might occur that would affect the outcomes. Unlike the clean and deterministic world of chess, our robot will be given jobs to do in the real world, and so it must be capable of reasoning about the uncertainties in this world. To reason effectively, our robot must have some way to represent the current and desired states of the world, the actions it might take to achieve its goals, and the types of events that might disrupt those goals. In this chapter we present the underlying data structures that are used to support this representation.

We will first introduce the data structure that we use to represent the state of the things in the world, which we call a `WorldSet`. The `WorldSet` is made up of a collection of individual descriptors that capture the knowledge about each thing that is salient to the problem at hand. These representations are designed to provide multiple layers of support for our deliberation system as it reasons about the world.

In the rest of this chapter we describe in detail the data structures that are used to represent the world, the goals, and the actions and events that can change the world. These representations will become the foundation of the tools that our robot uses to reason, and form the basis of the memory systems used to store knowledge about the world and its history. In much of this chapter we use an extended example involving our unnamed humanoid robot. For this example, we have given our robot a task "Get me the copy of 'Robots, Reasoning, and Reification' that I left on the top of the tall bookcase in the library." This will require the robot to walk into the other room (first opening the door), then the robot will need to figure out how to grasp the book, which is just out of reach on the top of the book shelf. There are several possible solutions, such as positioning a chair and standing on it, grabbing a pointer and pushing the book off the top of the shelf, or going into the closet to grab a ladder (See figure 4.1 for a idea of the layout). One must keep in mind that while the physical capabilities of our hypothetical robot far exceed what is available, for over fifty years symbolic planning systems have been able to solve these kinds of problems in simulated worlds. One key difference between the real world and these simulated worlds is that all the needed information is already provided in symbolic form - no reification is required.

The planning and execution system is based on a simple observe – orient – decide – act loop[15]. In the observe phase, the robot uses its sensor to detect the state of the world, and the Reification Engine maps these data into a symbolic representation. The second stage of the loop is to orient – to place the state of the world into a context based on the goals and intentions of the robot. This is accomplished by using the semantic memory and goal states to extract a salient subset of the robot's knowledge and focus attention on the salient features. The decide phase is accomplished by using the deliberative system to generate and evaluate possible actions that might be used to achieve the robots goals. Finally, a decision is made and a plan of action is put into effect. This plan includes both what to do, and what to expect as as result of each action. This information is translated by the Reification Engine into sensor-specific expectations to enable monitoring by the Perception/Action system. This closes the loop, and the process of observing the results of the actions begins

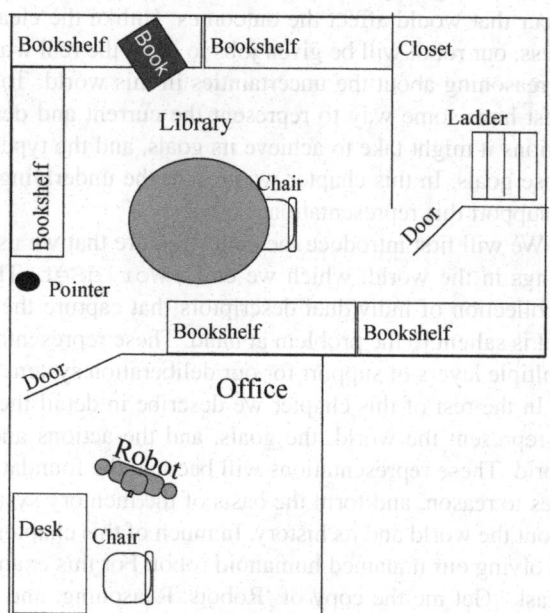

Fig. 4.1 The robot is given the task "Get me the book from the top of the bookcase." The book is out of reach, so the deliberative system must formulate a plan to reach the book. While this is beyond the capabilities of most autonomous robotics systems, the deliberative systems necessary to solve this kind of problem have been available for over half a century.

the cycle anew. All of this depends on having a effective way to represent the world, the goals, and the actions and events that can change then world. In the following text, we will explore the representation of the state of the world.

If our robot is going to solve this problem, it must be able to sense the world to assess the current situation. The robot relies on semantic memory to provide context for the goals and it relies on the `Reification Engine` to provide a symbolic representation of the current situation to orient itself. Beyond representing the state of the world, the robot must also represent the changes that can occur in the world, both those changes that the robot causes and the changes that occur beyond the actions of the robot. The effect of executing these actions in the real world must be modeled in the representation of the world as well. The format and mechanism of representing these actions is discussed in Section 4.3 below.

4.1 Representing Features of the World

There are several approaches to representing the state of the world. One of the easiest is to use the idea of a 'closed-world' assumption. In essence this states that anything that cannot be proved true, can be assumed to be false. Under this assumption the world can be represented as a collection of propositions, and, using the machinery of Boolean logic, theorems can be proved about the world. For example, in the example world described above, the door between the office and the Library can be represented as (Door, open) if the door is open. If this proposition is not present, then the system assumes that the door is not open, or closed. Alternatively, one might explicitly state that the door is closed by removing the proposition (Door, open) and replacing it with the proposition (Door, closed). If the door can be locked or unlocked as well as open or closed, the machinery needed to maintain consistency starts to get complex. and these complexities arise from simply trying to represent a static, deterministic world.

However, given the uncertain and non-deterministic nature of the world, this representation scheme has further problems. Some things that may be true at one moment may become false later. It is also difficult to represent the lack of knowledge that a robot must deal with, since there is no way to say "I don't know." The notion of boolean logic has been extended by many researchers using techniques such as continuous valued logic[57, 208] (the truth of a statement is a real number between 0 and 1), and three–valued logic where a proposition can be true, false, or unspecified.

Our representation uses a multi-state logic system in which the features that describe the things in the world can take on numerous values. Each feature has a name and a range of specified values that the feature can take on. Each feature also has an explicit representation of the "I don't know" state. This is critical in a world where the robot can not see through walls, and where the state of things might change over time. For example, in the case of the door we can explicitly represent the possible states of the door as being the set

Door : {Open,

```
HalfOpen,
Closed - Unlocked,
Closed - Locked,
DontKnow}
```

and any other possible states, provided that they are mutually exclusive. This allows
the robot to utilize a rich representation set, without requiring a large computational
overhead to check for inconsistencies.

The representation models the state of the world by defining a (Feature,Value)
pair, such as (Door, HalfOpen) to represent the door between the office and the
library in Figure 4.1. By defining the set of features and objects in the world, the
deliberation system can create a representation of the problem space as it currently
exists, and a representation of the goal state that it is attempting to achieve. By
utilizing the model of the world, it can record the state of the door even when it is
not actually looking at the door, and can represent the things that it does not know
by utilizing the DontKnow state.

Each Feature–Value pair represents the state of one aspect of the world at a specific point in time. The entire state of the world can be represented by a collection
of Feature–Value pairs, one for every salient aspect of the world. This collection is
called a WorldSet. The WorldSetcan be visualized as a list of Feature–Value
pairs that specify the state of each Feature that is salient to the problem at hand. If
the state of a feature is not salient the corresponding Feature–Value pair is simply
not included in the list. For example, the orientation of the Pointer in the Library
example might be upright or horizontal but if it is not salient to getting
the book, it can be left out of the WorldSet. Of course, if the pointer becomes
useful to solving the problem, perhaps by using it to push the book off the top of
the bookcase, the Feature–Value pair (PointerOrientation, Vertical)
can be added to the WorldSet.

4.2 Representing Goals

The model that is used to represent the current state of the world can be used directly
to represent future or alternate states of the world. This includes representing a desired state that the system wishes to achieve. By using a state based representation
of goals, we gain several powerful advantages. Since both current state and goals
states are built from the same type, or class, of representation it becomes possible
to do direct comparisons of the differences between the world as it exists and the
world as it is desired to be. This allows the extraction of the set of features that
need to be changed in order to transform the world to meet the goals, and it allows
the deliberative system to not expend computational resources on what does not
have to change. In Chapter 10 a number of specific comparative operators are described, which can be used to compare existing and forecast WorldSets against
the WorldSet that represents the goal state of the system.

4.3 Representing Actions in the World

An action is something that changes the state of the world. If a door is closed, and the robot opens the door, this action will result in a physical change in the world, and there must be a way to represent this action in the internal representation of the world. In the real world, there are three significant components associated with an action: the conditions under which the action can be taken, the possible results of taking the action, and the likelihood associated with these results. To allow the deliberation system to reason about the world, it must also have representations of these three components.

4.3.1 Enabling Conditions

The physics of the real world make it impossible to close a door that is already closed; if a door is closed and locked, the door must be unlocked before it can be opened. These are physically imposed preconditions that determine if an action is possible, and they must be faithfully preserved in our representation of the actions. There are additional benefits to modeling these preconditions for the deliberation system. One of these is that we do not waste time and energy examining actions that we cannot apply to the given world. This reduces the amount of computation that our robot must undertake. We can represent these 'enabling' conditions by using the same world state representations that were described above. For example if we had an action such as OpenTheDoor we can say that the preconditions are that the door is either HalfOpen or Closed(Unlocked). In any worlds where these conditions are met, our robot can consider taking the action OpenTheDoor. The WorldSet representation can be used to capture the preconditions of any action. To do this, we deliberately overload the semantics of the DontKnow flag that is available for any feature in the world. When representing the current state of a feature, the flag meant that we did not know what the actual value was. When representing a precondition this same flag has the meaning of "I don't care." This means that the action does not depend on this particular feature being in a specific state. For example, if the action is to open the door, the color of the door has no bearing on whether the door can be opened. Brown doors open just as easily as blue doors. It is only necessary to include in the WorldSet those feature that can impact the ability to undertake an action, it is not necessary to list all the features which are irrelevant. This gives us a very parsimonious representation

4.3.2 Outcomes

Once we have the preconditions represented we will also need to represent the results (or outcomes) of taking the action. In the case of OpenTheDoor, clearly one outcome might be that the door is now open, and we would expect this outcome in the majority of cases. However, in the real world, nothing is certain. So there are other possibilities that can result. Our hand might slip off the knob, and the door would still be closed or the hinges might stick, leaving the door only half open, or, possibly, we might pull too hard and the door would swing open, hit the wall, and bounce shut again. Any of these are possibilities, and most of us have experienced all of them at one time or another. If our robot is to be functional in the real world, it, too, must be aware that these are possibilities, and take them into account. To represent these in the deliberation system we can utilize the WorldSet in a third way, we can use them to indicate what features in the world will change in what ways when an action is applied.

In this application of the WorldSet, we overload the DontKnow/DontCare flag to have a third meaning. When it is in an outcome, it means DontChange. Once again we have a very parsimonious structure, since the absence of a specific Feature-Value pair in a WorldSet means that this feature is unaffected by the action, and it will retain whatever value it had before the action occurred.

4.3.3 Representing Likelihoods

While we have the ability to represent different possible outcomes, we have yet to encode the relative frequency with which these outcomes occur. In the door opening example we specified four possible outcomes, two of which left us with the door still closed (the slipping hand and the rebound from the wall), one which left the door partially open (the sticking hinge), and one which accomplished our intended result of an open door. From personal experience, it is clear that these outcomes have different likelihoods. Perhaps ninety-nine percent of the time the door actually opens, and the remaining one percent one of the others occurs. If the robot is going to be able to function effectively, it must be able to reason about these likelihoods. In order to reason about them, there must be some representation of the relative frequency of the possible outcomes.

The traditional approach might be to exhaustively enumerate every possible outcome, and assign to each some empirical probability. This has the drawback of requiring our system to be more than human, since in the real world, no matter how many outcomes we enumerate, we will find some other possibility occurring, if we wait long enough. Not only is this enumeration effectively impossible, it is also extremely computationally expensive to reason about. Biological systems can not, and do not attempt to analyze every possible outcome of every possible action they might undertake. At best, they might consider one or two likely outcomes and then lump every other possibility into an ill specified "Or something else might happen." Our robot uses the same approach, by enumerating a few possible outcomes, and accepting that beyond these there is a possibility of something else going wrong.

Putting these three pieces together we can define the data structure of an Action within the representation. An Action consists of:

1. An identifier
2. A `WorldSet` that defines the necessary preconditions to enable the `Action`
3. A list of possible outcomes consisting of

   a. The likelihood of this outcome occurring
   b. A `WorldSet` defining what changes if the outcome occurs

4.4 Exogenous Events

As we have said before, the world is not a static place. While our robot is busy
planning and taking steps to achieve its goals, the world is changing. Other entities
are making changes to the state of the world to achieve their goals, and other, less
intentional events are affecting the world - doors swing shut, light bulbs burn out,
cars run out of gas. All of these events are outside the direct control of our robot,
yet they cannot be ignored during our deliberations.

Since the exogenous events are outside the control of our robot, the robot does
not know when these events will occur. If these events are caused by another agent,
the events occur when the other agent causes them to occur, and the robot has no real
way of modeling that process. Alternatively, if the events are non-intentional (e.g., if
the vacuum cleaner breaks a belt, it becomes impossible to vacuum the floor) there
is no effective way to model the complex physics that result in the event occurring.

As a result, we treat all these exogenous events the same, whether they are intentional acts by another entity or are less intentional events. These events cause
changes in the state of the world, exactly the same as an `Action` (defined above).
In the interests of parsimony, we use the same basic `Action` data structure to
represent exogenous events. While an `Event` typically has a single outcome, the
`Action` data structure can support this. The key difference between An `Action`
and an `Event` is that an `Action` is invoked by the intention of the actor, in this
case our robot, whereas an `Event` is triggered outside the control of our robot.

To capture this independent nature of the trigger, we represent an `Event` as a
Poisson distributed random variable. Thus the representation of the vacuum cleaner
belt breaking and disabling the vacuum cleaner has an estimated frequency of occurrence. Since the outcome section of an `Action` has an associated likelihood,
we relabel the likelihood of occurrence as the event frequency. In addition, some
`Events` have necessary enabling conditions, which are captured in the preconditions field of the `Event`.

Chapter 5
Perception/Action System

When one thinks of a robot, one typically envisions the physical manifestation of the robot. The focus is on the hardware that allows the robot to interact with the world. In this chapter we focus on the hardware: the physical chassis, the sensors, and the effectors - the components that allow the robot to change the world. These components as a group are called the Perception/Action system, since they provide the ability to perceive the world and act on it. Without this the system may be intelligent, it may be autonomous, it may be goal driven; but it is just software, not a robot. A classical example of the Perception/Action system of a robot is "Rosie the Robot" from the Hanna-Barbera cartoon series "the Jetsons." This robotic maid was capable of interacting with the environment to achieve the tasks assigned by the family, whether that was cleaning up, washing dishes, or walking the dog. For many people the vision of the future is incomplete without these human-like robotic servants, whether they are robotic maids or the robots made popular in the Star Wars movies. In all these cases, the vision of the robot is the chassis, the manipulators, and the sensors.

But, the robot is the chassis not the brain. If the system has no ability to reason symbolically, or even no ability to reify the sensed data into a symbolic form, it is considered a robot as long as it can move about and make changes to the environment . Thus, a insensate welding robot is a robot. A bomb disposal robot that simply relays images to the human operator and follows commands issued via a joystick is a robot. The Perception/Action system, the hardware that embodies the system and interacts with the world is what makes the robot a *robot*, not all the fancy reasoning that takes place invisibly, inside the system. In this chapter we discuss some of the theoretical aspects of the Perception/Action system. Then we explain how the theory is used by introducing two of the robots from our lab, Fred and Basil.

5.1 Robot as Perception/Action System

The Perception/Action system anchors one end of our schematic model of the complete robotics system (See Figure 5.1) since it is the interface between the robotic system and the outside world. The Perception/Action system of any robot can be viewed as three distinct subsystems:

1. The physical body, or chassis;
2. The perception subsystem; and,
3. The action subsystem.

Each of these subsystems is dependent on the others to some degree (for example the chassis normally is responsible for providing the power to the sensors and motors) yet each is responsible for providing different abilities to the robot as a whole.

The robot body provides the structural system that supports and powers the other subsystems. The perception subsystem includes sensors such as the eyes, the ears, the radio system, as well as systems for balance, motion, grip strength, and so forth. The action subsystem might include a wheeled base or legs for mobility, arms for manipulating objects in the world, additional appendages and devices for informational manipulation such as the voice, and radio transmission.

While these subsystems will vary considerably from one robot to another, each has a specific role to play if the robot is going to be able to achieve goals in the physical world. For example, many current teleoperated systems use a complete Perception/Action system, but rely on the reasoning and reification provided by the human at the other end of the control system.

Fig. 5.1 The Perception/Action system is the physically embodied aspect of the robot. It includes all the hardware necessary to sense the world, and to take the actions that will change the world. It must also provide protection for the electronic and mechanical components that enable the robot to reason, and provide power to all the subsystems that require power.

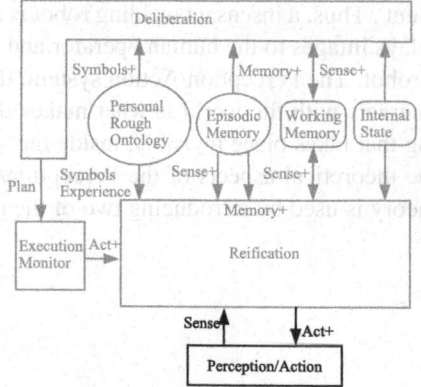

5.1.1 Robot as Body

The primary function of the body, or chassis, of the robot is to act as the support for the Perception/Action systems. The actual shape of the chassis will be driven by the tasks that the specific robot is intended to complete. It might be a generally humanoid shape, an aircraft, a surface ship or submersible, or any number of wheeled vehicles, traveling on any number of surfaces. Typically, the chassis of a robot is designed to meet several needs:

1. protection;
2. power;
3. structural support; and
4. mobility.

The function of protection ranges from simply shielding the electronic and mechanical systems from everyday damage from bumps, dust, and liquids to complete protection from hostile environments. Since the control components, the sensors, and motors are often designed to be enclosed in a relatively safe environment, the chassis provides that protection. For some robots this protection function is more extensive. Many robotic systems are employed in underwater exploration and research and for these robot chassis must protect the electronics from water under significant pressure. Consider the use of robotics systems by the National Aeronautics and Space Administration (NASA). These systems are deployed into extremely harsh environments and depend on the chassis for critical protection from heat, cold, radiation, as well as dust when deployed onto extraterrestrial surfaces. In these extreme environments, as well as in more mundane settings, the protections offered by the chassis are critical if the robot is going to get its work done.

At the other extreme are robots that are designed to be industrial machines. These chassis are often stripped down with little or no protection of the internal space. These robots provide structural support for the components, without impeding access. In an industrial setting, the costs associated with downtime can be significant and so for these chassis, the ability to access the hardware is more important than the protection provided by an external skin. This is also true for robot platforms that are designed as systems to test the robots themselves. The ability to rapidly modify the sensors, the effectors and so on is a primary design goal.

Beyond merely protecting the electronic and mechanical components, the chassis is typically responsible for providing power to enable these components to function. This can be a complex task in itself, since many robotics systems utilize combinations of electrical, hydraulic, and pneumatic power, which may be provided by battery storage, fuel cells, internal combustion engines, or even biological sources[111]. Even in a simple, all electric powered system there are potential problems. Electric motors can create large levels of noise on the power bus, noise that can disrupt the sensors, and can cause problems with the microprocessors that are controlling the robot. Even when these issues are addressed, there is a limit to the total available energy, and the power available at any one time. NASA has developed complex artificial intelligence solutions to solve the problems of load balancing, and task scheduling on spacecraft[179] - problems driven by the limited power available on these platforms.

To enable the robot to sense and act, the chassis must also provide structural support for the sensors and actuators. The required support varies greatly from one robot to another, again driven by the tasks that the robot must complete. It is also dependent on the nature of the sensors and actuators. A simple sonar mounted to the chassis may require little structural stability beyond that which is required to protect the electronics inside the body; however, a complex pan-tilt mechanism that is holding a 10 kilogram laser scanner may require significant structural support to preserve the accuracy of the scanning while traversing across a grassy field. The need for structure is at least as significant when actuators are involved. If the task of the robot is to carry a load, or to extend an arm and pick up a heavy object, the physical forces involved can require a correspondingly strong and well balanced structural system.

Finally, many robots outside the factory floor are mobile. To achieve their assigned tasks they must be able to move about the workspace. This can be as easy as rolling from one office to another in a modern building, to having to navigate up and down stairs that have been designed for humans, to traversing across a rocky field on Mars.

5.1.2 Robot as Sensor

Regardless of the domain and the tasks, if a robot is going to take deliberative action to achieve a goal it must be able to sense the state of the domain. At the most basic levels, if it cannot sense the state of the world, it cannot determine which, if any, goals have not been achieved. As a result, the two most common models for deliberate behavior: the Sense - Plan - Act model, and the Observe - Orient - Decide - Act (OODA) model, place a sensory stage at the beginning of the loop.

The nature of the sensing is task dependent. A robot that is responsible for delivering mail in an office setting, must be able to detect that it has mail to be delivered, sense to whom the mail must go, and perceive any potential obstacles along the route to the recipient[10]. However, a robot that is given the task of deploying a sensor package to an underwater thermal vent needs very different sensors to localize itself, detect the heat of the vent, and adjust and maintain its orientation and position in the face of underwater currents[11, 112, 126]. Regardless of the task and the domain, before the robot can reason about how to achieve its goals, it must be capable of sensing the salient aspects of its environment.

As we have indicated above, it is not sufficient to simply sense the environment. The sensors are the first stage in a complex path that leads from raw sensory data to a collection of reified symbols that are embedded in a context. It is this symbolic representation that a goal directed deliberative system (whether biological or cybernetic) reasons about. It is the responsibility of the Perception/Action system to gather the raw materials from which this symbolic representation will be built.

5.1.3 Robot as Agent of Change

Finally we have the most immediate of the roles - the robot must do things. Ultimately, unless the robot can make changes to the world - unless the robot can undertake actions, it is not a robot. There are many models of how entities interact with the world, but they must interact. Both the Sense - Plan -Act model and the OODA[15] loop, end in the same stage: Act. This is the most visible attribute of deliberative behavior. We, as humans, make many of our assessments of intelligence, intentionality, and goal directed behavior by the actions taken by the entity. Indeed if the entity does not act, it is unclear how it can be considered to have achieved its goals. In this section we focus on what the action portion of a Perception/Action system must include, and how these capabilities must also be represented in the reasoning on the robot.

5.1.3.1 Mobile and Autonomous

In many ways the utility of any robot is determined by the ways in which it can affect the world in which it is deployed. Since the early 1950's research laboratories around the world have had robots wandering the hallways. These robots were typically small wheeled systems that could maneuver on flat indoor surfaces such as the floors of hallways and rooms. Unfortunately, their utility was limited since they could do little more than wander around. While these robots could often be directed to go to a specific place, there was little or nothing that the robot could do once it got there. As late as 1997 one of the premier robotics research centers reported on their robot Xavier, which functions as an office delivery robot, and described the functionality as:

> A basic function of office delivery robots is to satisfy requests of the form "Go to X, then go to Y." When the robots arrive at location X, an item, such as a document, is given to them, which is then removed when they arrive at location Y[186]. (Introduction)

Since Xavier has no arms, this is potentially misleading. The only action that this robot can take in the world is to move. Great innovation has been applied to the question "If all the robot can do is go from place to place, how do we make it useful?" Some of the solutions have been:

1. Robot as service robot (delivery, messenger, etc.);
2. Robot as mobile sensor platform - used for security[135], chemical/biological survey, cartography, exploration;
3. Robot as mobile joke teller, a web based demonstration project; and,
4. Robot as toy.

In general the model is still "Go to X, do something, go to Y". Many attempts have been made to commercialize these autonomous robots, and there have been some successes[181]. While in some areas, such as mapping of biological and chemical data in undersea applications[174] the robots are of significant value, the most successful deployments of mobile autonomous robots have been in the last category listed: toys. There are literally thousands of robotic toys available, all with the same problem. While they have Perception/Action systems that can navigate and they have sounds and lights, they simply do not do much. Contrast this with the immense strides that have been made in industrial, factory, and laboratory automation.

5.1.3.2 Industrial Automation

There are many robots that have manipulators, and other end effectors for changing the environment, however many of these robots are not mobile. Industrial robots, factory and laboratory automation robots and others have very precise tools to change the world, but they often need to be in tightly controlled environments. Each action is carefully programmed, and each object which is affected (such as a automobile body being welded) is precisely positioned. This is due, in part, to the fact that this type of precise, repetitive action is exactly what is most efficient in a production setting, but it is also due to the inability of the robots to effectively make sense of the world that they are operating in. As a result, any deviation from the precisely scripted actions can be disastrous. People are kept carefully out of the range of the robotic manipulators.

Industrial robotics utilizes the Perception/Action system as the front end for a very tightly controlled machine that performs the programmed manipulations of the environment. Many of these robots utilize little, if any, direct sensing of the environment. The parts that they are working on are very precisely placed into well defined positions, and the actions that are performed have been carefully programmed in advance. See "The Handbook of Industrial Robots"[148] for an overview. The robots have very little discretion in what they do, other that a rudimentary level of failure detection. There has been recent work in using networks of external sensors to detect and address unpredicted motion in grippers in industrial workcells[203], but this is still in the research stage.

5.1.3.3 Teleoperated Robots

Another class of successful robots that also have complex and useful manipulators are the teleoperated robots. These systems utilize the abilities of the human in the loop to understand what the cameras are showing, and to control the manipulators to achieve the changes to the world.

Referring back to Figure 5.1, in a pure teleoperated system all of the functionality that is outside the Perception/Action system (the grayed out portion of the diagram) is provided by the human operator. The robot is nothing more than an end effector for the operator. One of the problems experienced by pure teleoperated robots is the lag between the robot and the operator. Also, the operator of a teleoperated robot can quickly become overloaded with the details of manipulating the robot and maintaining a good situational awareness. This has resulted in the incorporation of low-level intelligence into the robot to act much like reflexes in a biological system. For example, NASA's Sojourner vehicle deployed on Mars during the 1997 Mars Pathfinder mission was primarily a remotely operated vehicle. The robot would send current sensor data to the ground station, and the operators would develop a sequence of operations that would move the robot a short distance, or position an instrument and collect data. This plan would be uploaded to the robot, and it would be executed. However, a few on-board sensors and safety routines monitored the execution and were capable of interrupting the planned sequence. This increase in local control within the primarily teleoperated robotic platform has been driven by growing mission duration needs (such as within the Predator unmanned aerial vehicle[157]), and increased mission complexity.

5.1.4 Low Level Control Loop - Procedural Memory

The Perception/Action system is more than a set of sensors and a collection of effectors. To support reflex-like behaviors and the execution of simple preprogrammed responses (equivalent to the 'muscle-memory' or *motor learning* of a trained athlete, there must be a low-level control loop. This control loop would correspond to the control functions supplied by the reflex arcs in the somatic nervous system and in the metencephalon of the CNS[36].

This control loop allows the Perception/Action system to respond immediately when specific sensory triggers are detected, without having to pass information through the reification process to the deliberative system. This pathway is shown in Figure 5.2.

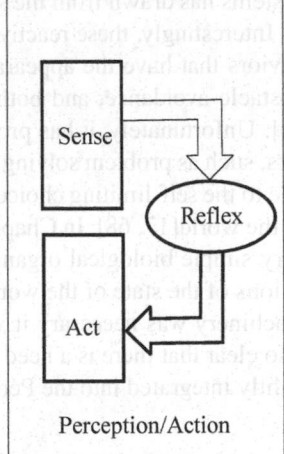

Fig. 5.2 The internal structure of the Perception/Action subsystem includes the mechanisms for sensing the world and for manipulating the world to achieve goals. In addition, it also contains a low-level control loop that functions analogously to the reflex mechanisms of biological systems.

This reflex arc is embedded in the Perception/Action system for a number of reasons. First, in biological systems reflexes are non-conscious actions that are effectively hardwired. They are typically associated with mechanisms that directly increase the survival of the organism, either by reacting to dangerous situations or be increasing the ability to acquire food. As most graduates of high school biology class remember, frogs and amphibians show reflex activity even when their brains have been removed. Anyone who has visited the doctor's office and been struck on the knee with that little hammer has also experienced non-conscious reflexes first hand. The reflexes are often responses to painful stimulus. The way in which these reflexes are constructed in robots is discussed below.

5.1.4.1 Reflexes and Reactive Systems

In biological systems numerous reflex arcs are external to the CNS. These control loops are located close to the sensory organs and muscles to reduce the time lag between the detection of a critical signal and the execution of the reaction. This corresponds in many ways to a purely reactive system in the robotics literature. Originally proposed by Brooks[20], the concept of a reactive system is driven in large part by the computational complexity of maintaining a detailed and current model of the world. The core concept was "Intelligence without Representation[22]."

Rather than maintaining a complex model of the world, the idea is to use the world as its own model. Use direct sensing of the environment to trigger specific behaviors that would achieve the systems goals. In addition, it is possible to use additional sensory data to inhibit some behaviors, while enabling others. In this way, it was felt, complex networks of inhibitory and excitatory interactions would be capable of producing complex, intelligent behaviors. For an overview of reactive systems, see Behavior Based Robotics, especially[3]. Much of the work in reactive systems has drawn from the same biological research that has driven our research.

Interestingly, these reactive system based robots can, rather quickly, achieve behaviors that have the appearance of living systems. Behaviors such as navigation, obstacle avoidance, and both foraging and predation have been demonstrated[13, 74]. Unfortunately, it has proved difficult to demonstrate more deliberative behaviors, such as problem solving and complex goal satisfaction. In part this seems to be due to the self-limiting choice of not maintaining a complex, representational model of the world[17, 68]. In Chapter 3, we presented data to support the notion that even very simple biological organisms do in fact maintain relatively complex representations of the state of the world, and we argued that unless this expensive cognitive machinery was necessary it would not be evolutionarily conserved. However, it is also clear that there is a need for systems to have these low-level reactive behaviors tightly integrated into the Perception/Action systems.

5.1.5 System Safety and Routine Actions

In deployed robotic systems, the use of safety critical reflex circuits has been seen in systems such as the Sojourner Rover deployed on Mars. In this robotic system (primarily a teleoperated device) several safety reflex circuits were employed. These included a tilt sensor that measured the angle of the rover body with respect to the gravitational field. In at least one programmed action sequence, the tilt sensor detected an excessive angle, and shut down the drive systems before the rover flipped. This reflex circuit was beyond the control of the operators on Earth, and prevented a fatal error. The use of these reflex circuits in the Perception/Action systems of deployed robots has proved its worth, and is included in most future designs[99].

An additional safety function that is commonly incorporated into the Perception/Action system is obstacle and collision avoidance. These reflexes depend on directly monitoring the sensory systems for indications of potential or impending collisions. At the simplest, touch sensors and/or proximity sensors can be monitored and the drive systems can be immediately shutdown upon a detected collision. This type of reflex requires no real deliberation, nor does it require a world model. These can be extended into systems that detect a void (often called a 'negative obstacle') such as the drop-off associated with a curb, or, for many robotic toys, the edge of a table. When a drop-off is detected, the system can rapidly steer away from the drop-off, or back away. These types of reflex arcs clearly mimic the reflexive behavior of jerking one's hand away from a hot surface.

In addition to the use of reflex arcs for system safety, it is also common to reduce the cognitive load on the operators of teleoperated robots by incorporating control loops for routine operations into the Perception/Action system. For example many unmanned aerial vehicles (UAVs) have control systems for maintaining altitude and heading (autopilot), controls for flying a preprogrammed circuit around a specific location[2] (loiter), or automated takeoff and landing[170]. In addition some sensors such as video cameras can have automated target tracking controls[199], which will pan and tilt the camera to keep a designated object in the field of view. Just as with biological systems, the line between reflex and deliberative action is determined not by the complexity of the task, but by the volitional nature of the activity. Many biological organisms have complex activity sequences that are non-volitional, and exhibit some very simple actions that are not reflexive.

5.2 Examples of Perception/Action Systems

5.2.1 Fred - a simple test robot

Fred is a simple wheeled robot that is designed for indoor tasks such as delivering objects or patrolling areas. The chassis has two co-axial drive wheels, with non-driven casters to provide support. The primary controller for the chassis is a Javelin chip from Parallax Corporation, running their subset of the Java programming language.

The chassis is open, and provides little or no protection from the environment. This is primarily due the the use of the robot as a test and development system. Having easy access to the internal components simplifies the task of modifying the hardware. However, since Fred is designed to only function in a controlled test environment, there is less of a need to provide protection from the environment.

5.2.1.1 Power

Fred is powered by a single 7.5 amp-hour 12V battery, with internal power buses providing 5V lines for sensors and micro-controller power. The primary battery provides unconditioned 12V power to the drive motors, and supplies power to a conditioned 5V power supply shared by the sensors. The hardware for the cortical stack on Fred has an internal voltage regulator and line conditioner to handle line noise from the drive motors.

5.2.1.2 Drive

The drive system for Fred consists of two co-axial drive wheels. These are roughly placed under the center of mass of the entire robot, and there are two non-drive casters arranged perpendicular to the drive axis. These casters provide support when the robot chassis is at rest, or when transient forces (due to acceleration and decelera-

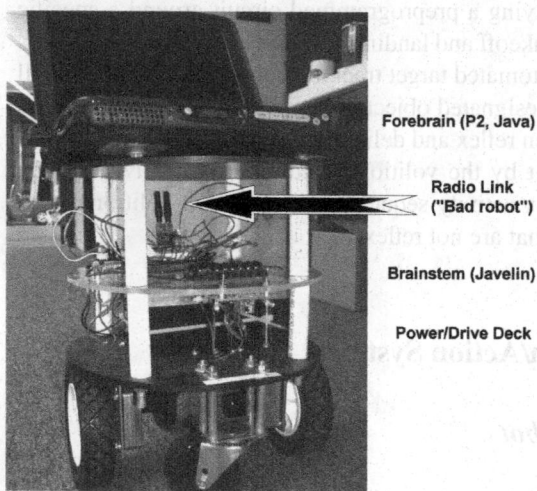

Forebrain (P2, Java)

Radio Link
("Bad robot")

Brainstem (Javelin)

Power/Drive Deck

Fig. 5.3 Fred is a simple indoor service robot.

tion) affect the balance point. The system is not self balancing, so generally one of the two casters provides the third point of support for the chassis.

The drive wheels are coupled to reduction gear boxes which are driven by independent 12V motors. These provide ample power for moving the chassis across floors, and up and down inclines. There is no capability for traveling up or down stairs, or over rough terrain. The robot is capable of transiting across typical indoor discontinuities, such as the transition from carpet to hard floors.

5.2.1.3 Sensors

Fred has a number of active infra-red ranging sensors for close-in sensing, and has a set of short range ultrasonic ranging modules for obstacle detection. The close-in sensors are monitored by the main control board, to reduce the response time when detecting obstacles. The ultrasonic sensors are controlled by in independent sensor board.

The close-in infra-red ranging sensors are IRODS from HVW Technologies. They have an effective range of 10cm - 80cm They are based on the Sharp GP2D05 sensors. The field of view for the sensors is approximately 10cm at 50cm range, or approximately 10 deg. They are mounted vertically to provide coverage from approximately 5cm above the floor to about 15cm above the floor. They are primarily intended to provide coverage directly in front of the drive wheels. These sensors provide the detailed detection of obstacles immediately in front of, and to the sides of, the robot chassis.

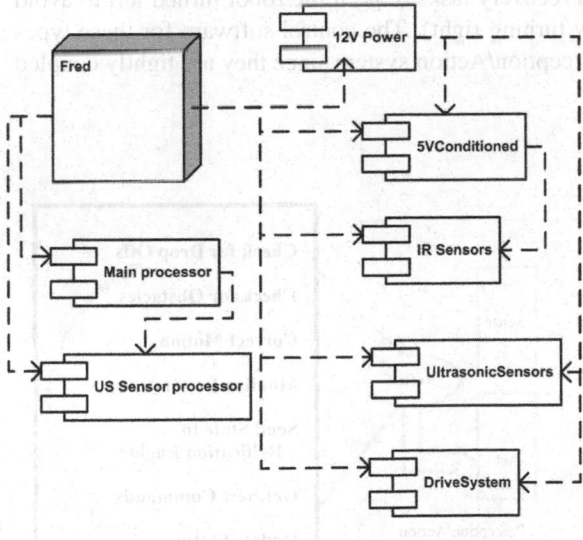

Fig. 5.4 A UML style deployment diagram of the primary sub-systems of the physical components of the robot.

5.2.1.4 Effectors

At present, Fred has no actuators other than simple movement. Figure 5.4 shows an overview of the hardware components that make up the Perception/Action system of Fred. We use a UML style representation to show the hardware dependencies between the components.

5.2.1.5 Control

Control for the Perception/Action sub-system in Fred is primarily focused on four aspects:

1. Safety;
2. Homeostasis;
3. Health; and,
4. Communication.

The safety aspect is designed to respond to the close-in IR sensors, and stop the robot before it hits any obstacles. This is a tight sense-react loop that runs directly in the drive motor control software. The IR sensors are also used to detect sudden drop offs in front of the drive wheels, and so prevent the robot from falling down stairs.

The homeostasis aspect is designed to implement procedural memory, and simple tasks such as maintaining speed. Procedural memory is the repository of simple action sequences, such as turning, accelerations, etc.)The procedural memory includes obstacle avoidance and recovery tasks (e.g., it the robot turned left to avoid an obstacle, it must correct by turning right). The control software for these types of tasks are loaded into the Perception/Action system since they are tightly coupled with the motor control.

Fig. 5.5 The control flow for the Perception/Action sub-system of the robot called Fred. The core of this low-level loop is: 1) check for conditions that threaten the robot (Drop offs, Obstacles), 2) maintain the current intended behavior (correct motion), 3) monitor slowly changing states (battery), 4) pass the current enteroception and proprioception data to the Reification Engine, and 5) integrate new command into the current status.

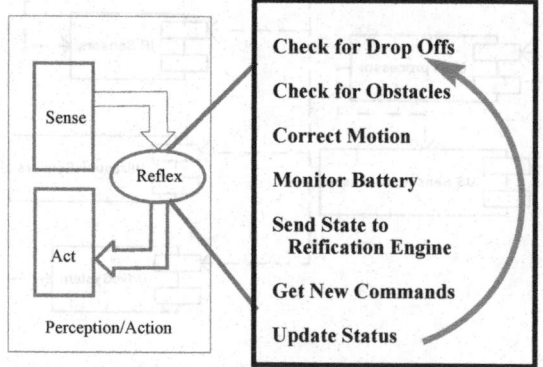

The health aspect of the control software handles issues such as monitoring battery state, and confirming connectivity within the internal hardware of the Perception/Action sub-system.

The Communications aspect provides two way communications with the reification and deliberative systems of the robot. This communication includes receiving new commands and sending current state information.

Fred is a traditional "trash can" robot, functionally equivalent to thousands of other roughly cylindrical robots roaming the hallways in laboratories around the world. Any design that claims to be general purpose must be capable of functioning on this class of robotic hardware. If the same basic control structures can also be applied to other robot chassis designs, then there is some merit to a claim of generality.

5.2.2 Basil

Basil is designed to be an indoor service robot. His primary function is to offer food and drinks at parties, interact with the people, and to deliver small packages. The environments in which Basil must operate are often crowded and are very dynamic. The robot must be able to address changing layouts, obstacles such as tables and chairs that are frequently moved, and avoid bumping into people that are moving through the space. This places different demands on most of the systems than the demands on a simple test robot such as Fred.

5.2.2.1 Power and Drive

In the areas of power and drive systems, there are few differences between Basil and Fred, other than increased battery capacity, and a chassis that has been increased in

Fig. 5.6 Basil is a simple indoor service robot. His exterior is enclosed to protect the electronics against spills, and accidental impacts, since he is designed to work in and around humans. He also utilizes a sonar based sensory system that allows him to build images similar to that provided by LIDAR.

strength. One obvious difference is that Basil's chassis is enclosed. Unlike a test robot, Basil requires significant protection from the outside world. One of his tasks it to serve food and drinks, which requires that the outer skin of the robot be waterproof, and that there are no easy routes for debris to enter the interior.

In addition, the chassis must be structurally sound. The upper surface of the robot must be capable of supporting the payloads that are required. These payloads (trays of food, drinks, or (in the case of the photo in Figure 5.6 the tea pot, cups, and the associated supplies and equipment) range from a few hundred grams to several kilograms.

Basil is a tapered octagonal column approximately 1m tall, and the top surface is approximately 400mm from face to face. His drive system is aligned so that one face of the octagon is forward, this face provides support for the primary sensors. Each of the side panels provides protection to the interior of the robot chassis, and so the side panels also provide a structural component. These panels must be able to withstand the occasional bumps and impacts that are normal in a crowded dynamic environment. These panels are thin fiberboard, laminated to semi-rigid anodized aluminum skin. The resulting surface is waterproof, impact resistant, and looks pretty good.

5.2.2.2 Sensors

Basil uses an array of short range sonars to build an image of the surrounding obstacles. While the resolution of these sensors is low, the ability to reify the raw sonar data into semantic information allows the robot to function effectively. This process is discussed in more detail in Chapter 7 and the comparative performance is demonstrated in Chapter 12

The ultrasonic sensors are Parallax "Ping)))" sensors. These provide the general coverage for obstacle detection. Their effective range is 0.02m to approximately 3m, with an in-plane field of view of approximately 15 degrees. The sensors are arrayed across the forward surface of the robot.

5.2.2.3 Effectors

Much like the simple test robot, the only effector that Basil has is its ability to move itself and its payload from one point to another. However, for the design goals of this robot, that is sufficient.

5.2.2.4 Control

Control for the Perception/Action sub-system in Basil is primarily focused of four aspects:

1. Safety;
2. Proprioception;

3. Health; and
4. Communication.

The safety aspect is focused primarily on two things, not running into anything, and not spilling anything. On the surface these appear to be fairly simple goals. In the vacuous case Basil can achieve both of these by simply not moving, but that option is not viable if the robot is going to achieve its goals. To avoid running into anything, Basil has a relatively tight control loop that uses the sonars to build a simple map of the nearest obstacles. This map is always monitored by the Perception/Action system and in the case of an impending impact, the drive system is controlled by a reflex loop that stops the robot, and finds a clear path to travel. This low level control loop is not sophisticated enough to avoid moving objects which will impact the robot. This process requires the involvement of higher functions from the deliberative system.

The second safety aspect is to avoid spilling drinks. To handle this aspect, Basil is equipped with a drive control loop which moderates the acceleration of the drive motors, an avoids rapid changes in direction. This is accomplished by low level monitoring of the desired and actual velocities of the wheels, and performs a feedback control system to adjust the velocities. This system is not under the control of the deliberative system, or the `Execution Monitor`; it functions independently of these higher level systems.

The proprioception system focuses on maintaining a representation of the current state of the robot, with respect to the outside world. It primarily maintains an estimate of the velocity of the robot, and the direction that the robot is facing. These are maintained using directly available information, since the Perception/Action system has control of the drive motors, and is directly controlling the steering commands. Unlike many other systems, there is not a direct estimate of robot position. This estimate is maintained by the upper level control system, specifically the `Reification Engine`.

The Health aspect is quite limited in this robot. There is a basic monitoring of the battery state, but there are no sensors for tilt. In fact, Basil is, at present, almost devoid of internal sensors of any kind. Rather, the robot depends on its ability to reason about the world to avoid situations that might damage the robot.

From Figure 5.7 it is apparent that Basil might be susceptible to tipping over; especially with a significant payload. It should also be evident that if Basil were to tip, it would be impossible for the robot to right itself. This is not a problem for most biological entities (yes, even turtles and tortoises can right themselves, given enough time) because being unable to right oneself is not a survival characteristic. However, it is also clear that most biological systems solve the problem by avoiding situations in which they might be tipped over. Basil also relies on the ability to predict conditions in which tipping has a higher probability, and the deliberative system avoids putting the robot into those conditions.

5.3 Summary of Perception/Action Systems

The Perception/Action system is the physical manifestation of the robot. It is what makes the robot a *robot* and not just a computer. We presented a rough taxonomy of types of robotic systems. This taxonomy includes the large group of teleoperated robots, such as bomb-disposal robots, and unmanned air vehicles; it also includes the very tightly controlled laboratory and factory automation systems. It seems that (at present) robots can be mobile and autonomous, but restricted to limited manipulation of the world; or they can be sessile and dexterous, active actors in a tightly controlled world; or they can be mobile and dexterous, but must rely on a human in the loop to provide the ability to understand the dynamic world, and provide detailed control to make changes. Our focus is not on any of these classes, rather it is on mobile, autonomous robots. By autonomous robots we mean that class of robots that can operate without a hand on the joystick, and that are free to change their behaviors in response to changes in the environment, or to alterations in their internal goals.

We examined the necessary functions that the Perception/Action system must provide to the rest of the systems, the functions of support, and power, of sensors and actuators. These are the interface between the cybernetic brain and the outside world, the sources of the information about the world, and the mechanisms that allow the robot to change the world in order to achieve its goals.

Fig. 5.7 Basil suffers from a narrow base, with an outward tapering chassis. In addition, while efforts have been made to keep a low center of gravity in the chassis itself, the nature of the service role frequently places significant mass on the top surface of the robot. This increases the risk of the robot tipping over. The lower deck includes the drive system and the batteries. The next level has the low-level controllers, on the level above this is the main computer. Each level also has the short range sonars. Several of the fascia panels have been removed to allow access to the interior.

Finally we looked at some concrete examples of instantiated robots. Fred is a robot that was designed as a laboratory test platform, and Basil, a robot that is designed to be turned loose in a crowded room, carrying food and drink to the guests. This latter robot body was presented in some detail since it will act as one of the running examples throughout the rest of the book.

These robots have more than just the mechanical manifestation of the robot chassis and sensors. They also include a cybernetic component that must be capable of reasoning about changes to the environment, and deliberately doing something to achieve the systems goals. This points out the very tight coupling that is inherent in designing an autonomous robot. As we will point out in more detail in later chapters, the 'brain' cannot be divorced from the 'brawn.' If the brain is to control the robot, the brain must have detailed knowledge about the physical capabilities of the Perception/Action system, its strengths and its weaknesses. There is also a tight coupling between the sensors that provide the information and the reasoning system that uses that information. This coupling is both necessary and problematic. In biological organisms this problem has been addressed by a common physiologic structure that is conserved across a wide range of creatures, effectively the entire terrestrial vertebrate line. This physiologic structure both isolates the brain, and it connects it very closely to the rest of the body. In the following chapters we focus on the 'brains' behind the physical robot.

Chapter 6
Design of a Reification Engine

In the previous chapters we have briefly explored the current state of robotics, and looked at the lessons that can be learned from living systems that do the types of things we want our robots to do. These lessons have suggested that there is a significant component missing from many robotics systems, and supplied by humans in other types of robots. This component must provide the mapping that enables the deliberative system to reason about the world in which the robot finds itself, and must translate the intended actions of that reasoning into behaviors that the robot can execute.

This chapter focuses on the design of a reification system for mobile robots. Among the design issues are:

1. how to implement a biologically inspired model?
2. what data structures need to be used to provide an interface between these fundamentally different representations? and,
3. what kinds of services must be provided by the Reification Engine to enable the robot to function effectively?

We begin with defining the criteria that will guide us in the process of making the design decisions that lead to the Reification Engine.

6.1 Model Selection Criteria

Once we have decided that reification is needed to build a cybernetic brain, then we must decide how to build it. There are many possible algorithmic solutions to the reification problem. These range from the biologically inspired population model of cognitive function described by Freeman and Kozma[70][117] to models derived from Kahneman and Tversky's prospect theory[109]. In order to build the model, one of these must be selected. The selection process is made easier by considering the characteristics that any candidate algorithm should have. In the following section we consider a few characteristics that are important to the reification process.

First, the algorithm must support the concept of the salience of features. For any recognition process there are a number of possible features in the environment that could be used. For example, for the recognition of a block in the environment, the algorithm needs to ignore such features as block color, room temperature, wall color, floor color, and sound level. Unfortunately, there are many, many features that could be observed, and (in most judgments) only a small number of these are salient. One might suggest that the robot be programmed to ignore the aspects that are not salient. Daniel Dennett expounds on this in his essay "Cognitive Wheels: The Frame Problem of AI," which contains a story about a robot that needs to retrieve a spare battery from a room containing a bomb. After several (explosive) failures due to not paying attention to enough, or to too much, the designers hit upon the idea of having it ignore the irrelevant:

> "We must teach it the difference between relevant implications and irrelevant implications," said the designers, "and teach it to ignore the irrelevant ones." So they developed a method of tagging implications as either relevant or irrelevant to the project at hand, and installed the method in their next model... When they subjected the [the robot] to the test ... They were surprised to see it sitting outside the room...
> "Do something!" they yelled at it. "I am," it retorted. "I'm busy ignoring some thousands of implications I have determined are irrelevant. Just as soon as I find an irrelevant implication, I put it on the list of those I must ignore, and..." the bomb went off.[49]

Just as Dennett's hypothetical robot found far to many implications that had to be ignored, our robot must have some effective way to only pay attention to those features that are salient to the judgment.

Hopefully, we have demonstrated that in order for the algorithm to make the mapping in less than infinite time, it needs to be able to select only the features required for the decision. These features are the salient set of features for that problem. Studies on humans and their ability to focus on multiple features at the same time has shown, that humans can only hold seven plus or minus two features in working memory at one time[130]. Rather than being considered a deficit when compared to the millions of things that a simple computer can keep in working memory, this may be an incredible strength. This limitation has forced living systems to effectively classify features as salient or not to the task at hand. To be biologically principled the chosen algorithm must include the concept of salience, and can not require the consideration of all of the features in the environment at all times.

Another closely related requirement is that the algorithm must be able to handle uncertainty and error. All observations of the environment are probabilistic by definition, so uncertainty is inevitable. In addition to uncertainty, the algorithm must be stable in the presence of error. In a real system, while error can be minimized, it can not be avoided.

The algorithm must also be reasonably fast. While additional processing time can (usually) reduce error and uncertainty, for a robotic system in the real world, it also adds a significant element of danger. Taking the time to reduce the uncertainty in the speed of the approaching car poses a real danger.

In the interest of parsimony, a desired property would be the ability to use the same mechanism in both recognition and preafference. Also, since we are emphasizing a biologically principled model, It would also be good if there was some reason to assume that the algorithm was analogous to that used in biological brains.

6.2 Judgment Analysis

A model that satisfies all of these requirements is judgment analysis. Judgment analysis is concerned with the ways in which humans make judgments in a probabilistic and changing world. This theory comes from the field of cognitive psychology and is based on the work of Egon Brunswik, who viewed the decision-maker as being embedded in an ecology from which he received cues as to the true state of things [25]. The main problem faced by all living creatures is the overloading of perceptual channels. In Brunswik's work, the decision maker makes judgments using a lens model [29]. The lens model simplifies the problem, by allowing the decision maker to assess which cues have high salience to the decision, and pay attention only to those cues. In general, there is too much going on, too quickly for the system to pay complete attention to every aspect, and every implication. The lens model proposes a mechanism that allows the system to discard that which is not salient. The mathematical formulation of the lens model is described below. However, Brunswik's work consisted not just of theory, but of a careful and detailed observation of human perception, both the physical and social domains. One of the major advantages of the use of judgment analysis for reification is that the researchers in this field have built and extended the lens model by this type of careful observation and analysis. Since the models have been built and tested on humans, there is at least a colorable argument that a reification model based on judgment analysis will be biologically principled.

> As was pointed out by the writer in greater detail elsewhere, any organism has to cope with an environment full of uncertainties. Forced to react quickly or within reasonable limits of time, it must respond before direct contact with the relevant remote conditions in the environment, such as foodstuffs or traps, friends or enemies, can be established. *Egon Brunswik*[27]

The *lens model* is shown in Figure 6.1. To discuss this model, let us consider the simple example of our humanoid robot estimating the distance to a child's building block lying on a table. In this model, the actual distance to the block is an environmental (distal) state variable (D). The observer has a series of observable (proximal) cues (x_i) relating to this distal variable, such as the size of the retinal representation of the block, the differences in the image in the right and left eyes, and the blurring of the image. These cues have a probabilistic correlation to the actual state, this is their *ecological validity*. In experiments on judgment tasks, the error has been shown to be approximately gaussian with a mean that approximates the "true" value [153][89]. The robot weights each of the cues with its specific weight (w_i) and uses a function of these weighted cues to make a judgment as to the true state (d). Because of the errors in the observation of the cues, the judgment also contains an error term. This set of cues and weights also has a correlation with the perfect cue and cue weight set, *cue utilization validity*. The relationship between the judgment and the correct value must then be defined as a statistical correlation, which Brunswik named *functional validity*. This can be used to update the weights placed on the cues in future judgment tasks[25][28]. This model was based on observation of natural perception and as such was designed to handle both uncertainty, salience, and speed.

Brunswik's initial model is described by the equation:

$$D = \sum_{i=1}^{n} w_i x_i + \varepsilon \qquad (6.1)$$

where: D is the environmental state variable
x_i is the raw value of the observed feature i
w_i is the weight applied to the feature i
ε_i is the error

This equation reduces to:

$$D = d + \varepsilon \qquad (6.2)$$

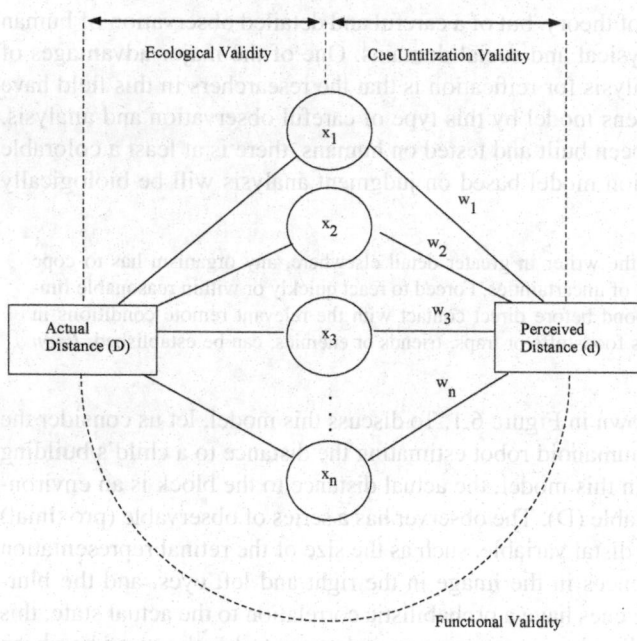

Fig. 6.1 Brunswik's Lens Model.

where: D is the environmental state variable
         d is the estimate of the environmental state variable
         ε_i is the error

In later work, the input to the lens model was extended past raw numbers. The lens model was extended to replace the raw observed value (x_i) with a function form $f(x_i)$ This function form may be linear, inversely linear, or non linear [190]. The input to the the lens model may also be categorical or probabilistic [37]. The outcome from one lens may also be used to form the cues for the next. This is called a hierarchical judgment decision and became the basis for social judgment theory (SJT) [91]. For the interested reader more information about Egon Brunswik and judgment analysis can be found in [88], [37] and [92].

Before we dive into the details involved in using the lens model to construct a Reification Engine, we need to consider the role of probability in judgment analysis. As mentioned above, ecological validity is the probabilistic relationship between the actual state of the observed object and the perceived state of the observed object. Functional validity is the organism's ability to use these observed cues to make a correct judgment as to the state of the observed objects [29]. This functional validity must be learned in a probabilistic way by each organism. Brunswik considered that there was a correlation between the state of the cues and the judgment of the observer [24]. Living organisms are not omniscient, there are many ways in which the cues and the real state of the world can be connected. Each organism uses its own assessment of the relevance of cues, based on the perceived success of judgments based on those cues over the course of its experience [28]. This means that it may not be obvious to an observer which cues in the environment are important to the decision maker and further, that the very form of the lens model may be different from observer to observer. An example of this difference can be found in the comparison of the judgments of criminals and householder with respect to security. In this study, criminals and householders were asked to assess the vulnerability of a house from a photograph. For some features, such as the presence of fences, they were in agreement. But, probably because of the different life experiences of the two groups, they disagreed on the importance of some cues. For example, 44% of the criminals used a "Beware of Dog" sign as a reason not to consider a house, while only 18% of the residents did. Criminals also rated the cue "House value" more highly than residents [184]. While we will address the process of teaching robots to learn in future work, clearly the learning loop must begin with the assessment of functional validity.

The relative lack of transparency and uniformity of the judgment process leads directly to the concept of representative design, which states that appropriate observations can only be made in the appropriate environment [25]. Observation of a robot in a laboratory may not tell you anything about the cues that robot will need to use on a busy street. In the case of training, any dog trainer or nanny can explain that humans (and dogs) respond to positive reinforcement. But, it not always clear to the trainer what behavior is being reinforced.

The giving of Latin before chocolate may result, not in the child's coming to love Latin, but merely in an unpleasant propensity to secrete saliva while studying Latin[196].

This means that training and testing must occur in an environment that is as close as possible to the environment that the robot will be deployed in. The reification process for a robot will be dependent on the environment it is to be deployed in, the sensors that it has, and the tasks it is to do. The reification process needed for the drink serving robot to determine a clump of humans to approach will be very different from the reification process for a security robot to determine the difference between a herd of deer and a group of humans.

Another problem is posed by the richness of the sensory environment. The recognition problem is, at its heart, a type of classification problem. Only some of the observable features will be relevant to the classification problem. While it may seem counterintuitive, the addition of additional features generally degrades the performance of classification algorithms [58]. The lens model deals with this problem by allowing the organism to, through trial and error, allow the weights of some of the features to approach zero. While this may seem like the organism is discarding potentially important information, the functional validity loop allows for correction of the weight, if the feature turns out to be important in judgment. This is no accident, as Brunswik states explicitly that the organism will always depend on overloaded channels of information [26].

6.3 Designing the Reification Engine

Based on the above, the use of a lens as the primary structure for reification meets the design criteria. So, now that we have decided on the type of model, what is needed is a design that can be implemented. In order to be biologically principled, this design needs to consider the brain. In order to construct this model, we will bring in another concept from neurology, that of the *percept*. A percept is the representation, in the brain, of something perceived by the senses. In fMRI studies, the creation and maintenance of percepts can be seen in the brains of human subjects[160]. For this model, the percept is an instantiation of a lens model. In order to differentiate between the percept in the brain and our creation in code, the software data structure will be called a PerCept. This PerCept will use raw sensory data to generate symbols in the recognition process, then the same PerCept will be used to create the expected sensory data from the symbol in the preafference process. While the technical details are reserved for the next chapter, it should be noted that the PerCept does not use an analytic solution, rather it uses a data driven process. This will allow the robot to learn new percepts, without having to construct an analytical form.

The recognition process is made easier, because the robot will not be recognizing objects in a vacuum. In general, even on suddenly awaking, organisms have some awareness of the state that the environment was in when they last saw it. This means that, while the position of some things may have changed, the position of stable objects such as walls, trees, and rocks, generally will not have changed [1] As will be described in 9.1.1.2 the permanence and mobility of objects in the environment is coded into the Personal Rough Ontology. This means that, when the robot is confronted with a chair, in a specific location, it knows that there was a chair in the room, if not in that specific place. It would start by using the PerCept of the objects that it would be most likely to find in that location. An unusual PerCept, such as the PerCept for *zebra*, is likely to get used late in the process, if at all.

The next question is, how are the percepts related? One evocative fact is that, in human brains, different types of damage can damage different types of visual perception. Depending on the nature of the trauma there may be damage to the perception of color, form, or motion[168]. This suggests that the processing of these different modalities of visual perception may be independent. However, at some point in the processing, these independent properties must be merged, since a healthy brain perceives objects with both color and shape. This set of facts suggests the following nested lens model design, which is shown in Figure 6.2. As with all of the other models in this text, this is intended to be a high level model, that is a very simplified sketch of brain function.

In this model, the sensorium of the external world is sensed through the Perception/Action module. Starting with recognition, let us say that our previously mentioned humanoid robot is looking at a dog. The different observations would be processed by the different lens models. So the form lens might go through a series of lenses and return a high possibility on *quadruped*. The color lens might also go

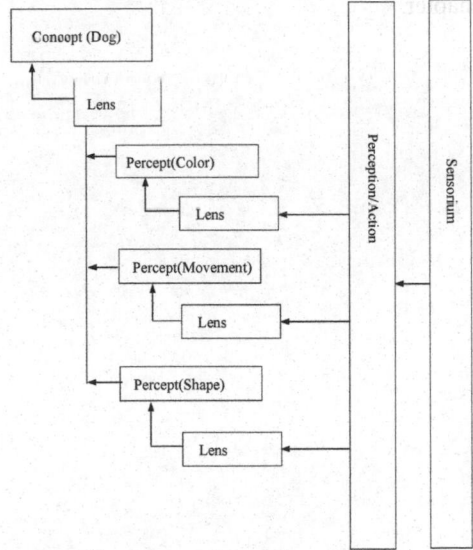

Fig. 6.2 In the nested lens model the data provided by the Perception/Action module is used by many independent lens models to judge the identity of the object. These PerCepts are then used in another lens model to determine the possibility of the objects being of the class of the concept.

---

[1] Certainly there are exceptions to this caused by tornadoes, tsunami, earthquakes, or sadistic roommates, but the very confusion shown by the victims shows how innately they expected the state of the world not to have changed as they slept.

through a series of lenses and return a high possibility on *brown*. The motion lens might return a high possibility on *fast*. These results and their probabilities would be stored as `PerCepts`. These `PerCepts` would then be available to a set of lens models that would finally result in a high possibility of the object being a dog. Possibly, if it was a Great Dane, there would be also be a high possibility on the class of horse. The results of this analysis would be stored as concepts. This would then give the robot access to additional information about the related concepts. This could be used to tell the difference between a large dog and a small horse.

Going to preafference, one of the most computationally expensive processes is making sense of sensor data. Research suggests that biological systems reduce the complexity of this task by pre-loading the appropriate sensory cortex with a low fidelity prediction of what the sensors should be detecting. In this way, the complex task of assigning meaning and correspondence to the data is simplified to one of matching the actual data with the expected data. If they agree sufficiently closely, the real world is assumed to be in the expected state. Needless to say, this process is failure prone, as optical illusions and sleight of hand magic effects remind us. However, in spite of the failure modes, it is apparently better for overall survival to quickly assess the state of the world. So, in this case the symbol *dog*, would have a percept with a set of lenses attached to it. For an abstract dog, they might be a large set of possible colors and sizes, but for a specific dog they would have both the percepts attached to dog, but also the smaller set of percepts related to the color and size of a specific dog. So the robot would, if it was expecting to see a specific dog, analyze the percepts related to that dog to answer the question, am I seeing the dog that I expect to see? The implementation details of this are described in the next chapter.

Chapter 7
Bridging the Sensor to Symbol Gap

In the introduction we presented a question, which has guided our research over the last several years. We observed that the state of deployed autonomous robots has been effectively static since the 1970's. At the same time, the deployment of teleoperated robotic systems (See Figure 7.1 for an example interface), such as remotely piloted aircraft, deep sea submersibles, and bomb disposal robots has seen extensive growth. This growth shows clearly that the hardware needed to support functional robots is available, but that the software to enable intelligent, autonomous operation is lacking. The question we asked was: "What is the human adding by looking at a low resolution display, and manipulating low precision joysticks that enables the robot to achieve the goals?"

We suggested that the role the human was filling was threefold. First, they translated the raw sensor data (in this case video images) into a semantic representation. Next, they reasoned about that semantic representation, and produced a symbolic plan that would achieve their goals. Finally, the human would translate the symbolic plan into expected sensory representations, and execute actions in the physical world to implement that plan. The middle step - the deliberative process of generating a symbolic solution to a symbolic problem has been demonstrated on computers since the early 1960's[64, 63, 67, 139]. It is the translation to and from the sensor domain that has been problematic.

In later chapters we will discuss the processes involved in reasoning about the symbolic representations of problems and the production of solutions. But, without the robot having the ability to turn the sensor data into symbolic representations, this deliberative process will have nothing to work on; and without the ability to translate the symbolic plans into sensor/effector based representation, the robot will be incapable of implementing the solutions. This bidirectional mapping is the core of reification.

7.1 Supporting Bidirectional Mapping

The mapping of sensor to symbol and back has been a focus of significant research over the last several decades. The ability to maintain the correspondence between the symbolic representations and their sensorium has been pursued from several different perspectives. It has long been a part of the discussion in philosophy[53, 54, 49], perception[25], cognitive science[168], and cybernetics[38, 182, 202].

There have been two general approaches to this problem. One begins with the symbols, and attempts to ground (or anchor) them in their sensorium and the other begins with the sensor data and builds more and more complex patterns from these, until the patterns have semantic value. The general consensus is that these two approaches would eventually overlap, and a complete solution would result. This is the traditional top-down versus bottom-up dialog. It has been pursued diligently, by very capable researchers for a very long time. However, in spite of the progress made, the predicted intersection of the two research paths has not occurred.

The general top-down approach suggests that since cognition involves the manipulation of symbols, one can build a dictionary of the necessary symbols. These symbols can be defined in terms of a collection of 'simpler' symbols, which in turn can be defined in terms of even simpler symbols. At some point, the symbols become so simple that they can be defined by direct sensory representations. A classic example would be reasoning about the manipulation of a "Red Block." The symbol *RED_BLOCK* can be decomposed into the intersection of the symbol *RED* and the symbol *BLOCK*. The symbol *RED* can be grounded in a direct sensory perception associated with a primary wavelength of light in some range around 650nm (nanometers). In a similar way the concept of *BLOCK* can be grounded in the array of visual or tactile representations that can be generated by a roughly rectilinear object with orthogonal faces.

The general bottom-up approach follows the reverse path, beginning with the recognition of the pattern generated by those roughly rectilinear orthogonal surfaces we can build up the symbol of a block, or cube. By building the sensory representa-

Fig. 7.1 In a teleoperated system, the human acts as a translator from the raw sensory images (provided by the video link) to a symbolic representation, and once a plan of action is determined, the operator translates that symbolic plan into a sensor/actuator based implementation using the joysticks and other controls. Shown here is one of the authors, using the teleoperation interface for a commercial robot.

tions of a range of reds, we can build support for the symbol *RED*. Then when we find a single object that is associated both of these sensory signatures, we can build up the composite symbol *RED_BLOCK*.

Steven Harnad presents the following conclusion in his paper on the symbol grounding problem:

> The expectation has often been voiced that "top-down" (symbolic) approaches to modeling cognition will somehow meet "bottom-up" (sensory) approaches somewhere in between. If the grounding considerations in this paper are valid, then this expectation is hopelessly modular and there is really only one viable route from sense to symbols: from the ground up. A free-floating symbolic level like the software level of a computer will never be reached by this route (or vice versa) – nor is it clear why we should even try to reach such a level, since it looks as if getting there would just amount to uprooting our symbols from their intrinsic meanings (thereby merely reducing ourselves to the functional equivalent of a programmable computer)[94].

In this conclusion, Harnad suggests that the reduction of the representations to a single, common structure is what limits the programmable computer. Biological systems, he suggests, are not so limited. Even relying on two representations (one from the top-down, and the other bottom-up, is significantly fewer than biological systems utilize. Ongoing research into cognition suggests that there several intervening mechanisms between the purely symbolic representation and the purely sensory based representations. Recent fMRI research has shown that there is not one single repository of neurological representations of concepts in the human brain. Rather there are as many as six spatially distinct representations for different aspects of a single visually presented object[197]. These representations include:

1. Object token - conscious viewpoint dependent representation;
2. Structural description - how it would look from other perspectives;
3. Object type - the class of the object (e.g. a chair);
4. Associated knowledge - the relationships with other concepts,
5. Emotional associations of the object; and
6. Affordances - the action-centered representation.

This suggests that there many different representations in use. Some are direct sensory components, others capture the general class-derived aspects, and the associated knowledge (what we reason about), and the knowledge associated with the actuators that can manipulate the object. These different representations are encoded into different structures within the biological brain, and we encode similar data structures into the cybernetic brain. The object token, structural description, and the affordances are maintained and manipulated by the `Reification Engine`, enabling it to function as the Sensor to Symbol bridge, while the Object Type, the Emotional Associations, and the Object Token are encoded into other portions of the cybernetic brain, just as they are spatially distinct in biological brains. Thus, our conclusions are based in the biological and neurophysiological data, but they are in accord with Harnad's.

7.1.1 A Third Approach

Rather than approaching the problem from either the top-down or bottom-up perspectives, we approach the problem from the middle out. The lens model described in the previous chapter is the guiding design. Brunswik's lens model suggests that there is a mechanism in the human brain that interprets the sensorium, evaluates the cues, and makes a judgment - assigns semantics to the data. This mechanism also must be capable of adjusting the weights on the cues based on experience. This capability is what we are looking for in the reification process. We can imagine the reification process as the middle component translating between the sensorium (Brunswik's 'cues') and the semantic representation (the judgment).

There is a tight coupling between the six distinct representations listed above. In the same manner there is a tight coupling between the representations used by the Reification Engine, and those used by the Perception/Action system, as well as those used by the Personal Rough Ontology (this is the mechanism that stores and manipulates the conceptual model of the world, and is described in Chapter 9). In Figure 7.2, we focus on the fact that there are several levels of representation, spanning from raw sensor data in the Perception/Action system, to the purely symbolic representations in the deliberative system, yet each of these representations may refer to the same object in the outside world. These representations are not embodied in the code of the various components of the brain, rather they are data. Biological brains utilize the same basic mechanisms, but apply these 'functions' to different data. Similarly, while the Reification Engine is general across robotic platforms, the representations that it manipulates are specific to a given platform; and even when they are on the same platform, the mission of the robot may change the underlying nature of the data as well.

7.2 Reification Architecture

To bridge from the symbolic domain into the sensor/actuator domain and back again, the Reification Engine must have one foot on each shore. The architecture of the Reification Engine is shown graphically in Figure 7.3. There are three main components in the Reification Engine. The core component is the library of PerCepts, which provide the grounding in the sensor domain. Recall that PerCept refers to the data structure, while percept is used slightly differently in cognitive science. Using these PerCepts, the Reification Engine maintains a model of the world, this Mental Model captures the sensor-derived knowledge about what things are out there, where they are, and how they are oriented. Finally, the Reification Engine manages a symbolic representation of the world. This Current World State is provided to the deliberative System, by way of the Personal Rough Ontology. The library of PerCepts capture the structural description of things in the world that are perceivable. In the following sections we will describe the PerCepts and their use. To simplify this description we will provide examples of PerCepts, drawn from one of the Perception/Action systems outlined earlier.

In Chapter 5 we described the hardware and sensors on Basil, the indoor service robot. In this section we will explore the Reification Engine as it is implemented on Basil, since that provides a good overview of the components that make up this critical aspect of the robot's brain. The customization of the Reification Engine to Basil is done by providing data that is specific to the chassis (the Perception/Action system) and the world that Basil inhabits (the Personal Rough Ontology and the system goals). The customization is not achieved by altering the software that makes up the Reification Engine. The architecture of the Reification Engine is constant across robots, only the 'knowledge' of the specific robot changes. We will focus on Basil's specifics only to illustrate the Reification Engine.

We use the term PerCept as our symbol for the representation of a perceived object. This is consistent with many of the working definitions. In our model a PerCept is the data structure used to hold the information associated with a perceived object. The PerCept has two components: a sensor derived signature that can be used to recognize the occurrence of the object, and a symbolic component that links to the semantic representation in the symbolic domain. In addition to these two data components, the PerCept provides some basic functionality to the Reification Engine. Each PerCept is associated with a single class of per-

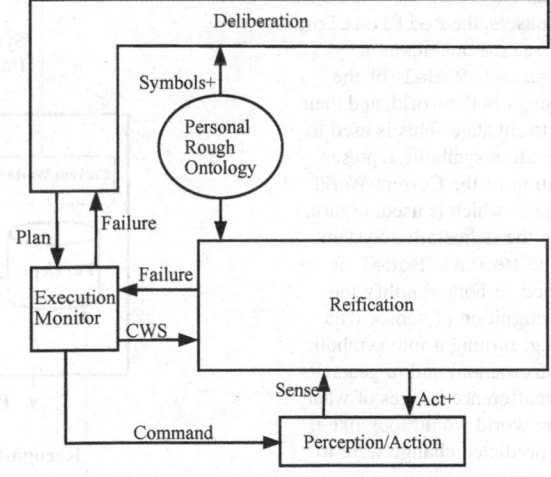

Fig. 7.2 The structure of the Reification Engine interaction with the Deliberative System, the Personal Rough Ontology, the Execution Monitor, and the Perception/Action System. Due to the tight coupling of these systems, and the central role played by the Reification Engine, the representations and services provided by this system are highly specific to the underlying sensors and actuator as well as the semantic representations needed by the deliberative system.

ceivable object. These `PerCepts` have a symbolic tag (think of it as a name) and the sensory definition of the object.

Imagine a chair. Many of us maintain a complex hierarchy of chair types in our minds. There are kitchen chairs, office chairs, recliners, chairs with wheels, chairs without backs, chairs with padded seats, chairs that creak ominously when we sit in them. There are specialized chairs: seats in automobiles, benches, couches, dentist's chairs, and the 'naughty chair' where children have to sit if they have misbehaved. Yet, in spite of the array of possible chairs, we seem to have a generalized concept of *chair*, at least enough to answer the question "Is that a chair?" Much as in Plato's notion of the Ideal, or the concept of a 'class' in object-oriented programming, we have a complex structure of symbols that correspond to the different types of chairs. We can utilize those symbols to reason about the types of chairs we encounter. The `PerCepts` have one foot in this complex symbolic structure. Each `PerCept` requires a symbolic tag that links into the semantic knowledge used by the deliberative system. If the ontology has information that there exists *Jim's_chair* which is a specific instance of a *short_wheeled_chair*; then there must be a `PerCept` that is identified by the semantic tag *short_wheeled_chair*, and there must be a thing in the `Mental Model` which corresponds to the current state (perhaps position and orientation) of *Jim's_chair*.

Fig. 7.3 Using the `PerCept` datasets, the `Reification Engine` maintains a `Mental Model` of the things in the world, and their current state. This is used to create a symbolic represen- tation of the Current World State, which is used, in turn, by the deliberative System. The `Mental Model` is used to both simplify the recognition of sensor data (e.g. turning it into symbolic information) and to generate preafference images of what the world would look like if a predicted change were to occur.

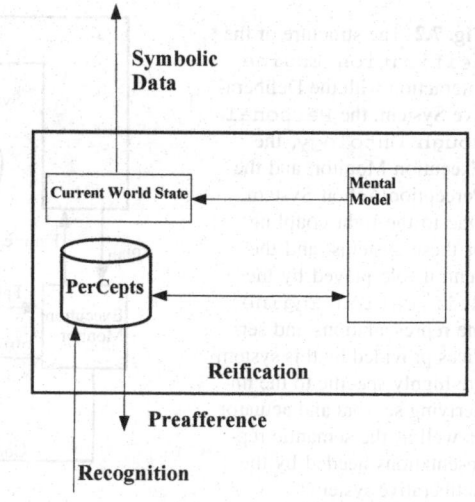

The PerCepts also have one foot deep in the sensor world. This sensor based representation is defined by the physical abilities of the body of the system. Each robot has its own types and placement of sensors, so the things that it perceives can and will have different sensor representations. This is true in biological systems as well. We, as humans, are very sight oriented[205], and so we attach visual representations to our semantics. We use vision as a primary metaphor for understanding - do you see what I mean? Look at it this way - at the beginning of the last paragraph, you read the words "Imagine a chair." For many of you, a visual image formed in your mind. However, other species have very different sensor modalities, and so their percepts will vary considerably. Imagine a human, a dog, and a bat encountering the same insect. While the human would focus on the appearance of the insect, the bat would more likely form an acoustically based 'image' of the bug, and the dog would generate a scent based model of great complexity.

We utilize a data-driven representation of the sensorium that corresponds to the object represented by the PerCept. There are two primary reasons for this approach, one is that it ensures a direct correspondence between the mental model of the thing and the perception of the thing. We create a dataset which can be used as a template. This template can be 'filled in' with the specifics of the location and orientation, and other details, to generate what the sensors would perceive. This contrasts with a more analytic representation of an object and the necessary transforms that could be used to generate the sensorium. There are several advantages to the dataset approach. Since the identifying characteristics are data, the Reification Engine can generate new PerCepts by creating new data representations. If the analytic representation were used, the system would need to generate new functions and add to its code. Of course, there is a significant disadvantage to the dataset approach: the datasets can get large, and are complex. The penalty we pay for the ability to learn is that much of the mechanism of the Reification Engine is dedicated to managing the PerCepts to provide the functions of preafference and recognition (See Figure 7.4).

7.3 PerCepts and Reification

The Reification Engine relies on the PerCepts to provide much of the capability for the two functions of recognition and preafference. The first function can be viewed as being able to as the question "Here is the sensor data, how likely is it that this data corresponds to the object you represent?" This enables the Reification Engine to perform one of its functions - recognition. The second function provided by the PerCept is the inverse: "If I (the thing represented by the PerCept) were here, in this orientation, what would I look like on the robot's sensors?" This supports the preafference function of the Reification Engine.

Each Reification Engine acts as a specific bridge for one Perception/Action system to a deliberative system. This is driven by the requirement that the Reification

Engine be grounded in the sensors and effectors of the Perception/Action system, and that the symbolic representations have the characteristics needed by the deliberative system. These symbolic representations must encode the semantics that are needed to reason about the goals of the system. The Reification Engine acts as a bridge, carrying traffic back and forth between two shores.

The translation between semantic and sensory representations must be specific to the sensors of the robot and the specific symbols used by the deliberative system. This has an analogy in humans. Individual humans have similar, but not identical, sensory systems. Some have more sensitivity to tastes, others are more sensitive to touch. Some people can sense colors that others cannot. For example, human genetics encode two different genes for sensitivity to the color red. These genes are encoded on the X chromosome. Most women have identical copies of the red receptor on both X chromosomes and see three colors, but some women have genes for both of the red receptors, and thus see, not three colors, but four[105]. This means that to make sense of their visual field, the reification process for vision is more complex for them than for individuals with only one type of the red receptors. Clearly, these Reification Engines are extremely personal. Therefore, for each type of robot, the Reification Engine is personalized by library of PerCepts.

Each PerCept is a template described by sensor related data. This means that while the Reification Engine for a specific robot must be personalized, the personalization does not mean that the software must be changed. Rather, the soft-

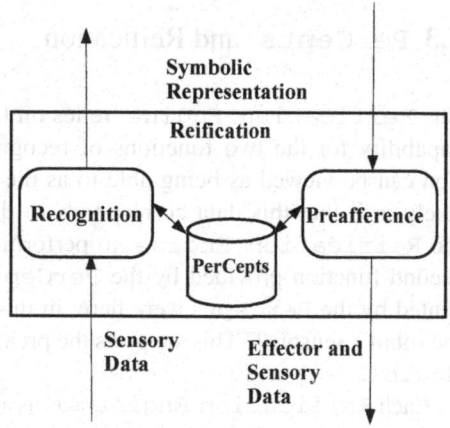

Fig. 7.4 The Reification Engine provides bidirectional mapping between the symbolic and the Perception/Action representations. It relies on a collection of PerCepts, which relate the sensorium to the symbolic.

ware supporting the recognition and preafference functions is common across many robot brains, only the data in the datasets change. This is true of both the semantic and the sensory aspects of a PerCept.

7.3.1 PerCept Data

Each PerCept corresponds to a class of perceptible things that the system can recognize and reason about. Since the main function of the PerCept is to bridge between the sensors and the symbolic representation, PerCepts are, first and foremost, a description of the structure of the thing. We have chosen to accept the possible size penalties associated with a data driven representation. Using the chair example begun earlier, let us look at the PerCept for a simple office chair.

The symbolic tag for the PerCept is *short_wheeled_chair*, this distinguishes it from the taller drafting table chairs (*tall_wheeled_chair*) and the *wooden_chairs* we use at the *round_table*[1] The templates for the sensorium are based on what the objects look like to the robot's sensors. In the case of many of our robots, we rely heavily on sonar imagery. These sonar images are built up from an array of individual, narrow field of view, sonars, each of which returns a distance from the robot to the closest surface of the object. This is functionally equivalent to the use of LIDAR, except it has far lower resolution and shorter range.

We represent the sensor image of the office chair with the expected values over the small number of sonars. See Figure 7.5 for a simple example. If the raw data were to be used to identify the object, it would necessary to store one template for every distance, however, it is apparent that all that matters is the relative offset from a reference point such as the center of the chair. Thus the chair-back in the figure would be offset behind the chair center by 250mm, while the front edge of the seat would be offset toward the sonar by about the same amount. With this center-relative encoding one template will work for a wide range of distances. In practice, as the robot gets closer to the chair, the side sonars (reporting infinity in the figure) will begin to show returns from the sides of the seat and the back. So we generate a set of templates based on the absolute range values. This gives us one view that is used for the range 300mm to 1249mm, a second for the range 1250mm to 1749mm, and a third for the range from 1750mm to 2500mm, which is the effective maximum of the sonars.

A second degree of freedom is the relative viewing angle of the chair. If we are viewing it from the front, the chair back is offset away from the chair center. However, if we are viewing the chair from behind, the chair back is offset toward the

---

[1] By this time, it has probably become apparent that our lab is nothing if not functionally oriented. This results in a certain amount of humor, both intentional and unintended. While in the book we use *type-faces* to distinguish between classes and instances and to denote the difference between the *symbol*, the **concept**, and the 'thing' itself; discussions at the white board rely on arm-gestures, facial expressions, and tone of voice. I'm afraid to think what a design meeting would look like if the video hit the Internet.

sonar. This relative pose angle is a critical feature in representing the sensor image of the chair. We address this by maintaining a collection of views from significantly different relative angles. Interestingly, this is where the relatively low resolution of our sensors shows an advantage. Since the range resolution is low, and the spatial resolution is also low, rather than maintaining templates for thousands of relative angles, a small number is all that is required - in the case of the *short_wheeled_chair* eight rotational views have been sufficient. In the case of objects with greater radial symmetry the number of angular views drops proportionally.

One of the benefits of the lens model approach is that the weights on the cues reflect the significance of a particular cue with respect to a specific lens (See Equation 6.2). We include a weight term in the templates to indicate that certain regions may have no impact on the judgment during recognition. In addition, the templates can also be used to encode voids in the object. In some cases the key signature of an object may be based on the absence of a return in a specific area. This can be critical in distinguishing between a chair (with a back) and a stool, for example. The template based models handle this by tagging specific returns with a 'must not exist' value attached to each element in the template. This is done by attaching a large negative value to the weight field.

Up to this point, the trade-offs between the data-driven template model, and a more formal analytical model of the object might seem to be in favor of the analytical model. After all, with a single analytical model every possible distance and relative viewing angle can be calculated on the fly, with no increase in the data needed. However, a simple 3D model of a wheeled chair that we used for the VR

Fig. 7.5 A simple example of a Sonar Image. The top section shows the elevation view of the robot 'pinging' an office chair. The middle panel shows the plan view, and in the lower section, the actual range values for each point are shown. Sonar images can be treated as extremely low resolution LIDAR. On the surface it would appear that this lower resolution and shorter range are disadvantages. However, in practice, biological systems take advantage of the much reduced bandwidth by automatically ignoring information about things that are not important. They have found an effective balance between too much data and too little.

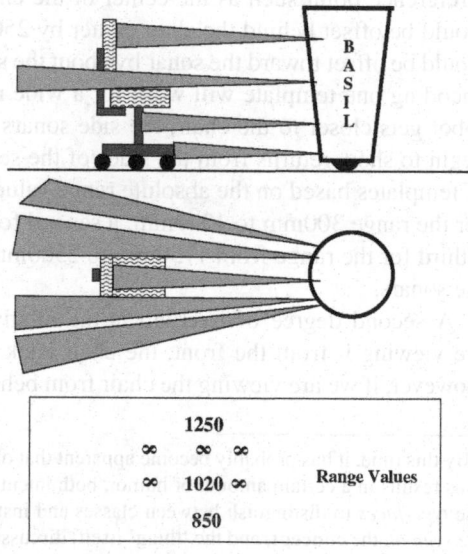

image in Figure 8.2 requires approximately 21KB of data, versus the 7KB needed for the templates of a similar (but shorter) chair.

Two aspects remain to be addressed before a final assessment can be made. Perhaps the most critical is the fact that real world objects rarely behave like their idealized analytic models would suggest. For example, for our *short_wheeled_chair*, the fabric on the seats is often sonar absorbent. As a result, where the analytic model would require a return, we often 'see' nothing. With the data-driven templates, we use the actual returns, as seen by the specific sonars in the robot, to generate not what the robot *should* see, but what the robot *does* see. In addition, since the real world is not deterministic, the sensor values are often close to, but not exactly what the analytical model would predict. As comforting as it might be to say that the real world is wrong, and we just need better, higher resolution sensors, and larger, more complex analytical models (along with more advanced processing to handle the additional variables, etc.), the harsh reality is that there will always be differences between the mathematical models and reality, and reality always wins.

The concept of increasing the fidelity of the analytical model brings us to the final, and most telling advantage to the data-driven, template based solution. Since the PerCepts are stored, not as software, but as data, it is possible for the robot itself to add additional PerCepts, adjust the values in the templates, and modify its knowledge of the world around it. By comparison, it is barely feasible to imagine a mobile robot able to sense an new object and then generate a new analytical description of the thing, a task that often takes a trained engineer hundreds of hours to complete. Giving the robot the ability to collect a number of sensory views of an object, at known distances and orientations is fairly simple. Since this collected data is already in the form required by the PerCepts, it requires little effort to translate it into a template. Thus, it is uncertain that the benefits of the analytical solution will outweigh the costs. The only real cost to the template based approach is the size of the representations. In Table 7.1 we show some of the actual PerCepts that the service robot uses. With the largest of these at under 10KB, even a modest computer has adequate storage capacity for thousands of PerCepts. In addition, since the data in each PerCept is shared by all instances of the class, this means that the cost of maintaining an understanding of the world is quite low.

Table 7.1 Sample Sizes of PerCepts

PerCept	PoseCount	ByteCode Size	Note
FauxChair	8	2K	Used for Testing
ShortWheeledChair	24	7K	office chair
WoodenChair	24	5K	office chair
Stool	8	2K	simple cubic shape
RoundTable	12	5K	5' diameter table
NorthWall	1	6K	North wall of the lab

7.3.2 PerCept Function

In addition to being a data structure, there is significant functionality associated with the PerCepts. To support the ability to transform the data driven template into the expected sensor image, the PerCept requires a significant number of geometric operations. The first task is to take the position-independent, pose-independent template, and generate from it a representation of the object in its correct position in three dimensional space, as well as in its correct orientation. The second task it to take this representation and determine the relative perspective that it has with relation to the robot's sensors. The final task is to take this perspective view, and generate the expected sensor image that would result. These three tasks define the majority of the machinery that the PerCept must provide.

The main data upon which the PerCepts mechanisms operate are produced by the specific sensors. In the case of Basil, the primary sensor data are sonar returns. The raw data is an array of distances. While this raw data is useful, Basil needs to reason, not about the distances, but about the things in the real world that caused the sonars to reflect. This is common across almost any type of sensor - the data produced by the sensor is caused by the thing being sensed, and it is the thing we are interested in, not the data. As a result, the first function provided by a PerCept is to utilize the knowledge about the sensor to generate a hypothetical 'thing' in the real world that could have generated the sensor data. These are ObstacleObservations which are spatially located volumes that correspond to the object (or objects) that might have caused the sensor data. They are encoded as three intervals, one in each of X, Y and Z, as well as the distance and time at which the sensing occurred (See Table 7.2). It also includes the confidence that the sensor has in the datum.

Needless to say, this suggests that the robot is equipped with 'smart sensors.' Smart sensors are sensors that do more than simply report data. They have additional capabilities to preprocess the data and provide additional information. The biological support for such smart sensors is widely available, ranging form recent research into the significant amount of preprocessing that is performed by the retina[205], to the preprocessing that enables us to understand speech, and suppress background noise[33]. Some of this occurs in the actual sensory organs, while other sensory organs depend on very specialized regions of the brain to provide the preprocessing.

Once the ObstacleObservations are available, each PerCept can operate on the data in several ways. However there is a common group of spatial functions that are shared across many types of reasoning. These generally fall into the class of spatial reasoning, answering questions like: "What would it look like?" and "Where is it in relation to me?" or "Should I be able to detect it at all?" Since the Reification Engine is grounded in the physical sensors of the robot, it has knowledge about the physical characteristics of those sensors.

In general, this knowledge must include the position and orientation of the sensors on the robot chassis, it must also include the range of the sensors, the field of view, and the data types that are returned, as well as the physical constants that relate the readings to the real world. These are stored in a parameters dataset, which

Table 7.2 ObstacleObservation Data Type

Data	Type	Description
XPosition	Interval	The global X range
YPosition	Interval	The global Y range
ZPosition	Interval	The global Z range
Sensed Distance	int	this is the raw data
Time of Observation	long	from the system clock
Weight	int	the weight of the observation in the judgment

is accessible to the PerCepts. This information is needed to enable the PerCept to generate the preafference images that are needed for reification, and to validate the existence of the object that the PerCept represents during recognition.

Any PerCept can use the spatial reasoning to translate the sensory data into a form that is consistent with its model of itself, as viewed by that specific sensor. It can place itself in space, determine the relative viewing angles from the sensors, generate the image that the sensors would have of it, and evaluate the actual sensor data to confirm its presence in the dataset. It can express a confidence that there is an object of the type that the PerCept represents located *here*, in this *orientation*, and explained by these *observations*. This is the output of one PerCept. The Reification Engine must weigh this against the outputs of other PerCepts, trying to explain themselves using the same sensory data set, to develop a Mental Model of the current state of the world - not in sensory terms, but as semantically tagged objects positioned in space.

7.4 Mental Model

The Mental Model used by the Reification Engine is based in the sensory domain. It contains knowledge about all the perceptual things of which the robot is aware. This is not limited to things which are immediately perceivable. If the robot turns its sensors away from a chair for example, it does not lose all knowledge of the chair. Rather, the chair remains in the Mental Model, along with the last recorded information about its position, and orientation. Thus, when the robot turns its sensors back toward the chair, it can use preafference to predict the sensor representation of the chair in its last known location. As time elapses with no referents to the chair, for example if the robot were to go into a different room for several hours, the detailed knowledge of the chairs position and orientation would be dropped from the Mental Model.

The Mental Model is a list of things. These are represented in a data structure called a PThing which indicates a perceivable Thing. Each PThing has information including:

- Symbolic Name - matching the corresponding name in the `Personal Rough Ontology`;
- Pose - the best estimate of the sensor derived position and orientation of the thing;
- LastUpdateTime - the timestamp of the cast confirmed detection by the Perception/action system; and
- `PerCept` - a link to the correct `PerCept` for the `PThings` class.

Each of these structures also supports a number of functions, most of which are used to support the preafference and recognition functions. Recall that the `PerCepts` are structural models of the class of things that they represent. Since these `PerCepts` do not have information about the specific instances of chairs or tables, the `PThing` must work with the general `PerCept` to produce the specific recognition of the instance, in its specific location, and its specific pose.

In addition, the `PThing` has functions to estimate if the sensor data indicate that the thing has moved relative to the robot. These functions are used by the `Reification Engine` to determine whether the thing has moved, or the robot has moved (either of which could account for the change in relative position). Finally, the `PThing` is responsible for updating its own pose, when the `Reification Engine` requests such an update.

As we discussed, the `Mental Model` is the collection of things that the `Reification Engine` is tracking at any specific time. As such, in addition to providing access to the `PThings`, the `Mental Model` also provides functionality on its own. The `Mental Model` maintains a representation of the current state of the robot as a special thing in its world. It is possible to treat the robot as just another thing in the `Mental Model`, but the robot is key to so many aspects of the reification process, it makes sense to give it special treatment. This eliminates having to search through the (possibly large) collection of other things in the world in order to get access to knowledge about the robot.

In addition to direct access to the knowledge of the robot, the `Mental Model` provides high level comparison functions between the expected state of the world and the actual, sensed, data. These functions include the ability to do a fast presumptive test of consistency, the ability to quickly extract the components of the sensor data that are inconsistent with the expected model, and a function that allows the `Mental Model` to update its estimate of the robot's position, based on the available data.

The presumptive consistency check utilizes the ability to quickly generate a view of how the world should look, given the robot's position and orientation, and the `Mental Model` of where the things in the world are presumed to be. This enables the `Reification Engine` to quickly assess that everything is going along pretty much as expected. If things are going as expected, the `Reification Engine` can provide that information to the `Execution Monitor`, and then update the more detailed model of the world.

If things are not consistent, the `Mental Model` has the capability to provide a detailed report of what things the Perception/Action system is reporting that are inconsistent, and the `Reification Engine` can focus on these problematic data, and attempt to understand them.

7.5 Current World State

The third main data structure in the `Reification Engine` is the Current World State. This is a persistent representation of the state of the world - specifically the placement and orientation of everything that the robot is tracking. This is more exhaustive than the immediate `Mental Model`. It includes things that the robot may not have encountered for a significant amount of time, and includes the information about when they were last experienced. The function of this repository is two-fold. First, it is used to provide specific information to the deliberative system, to enable that system to achieve its goals. Second, it is used to populate the `Mental Model` when returning to previously encountered environments. The Current World State is accessed less frequently than the `Mental Model`, and is generally just updated with current information.

The Current World State has the responsibility of providing semantic information to the deliberative system. The `Mental Model` needs to store very detailed state information about the objects it is tracking. It needs to represent the precise position of a chair, and the precise orientation of the door, if it is going to build a sensor based representation of the robot's perspective of that chair and that door. The deliberative system does not need to know (in general) the position of the chair to the nearest millimeter, nor does it (necessarily) know what to do with the angle of the door with respect to the wall. Rather, it needs to know that the chair is over by the assembly bench, and that the door is closed. This semantic information is what allows the Deliberative System to reason about the need to open the door, and that the chair is out of the way.

Table 7.3 Multiresolution views of the World

Thing	Mental Model	CWS
Chair1	Pose(10100,500, 128)*[a]	Assembly Bench Area, facing South
Table2	Pose(4500,5000,0)	Programming1, facing North
Robot	Pose(7000, 3200,224)	Room Center, facing NorthWest
Door2	Pose(2641,4115,0)	Door closed

[a] These are objects in the lab, in local coordinates

These two views of the state of the world are the same world, represented at different resolutions. Humans are extremely good at multi-resolution modeling (MRM) but it has proved difficult to develop effective MRM in machines[1, 165]. The Current World State structure provides support for both the semantic and the sensor-domain representations of the world.

7.6 Reification functionality

We began this chapter discussing the functions that the Reification Engine needed to provide to enable the robot to perform in the real world without a human in the loop. We dove deeply into the nuts and bolts of the mechanisms within the Reification Engine, and now we have returned to the surface. Once again we can talk about the bidirectional mapping of recognition and preafference. In the previous section we focused on the data that the Reification Engine maintains and depends upon. In this section we address the functions that the Reification Engine provides to the other systems in the cybernetic brain. There are primarily four functions:

- Initialization;
- Recognition;
- Preafference; and
- Maintaining the Current World State.

We will look at each of these in a little more detail. However, much of the detail has already been covered, since the Reification Engine relies on the services provided by its components to do most of the work.

7.6.1 Initialization

One can envision this coupling by following the path from the initialization of the Reification Engine through its delivery of a symbolic representation to the upper layers. Each of these stages will be addressed in more detail in the sections to follow, so this is a high-level tour.

The deliberative system relies on a complex web of semantic knowledge of the world. Every thing about which the robot has 'knowledge' is represented semantically in this ontology. Only a small part of this knowledge relates to thing that are perceptible. This small set of things which are perceivable can, and must be extracted from the ontology. Each must have a PerCept stored in the Reification Engine. For example, the specific short wheeled chair next to the conference table belongs to the class of *short_wheeled_chair*. This list is used to populate the Mental Model. Recall that, generally, the system is initialized very rarely. Initialization is much like waking up in a hospital room, with amnesia: one has no idea where one is, or what to expect. And so, general knowledge of chairs and tables is available, but there may be no knowledge of the current arrangement of the chairs. While the robot can begin the laborious process of building a mental model from scratch, having access to previous memories of the state of the world is beneficial.

Using the memory of the previous world state, each thing in the Mental Model can be initialized with its last known position and orientation. Now the Reification Engine can use the data from the Perception/Action system to confirm and update the `Mental Model`. The sensor data may show that a specific chair has been moved, or that the robot itself is in a different position. The `Reification Engine` uses preafference of the things in the `Mental Model` and the ability to recognize new things to build a more accurate model of the world, and this is used to update the symbolic representation of the Current World State.

7.6.2 Mapping the World onto its Model - Recognition

The `Reification Engine` uses the `PerCepts` to recognize the state of the outside world. A simple brute force approach would be to take the sensor data and attempt to match it against every possible `PerCept` in the library. Of course there might be a large number of `PerCepts` in the library, each of which could be at any possible distance and a number of possible orientations. The computational complexity of this task is daunting to say the least. We know that living systems perform this process quickly and (in general) reliably. We also know that computer-based recognition is (in general) neither.

There are arguments that the advantage of biological system is in the massive parallelism of the brain, that the same sensory data is presented to thousands or more recognition modules at once, and that the best match fires first. There are similar arguments that the brain is fundamentally operating on a quantum level, and that recognition has more in common with the collapse of the quantum wave, than any traditional computer algorithm. As we discussed before, since we are not attempting to build a structural model of the brain, we need to model only the functionality not the mechanisms.

We take advantage of the fact that sensing does not occur in a vacuum. Sensing and perception are one step in a continuous cycle, which was preceded by an earlier perception stage. One of the core functions of reification is to maintain a (more or less) continuous model of the `PerCepts` that correspond to the state of the world[160]. The `PerCepts` from the last perception, and the `Mental Model` built from them, can be used as a guide to shorten the following perceptual process. This is based on the concepts of 'thing constancy'[188] and 'object constancy'. In effect, the things that we perceive do not (in general) magically appear or disappear. Thus, we evolve the previous model of the world, based on our knowledge of what activities are occurring, and predict the ensuing state of the world. With this predicted model, we can confirm what we expect to see, at a far lower computational cost than approaching the perceived world *de nova*.

As an example imagine our robot traversing a room. At the start of the motion, the robot has a `Mental Model` of the room, its relative position to the walls, the distance to the table, the location of the chair. When the robot moves forward, the `Reification Engine` updates the expected world state, changing the position of the robot in the room. When the sensory data arrives from the Perception/Action system, the robot can ask the `PerCept` for the table "If I am in this position, and looking this way, am I seeing you?" Since the `PerCept` includes the necessary structural description, it can quickly confirm (or deny) whether the sensory data is consistent with the expectation. This can be continued with the chair, the walls, the picture on the wall; and if the world model is confirmed, it can be updated. This process does not require querying every possible PerCept, or even querying every expected PerCept for every possible position and orientation. Rather, it quickly attempts to confirm the expected world state.

7.6.2.1 Dealing with the Unexpected

Sure, but what if the world is not what the robot expects? What if someone sneaked in and moved the chair, or simply stepped into the robots field of view? In this case the presumptive confirmation of the world fails. Now the Reification Engine begins to expand the range over which the search occurs. If there are people (or other moving entities) in the world model, they are added to the search "Is it possible that this person stepped to the left?" "Is it possible that the chair moved?" "Am I really where I expect to be?" This increases significantly the computational overhead, but this is consistent with the fMRI data, which shows that it takes longer to recognize the unexpected. If this level of relaxation of the model fails to produce a consistent world model further relaxation may occur, less likely objects are added to the search list (although it will be a while before the robot considers the possibility that a zebra has suddenly appeared in the living room). This is consistent with the results of studies on humans in disasters. People who experience dramatic destruction (such as coming out of a storm cellar after a tornado) report that for several minutes they cannot place themselves in space, the permanent features that they expected to see, the buildings, the walls, the trees, have been altered to the point where they cannot perceive a frame of reference. Nor is this limited to humans, pets can also experience disorientation due to the disruption of their sensorium, notably the changes to the landscape of scents that they use to define space[145].

7.6.3 Projecting the Model onto the World - Preafference

The second function that the Reification Engine supports is the projection of the model onto the world. Preafference is the process of taking the Mental Model of the world, and generating the view that the robot would see, if everything were like the model. This process produces a *virtual reality*(VR) representation of the world as it is expected to be. In effect, the Reification Engine acts as a rendering engine for the mental model of the world. This rendered image is used to speed up the process of confirming that the world is pretty much what we expect. Fortunately, much of the machinery needed to perform this function is shared by the recognition task. The low-level functions needed to place objects into relative positions with each other, and to calculate the sensor images of these objects given the robot's pose and position were already described above in the sections on

PerCepts, PThings, and the Mental Model. It is only needed to use these functions in a different way to generate a preafference image, rather than to recognize the objects in the world. Just as a physical lens bends light regardless of the direction, our cybernetic lens can be used to either project the sensor domain into the symbolic, or project the symbolic domain into the sensorium.

To do this projection into the sensor domain, we take advantage of the fact that the Mental Model has a list of the objects that are expected to be in the world, and their positions, orientations and properties. With this information, and the machinery of the PerCepts, generating this rendered image is relatively straight forward. In the case of our example robot, Basil, this rendered image is a sonar image of what the sonars would return. The generation of this image is done in three stages:

1. Select the PThings that are in the field of view of the robot;
2. Use the PerCepts, the pose of the object, and the pose of the robot to generate individual images; and
3. Fuse these individual images into a composite image.

The first of these steps in simply done to reduce the computational burden of the full process. Rather than attempting to build the sensor images of objects that might be in another room (recall that the Mental Model tracks things that are not immediately perceivable), or even attempting to generate a complete 360° panoramic view, we only generate images for objects that are likely to be in view. This is the same process that is used in VR rendering systems in the form of bounding surfaces[154]. The Reification Engine uses the sensor parameters for the specific sensors, and slightly over estimates the field of view of the robot. This angular interval is compared with each of the individual objects. We take advantage of a function of the PerCept that calculates the perceived angular extent of an object, based on its position and orientation, and the position of the robot. A quick test to see if the two intervals overlap is sufficient to determine if this object is in the field of view.

For those PThings that are in the field of view, we can request the PThing to generate a view - the expected sensor image of the object. This method is specific to the object and the sensors that are in use. It generates the sensor image that would be returned by the object if it were viewed in isolation. Basil uses sonar sensors that are slightly smart, they produce a three dimensional volume that represents the area from which the sonar return reflected. This view is a collection of ObstacleObservation that are directly comparable to these sensor returns.

The final step is for the Reification Engine to fuse these individual views into a complete sensor image. If there is only one object generating a sensor image, this task is trivial. The difficulties arise when there are multiple objects in the field of view and there are occlusions (e.g., one object generates a return that blocks the view of another object). This is a common occurrence as the resolution of the sensor increases. However, the techniques for resolving occlusions have been well tested in visual rendering software. Utilizing the information encoded in the individual returns, and the relative positions of the robot and each item, it is fairly straight forward (if computationally intensive) to generate a final rendered sensor image.

This final preafference image can be quickly compared against the actual sensor image to see if there are major discrepancies.

7.6.4 Updating the Current World State

The final task of the Reification Engine is to take the changes that have been made to the Mental Model, and project them into the semantic space of the Current World State. This process requires the translation from the sensor driven, numerically based information in the Mental Model. The key support structures for this translation are representations that link the semantic terms utilized by the deliberative system - the world-state representations presented in Chapter 4, with representations that are consistent with the PerCepts. For example, The Mental Model maintains precise locations of the objects that the robot knows about. However, the deliberative system does not model the location of objects at this resolution. It keeps track of the fact that the chair is over by the assembly bench, not that it is at coordinates X=10,100, Y=500. So the Current World State must maintain information at the level of detail needed by the deliberative system, using the symbolic names of the locations in the ontology.

It is important to note that these symbolic names must match the symbolic names that are known locations in the ontology. The second point to note is that, once again, these are simply data that describe the space in two ways. When the system is deployed, it is possible that higher resolution may be required, and the system can add new locus points, with new symbolic names to its model of the world, and then reason about these new locations in exactly the same manner as those that are provided to jump-start the reasoning process. As we said in the introduction, we do not go into the details of how the system modifies its own representations in this book. However, it depends of having representations of the knowledge, both on a semantic, and a physical level that resides wholly in the form of data.

7.7 Wrapping Up Reification

Reification is a critical component necessary for autonomous systems to function effectively in a dynamic and uncertain world. Reification is the mechanism that translates between the sensor domain - the world of images, echoes, encoders, and force transducers - into the semantic domain of chairs and trees, rooms and fragile packages. In this chapter we looked at a specific implementation of a Reification Engine. We explored the details of the needed functionality, some underlying data structures, and presented them with examples for a deployed robot - Basil the drinks robot. In this section we sum up the various pieces, and look at how they work together to provide reification to the robot.

Reification can be viewed as a necessary middle-ware component for autonomous robots. While the technology for deliberative planning has been available to chess computers, planning systems, and other decision support software for over 50 years, it has not been well integrated into mobile robotics. At the same time, industrial and teleoperated robots have made major strides in capability - industrial robotics in tightly controlled domains, and teleoperated systems in more dynamic domains (provided there was a human in the loop). The reification bridge between the sensors and actuators on one side, and the sophisticated deliberative systems has not been available. It provides recognition services to map the sensorium into symbolic representations, and provides the complementary service preafference to map the expected state of the world into the anticipates sensor representations.

The `Reification Engine` presented here both anchors the deliberative symbols in the sensor domain, and attaches semantic tags to the patterns presented by those sensors. It does this, not by extensively hard-coding the patterns, but by associating the data derived patterns with the meanings used by the ontology. This data derived approach has several benefits, as well as costs in comparison to an analytic representation scheme. One of these benefits is that the data driven approach is based on the actual properties of the objects as viewed by the actual sensors, rather than an idealized model. As a result, if a given sensor has an idiosyncrasy (perhaps it is mounted at a slight angle), or if a specific object has a unique property (e.g., it absorbs both IR and ultrasonic pulses) that is reflected in the data derived pattern.

The second major benefit is that the patterns are simply data. There are several basic algorithms that are grounded in the physical relationships of the world: things like distance calculations, and the determination of relative angles. However, the representation of objects, sensors, and the structural descriptions of the world are simply data. This means that the cybernetic brain, and specifically the `Reification Engine`, can modify these patterns as it experiences more of the world, and can modify the parameters in response to the changes that the world will have on the robot's own structure. By using data structures for as much as possible, the robot can both stay synchronous with the dynamic world, and can update its mental representations as it experiences new things. How the recognition and preafference services of the `Reification Engine` are used in the creation and maintenance of personal experiences and memory are the subject of the next chapter.

Chapter 8
Working Memory and the Construction of Personal Experiences

In this chapter we focus on how we can generate and store the vast amount of knowledge that our humanoid robot will need to be able to do its job, and how we will represent the complex relationships that define that knowledge. We focus on three of the four areas of representation (See Figure 8.1). We describe the mechanisms of the representation of the current state of the world, the representation of the internal state of the robot, and how these provide the basis for the generation of episodic memory. We describe the remaining component of memory - semantic memory, and its implementation as a Personal Rough Ontology in Chapter 9.

As described in Chapter 3 these categories of memory can be classified into two broad classes, long-term and short-term memory. A functionally equivalent way of looking at the classes is Persistent and Transient memory. Persistent memory includes the facts and concepts that are used to represent one's knowledge about the

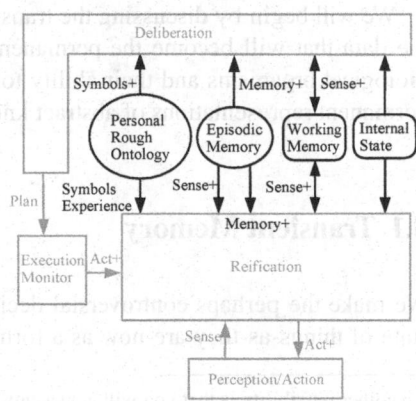

Fig. 8.1 These are the four primary memory structures that are utilized by the cognitive system of our robot. The Personal Rough Ontology and the Episodic Memory are persistent data structures, while the Working Memory and the Internal State are transient.

world, knowledge about procedures and common activities, as well as one's memories of activities and events that have been personally experienced. The transient memory is more of an instantaneous representation of the immediate state. This transient snapshot contains both knowledge of the outside world (where the coffee cup is) and knowledge of the internal state of the robot. This includes both physical state (proprioceptic and enteroceptic knowledge) and the current goals, plans, intentions, and expectations.

There is a constant interplay between persistent and transient memory. The current state of the living system is transformed into a more permanent record as one's episodic memory. In turn, episodic memories are accessed when new, but similar states are encountered, and these previous experiences affect how one responds to the current situation. Finally, living systems learn from their experiences, and most humans are capable of extracting information from their episodic memory to build semantic memory. Thus, there is a continual flow between past and present, between what happened then, what is happening now, and what is expected to happen in the future. For example, perhaps when one is experiencing a severe storm in the fall, one's expectations of the outcome and the instantaneous experience is moderated by the memories of how you felt while riding the roller coaster that day in June when a severe storm occurred and it started hailing. The fear and panic, that you felt at that time, may carry over to the current storm. [1] In this chapter we focus on the transient memory and how it can be used to generate the more persistent episodic memory.

The two broad categories of persistent and transient memory are broken down into two subdivisions as follows:

1. Transient Memory
   a. Working Memory
   b. Internal Memory

2. Persistent Memory
   a. Episodic Memory
   b. Semantic Memory

We will begin by discussing the transient memory since it acts as the source for the data that will become the permanent records. This is driven by the nature of biological organisms and their ability to learn from experience and build complex permanent representations of abstract knowledge.

8.1 Transient Memory

We make the perhaps controversial decision to define the instantaneous, dynamic state of things-as-they-are-now as a form of memory. This is driven by three pres-

---

[1] Another possibility is that you will get sweaty when smelling cotton candy.

sures. The first of these is that when we build our memories, especially episodic memory, these transitive states are part of those memories. Arguing from the perspective of parsimony, there is no need for two different types of representation, if we can make do with one. The second pressure is the need to have access to both the Current World State (CWS) and the current internal state of the robot when reasoning about what goals to pursue, and what behaviors are being used to successfully achieve those goals. Finally, these transient states are the raw material of procedural memory - the transient states that the Perception/Action system goes through in the process of acquiring a new behavior must be incorporated into procedural memory such as the necessary steps to make a cappuccino or to prove a theorem.

From a historical robotics perspective, a system with only transient memory corresponds closely to a reactive system. A purely reactive system is one that holds no representation of the previous states of the world, and only responds to the current sensor inputs. In the classical definition, if there is no need to store previous states, then there is no need for any kind of representation. The world is its own best model, and the overhead of maintaining a consistent, accurate representation is unwarranted. While this is compelling from a mathematical perspective, and perhaps from an engineering perspective; it is clear that from the biological perspective there are significant benefits to having more than a simple, stateless, input – react system. In addition, our humanoid robot will need to learn from its experiences, and so, it must be able to represent those experiences in memory. So some form of representation is required for our robot to function effectively.

8.1.1 Working Memory and the Current World State

Some of the simplest of biological organisms have been shown to maintain models of the the state of the the world. As discussed above, even simple one celled organisms such as bacteria maintain a primitive model of the intensity of chemical signals so that they can determine a gradient that will lead them toward food. As humans, we maintain a very complex model of the current state of the world, to enable us to both reason about and to act in the pursuit of goals. Research by cognitive scientists has shown that the working memory used by humans is very limited (in comparison to more persistent memory) and it appears to be clearly separate from both semantic and episodic memory[6, 45].

The idea of a separate working memory was adopted fairly early by artificial intelligence researchers, perhaps not so much due to the biological inspiration, but due to the hardware constraints of the computers. During the early years of computers random access memory (RAM) was extremely limited in capacity, and expensive. Disk storage on the other hand, was less limited, but significantly slower to access. This led to a natural devision of long-term storage in one memory structure (the disk), and working memory in another (RAM) structure. Researchers were effectively forced into developing designs that closely mapped the biological systems.

Short-term working memory is used in two primary ways: storing the intermediate products of the deliberative process (which will be discussed in Chapter 10) and to store the model of the CWS, as far as it is known. The actual data structures used for storing the CWS were described in more detail in Chapter 4, however a brief overview is presented here.

As was discussed above, there has been a significant debate in the field of robotics as to whether any model of the world is necessary, and if some representation is needed, how complex it needs to be. In addition, there is some debate in the cognitive science community as to how much representation (e.g., modeling) of the world goes on, and to what degree it is symbolic. Since it has been shown that even simple biological organisms maintain models of the world, there must be some value to modeling the outside world. Thus a major component of our transient memory structure is devoted to maintaining a world model. The world model consists of both representations of the external state of the world, and representations of the internal state of the robot.

The primary source of data about the current world state comes from the Perception/Action system by way of the Reification Engine . The current information from the sensors is processed by the Reification Engine into a symbolic representation of the world. For example, if the sensors are directed at a door, the Reification Engine generates the appropriate symbolic representation of the door, and the symbols are provided as input to the working memory. These symbols are maintained by the working memory as part of the CWS. However, unlike a purely reactive system, when the robot turns its sensors away from the door, the knowledge that a door exists, its location, and any other salient information does not vanish from the working memory. This enables the deliberative system to reason about the door, and to take the door into account when planning.

As many researchers have pointed out[21, 65, 77], there are problems with maintaining a model of the current world state. It can become 'out of sync' with the real world - resulting in plans that fail because they depended on a door being open (as indicated by the memory of the current world state), but in the meantime the door has been closed. Of course, these problems occur with any biological organism, humans included. In part this is due to the limited cognitive capacity of any physical system, and in part to the fact that the real world is not a static, deterministic place. A second concern with maintaining a model of the CWS is the computational burden associated with keeping it up to date, and in simply sorting through the large number of possible facts about the world and selecting the ones that are salient. As Dreyfus wrote in "What Computers *Still* Can't Do:"

> It turned out to be very difficult to reproduce in an internal representation for a computer the necessary richness of environment that would give rise to interesting behavior by a highly adaptive robot.[53]

Achieving this 'necessary richness of representation' is challenging in two ways. It seems to be necessary to have a wide and deep representation to handle complex goals, yet only a relatively small subset of this representation is required for any given problem. If the deliberative system has too many symbols to deal with, it quickly becomes overloaded, simply managing the representations. There is current research in neurodynamics that suggests organic brains utilize a non-representational activation mechanism that is triggered directly by sensory input, but activates a context-like structure that focuses on the problem at hand[54, 71]. Such a mechanism operates like a hologram, where there is no direct mapping of a specific place to a specific bit of knowledge. Rather the sensory input activates memory structures with similar structure, resulting in the recall of salient knowledge.

In the cybernetic brain the actual memory structure for the CWS is a list of facts that describe the world-as-it-is, or at least as accurate a picture as the sensors and `Reification Engine` can provide. These facts are represented using a list of predicates of the form: (*Feature,Value*), where features are the characteristics and things that make up the world, and the values are the current state of those things. To use a classical example, let us suppose that our universe is made up of a table, and a set of colored blocks. This Blocks World example has been used since the late 1960's. In this classic form, the state of the world can be represented with a series of statements like (*RedBlock, OnTable*), (*BlueBlock, OnRed*), (*GreenBlock, OnTable*). In general, the robot is presumed to have complete and accurate knowledge of the world, and so, the CWS would always have a statement for the condition of every block. Traditionally, the world model would be boolean, so that every fact about the world would have a statement indicating that it was true. In addition, the deliberative systems worked under what is referred to as the *Closed World Assumption*[166] which means that anything that is not stated as true can be assumed to be false. In the real world we need more complex representation than these simple predicates, and we cannot make the closed world assumption, since there are many things for which we will not know if they are true or false at any given point in time.

To limit the size of the Current World State, we restrict our representation to currently supplied representational symbols from the `Reification Engine` and the working memory from the deliberative system. As a result our robot will 'forget' the current state of objects like doors unless either it has perceived the door recently, or has been referring to the door in its recent deliberations. The CWS captures what is known about the current state of the world. With every input from the `Reification Engine`, the CWS is updated with new information, and without any reinforcement, older information is discarded. As a result, the working memory becomes a self organizing structure, with the symbols that correspond to current sensory experience and current deliberation being kept current. This begins to act as a focus or attention mechanism, preventing the deliberative system from becoming mired down in facts, plans, and goals that are no longer of current interest.

It has been long accepted that there is a critical need for some way to narrow down the focus of cybernetic reasoning system. The wealth of information that is required by a system to be reasonably knowledgeable about the world quickly becomes overwhelming to the computational resources available to a computer. The development of some way to focus attention[195] to the subset of information that is germane to the situation at hand is a critical aspect of reasoning. In addition, the ability to provide context sensitive subsets of the total knowledge provides a mechanism to address the frame problem[23, 95, 121, 129], by eliminating inappropriate contexts. Thus the ability to keep a current world state that both has memory of past states, and also allows world states that are no longer important to drop from the current awareness is a necessary component of our transient memory.

8.1.2 Internal State

Unlike the CWS and the working memory, where information dynamically appears and disappears depending on the directed attention of the system, the internal state is always complete. It is clear that biological systems maintain an accessible model of their internal state at all times. This information is used both to drive behaviors and it affects the cognitive and decision making process. In terms of a biological organism, imagine a rabbit, driven by any one of a number of possible goals: fear, reproduction, hunger, and so on. If the rabbit is being chased by a fox it will run past that tempting carrot rather than stop for a bite - regardless of how hungry it is. However, if a starving rabbit senses both a potential mate and the tempting carrot, the hunger may impact the behavior or the rabbit. Thus the internal state of the organism affects the decision making process, which, in turn, affects the behaviors that are enacted. The internal state consists of a combination of several components. In Chapter 5 we discussed a number of the functions of the Perception/Action system. Many of the hardware components that are necessary to fulfill these functions have time varying state. The proprioceptive systems have information about the current position of joints and effectors, as well as the current power being consumed; the enteroceptic systems have information about the level of energy in batteries or the amount of fuel remaining. These data make up a significant part of the internal state of the robot at any point in time. Biological organisms include this (contrast the state of hunger of the rabbit discussed above with the fuel reserves of an autonomous aerial vehicle) as well as the current state of broadband neurotransmitters[42] affecting the central nervous system. The four basic emotions were discussed in Section 3.3. There are be analogs to these neurotransmitters in our robot, and to be effective in the real world, there should be. Consider the rabbit example above, but replace the rabbit with a UAV, and the fox with a surface to air missile (SAM). Should the UAV pause to take a tempting photograph of a convoy moving down the road while the SAM is closing, or should some analog of fear cause the UAV to skip the photo shoot until the threat is gone?

8.2 Episodic Memory

Episodic memory is the mechanism used to store experience and events. From the biological evidence it is clear that the mechanisms and nature of episodic memory differ from semantic memory. Episodic memory is a system that retains prior experience and makes those experiences available for current reasoning[82]. It has been shown to influence the cognitive mechanisms of attention, decision making, and the categorization of new information. In cases of amnesia, it is common for episodic memory to be disrupted, while semantic memory continues to function normally. In addition, recent research by Rosenbaum *et al* indicate that episodic memory is independent from the ability of one human to infer other people's mental state (Theory of Mind)[171]. From these data it is clear that episodic memory is a distinct mechanism in biological systems.

Numerous mechanisms have been proposed for representing episodic memory in computer based models of cognition. These models often place episodic memory into the same storage as semantic memory. In deriving a biologically inspired model, we have no choice but to separate these memory stores. But, this does not mean that we must discard previous work. Regardless of where these memories of experienced events are stored, the mechanisms and representational schema have been well researched, and several effective proposals are available.

One of the earliest attempts to formalize representing episodic memories was done by Rumelhart, Lindsay and Norman[173]. While this work was primarily focusing on the encoding of textual material (e.g., inputs like "Yesterday at school, the boy hit the window with a stone. The man scolded him") the encoding that they proposed is equally effective for any sequence of events, with one modification. Unlike a dry recitation of a sequence of events, episodic memory contains complex emotive information. Since episodic memory is personal, it is the memory of what happened in the life of the individual who experienced the events, the internal state of the experiencer is also encoded along with the events themselves.

So in addition to the encoding of the sequence of current world states, these memories must also encode the internal states that were coincident to the external events. Thus in the episodic memory of the boy who hit the window with a stone there would be an association perhaps of fear; while in the episodic memory of the man who scolded the boy, there might be an association of anger.

The analogy of a log file is frequently used as a model for episodic memory. In this model the episodic memory is viewed as a time sequenced series of snapshots of the state of the system. While this captures a high fidelity record of the events, it also contains significant levels of redundancy. Consider such a system logging the state of an autonomous robot. This robot has obstacle detection using active sonars and it has navigational data provided by GPS and a digital compass. It has a traditional drive system with two drive wheels, and front wheel steering, so it must maintain information about the power sent to the drive wheels, the actual speed of the drive wheels, and the position of the steering. Finally, it has general information about the state of the batteries, and possibly sensors monitoring the internal network capacity, the CPU load, and so on - what NASA refers to as health and safety data[98]:

$$\mathbf{RobotState(RS)} \equiv (time, sonar, navigation, drive, health) \qquad (8.1)$$

where: *time* is the timestamp of the observation;
         sonar is the current sonar data;
         navigation contains the GPS and compass data;
         drive contains the drive power, wheel speed, steering; and
         health includes the state of the batteries, etc.

If the entire state *RS* were to be logged with any frequency, the log would be filled with redundant values that changed slowly. Envision such a robot crossing an open field - the sonars would be recording the robotic equivalent of "all clear" hundreds, perhaps thousands of times, while the overall battery state might change once or twice, if at all. In addition to being inefficient, it does not match our intuitive notion of episodic memory, which is based not on state but on events that change the state in a salient way. Recall the brief story of the boy, the stones, and the scolding man. There is no notion of the continuous recording of where they were, once the scene in the schoolyard is set. This suggests that only things that have changed are represented. In addition, there is no description of the weather, the trees, or the cracks in the pavement; these may have been experienced, but they are not salient to the memory, and so they are not represented. From this we can conclude that the episodic memory of living systems is not a long, dull, redundant recording of the state of every variable, rather it is the record of the events (changes) that were significant in some way to the episode.

From this it is clear that something more like a change log is required, the elements of the episodic memory would capture not the entire state of the system, but only those things which changed during the episode. This places the focus onto the events that comprise the episode. However, unlike a long running series of differences, an episode has a beginning, a point in time or space when the episode starts. In our story, it was "Yesterday, at school." So an episode begins with a description of the initial state from which the story begins, and then begins to detail the salient changes that capture the essence of the story.

$$\textbf{Episode} \equiv (RS, \{Event_1, Event_2, ..., Event_n\}) \qquad (8.2)$$

where: *RS* is the initial Robot state; and
         Event_x are the changes that occurred in sequence.

On the surface this seems fairly straight forward, we have a stream of current world state data, each entry carefully time stamped to maintain sequence, and we extract the significant changes as events. These events are stripped of redundant information so that only the salient changes are represented in the events. And this, of course, is the difficulty. The question of what constitutes a 'significant change' and what criteria are used to detect a 'salient change' is fundamentally hard.

As a first pass, one might consider specifying a significant change as one that exceeds some threshold, but this simply begs several questions. What thresholds are significant? Are these thresholds constant or do they vary depending on the task? What if the change is large, but it is one that is predicted to happen? What if the change is small, but critical for one task, while the same change in the same variable is immaterial for a different task? This problem is another version of a core open question in artificial intelligence research; it is the same problem that Shank and Abelson addressed with scripts, it lies at the back of the frame problem[128, 49, 131], and others.

The difficulty arises, in part, from the lack of context in a simple log file. The recording of sensor state does not include any association of the semantic information. Rather than relying on some numeric or syntactic attempt to classify the application of a threshold, we rely on the mapping capability provided by the Reification Engine. The events that are logged are not simple positions and sensor data, rather they are mapped onto symbolic representations. These symbolic representations are instances of the complex web of knowledge that makes up the Personal Rough Ontology, and thus the relationships that are expressed in that structure can be used to assess salience.

From this structure, it becomes possible to imagine our robot storing an episode associated with a specific task such as being directed to travel to a location and begin monitoring for a toxic plume. While the actual episode might be unreadable to a human, we can imagine the salient events recorded somewhat like:

- Time X, Location: Parking lot facing north, Speed: 0, Sonar clear, Detector off
- Time X+1, Goal added: travel to field 300m east, monitor for chlorine gas
- Time X+2, Steer right, Set speed: 10
- Time X+3, Heading: NorthEast
- Time X+4, Heading: East, Steer Straight
- Time X+5, Location: 10m east, Sonar: vehicle (V0031:Class Truck, subclass Pickup truck) detected ahead, Closing speed: Extreme
- Time X+6, Emergency Stop
- Time X+7, Speed:0, Sonar: vehicle (V0031) detected ahead, closing speed: zero
- Time X+8, Steer: Left, Set Speed: 5
- Time X+9, Steer: Straight, Set Speed: 10, Sonar: vehicle (V0031) detected to right, Closing speed: negative
- Time X+10, Heading: NE, Steer: Right, Location 20m ENE, Sonar: clear
- Time X+11, Heading: E, Steer: Straight, Set Speed: 20
- Time X+12, Location 100m East
- Time X+13, Location 200m East
- Time X+14, Location 280m East, Set Speed 10
- Time X+15, Location 295m East, Detector: on, Set Speed 5
- Time X+16, Location 300m East, Set Speed: 0
- Time X+17, Detector: Activated level: 9, Send Message: "Chlorine detected 300M east of Parking lot"

To summarize in an anthropomorphic sense, the story would be told as:

I was in the parking lot that was the staging area for the HazMat response last Tuesday. They told me to head out to the east 300m to make sure that the chlorine gas wasn't drifting toward the staging area. I no sooner started heading out, than some bozo in a pickup truck cut right in front of me, and I had to slam on the brakes. After they skidded to a stop, I had to detour around them. Once I got past them, I went out into the field, and turned on the detector. The buzzer went off, and the reading was a nine on the scale, so I radioed it in to the command post, and they cleared the parking lot.

One difference between the story and the list of events should be clear - the list is a fairly dry, dare we say mechanical, recitation of changes that the robot detected, while the story format has a more emotional flavor. In the next section we will discuss those emotive tags.

8.2.1 Emotive Tags

As we have discussed above, for a biological entity to function effectively in the world, the emotional states that are influenced by broadband neurotransmitters must affect the deliberative process, and have been shown to modify the decisions that are considered to be 'intelligent'. These emotional states are part of the record and are embodied in the episodic memories. One of the key aspects of episodic memory in biological organisms (at least in humans) is that these memories include emotive tags[155], and the recounting of them can, and does, re-invoke the emotional states that were part of the experience. It is also clear that the emotive tags associated with episodic memory affect how these memories generate semantic knowledge. To support these functions it is necessary to record the emotive tags along with the dry state changes that make up the list above. The entries around Time X+6 should be amended to be:

- ...
- Time X+5,(FEAR: HIGH) Location: 10m east, Sonar: obstacle detected ahead, Closing speed: Extreme
- Time X+6,(FEAR: HIGH)Emergency Stop
- Time X+7,(FEAR: NORMAL) Speed:0, Sonar: obstacle detected ahead, closing speed: zero
- ...

The addition of these emotive tags is also critical for the system to learn effectively, since they are used to filter the important events from the huge amount of episodic memory that accumulates from day to day. So the final structure for the Events in the episodic memory (described in Equation 8.2) becomes:

$$\textbf{Event} \equiv ((F, R, S, P), \{WS_1, WS_2, ..., WS_n\}) \qquad (8.3)$$

where: F is the FEAR index;
R is the RAGE index;
S is the SEEK index;
P is the PANIC index; and
WS_1 - WS_n are the changes to apply (using the WorldSet notation).

As we discussed earlier, these four emotive tags seem to be common across a large range of vertebrate species, and are almost the defining characteristics of mammals. A seeking drive has clear applications to robotics, in fact some of the earliest autonomous robots were hard coded with the behavior of finding a charging station when the batteries ran low. One early example was the turtles of W. Gray Walter. These robots were built in the 1950's utilizing vacuum tube technology for their cognitive ability, and had the ability to learn from their experiences[204]. The key behavior built into these robots was a seeking behavior.

Fear, at least in the form of some kind of protection drive is a common drive in most robots. After all, with robots costing upwards of tens of thousands of dollars, some sort of self protection is a good investment. Yet even low cost robots are frequently setup with self protection drives. A common early task for hobbyists starting in robotics is to build the robot that can detect and avoid the edge of the table - FEAR at its most basic.

It is less clear why panic is conserved across a wide range of biological organisms, yet it is. Panic can have many forms, from a deer freezing in the headlights, to shortened planning horizons, to a frantic 'try anything, but do it quickly' response. In our robots we tend to focus on the latter two effects, reducing the depth of planning to more quickly produce a solution, and to lower the acceptability threshold for plan success probability.

The final emotive tag is rage. Needless to say, giving a robot the ability to become angry is somewhat controversial. It is also unclear what benefit would derive from the ability. For the moment, we will include the capacity, but not enable the application.

8.3 Memory Services

The four types of memory are utilized by both the deliberative process and the Reification Engine. The services provided to each are different, yet they must be in sync with each other. We will look first at the services provided to the deliberative system, and then address the services provided to the Reification Engine.

The deliberative process works from the symbolic model of the current world state, and the representation of the desired goal states. It also relies on the semantic knowledge of what things can be done to change the state of the world. All of these are maintained by the memory system - the ontology provides knowledge of the things in the world and actions that can be taken, and the transient memory provides specific knowledge of the state of the world.

These instantiated representations are used to populate the symbolic world model which is reasoned about by the deliberative system. This knowledge is extracted and provided to the deliberative system to be reasoned about, and (if possible) the deliberative system can generate a sequence of actions which can be used to achieve the goals. If the deliberative system generates a plan to achieve a goal, or goals, each step in the plan has an associated symbolic representation of the expected state of the world. This plan, along with the expected intermediate states become part of the transient memory, and can be utilized by the Reification Engine during the preafference step.

8.4 Providing Memory Services to the Reification Process

Reification is the mapping of sensor data onto a symbolic representation, and then mapping of the symbolic representation of the expectations onto the equivalent sensor-based expectation. Clearly, there must be a direct connection from the symbolic representations to the sensor-based representations. The memory structures presented here must support those connections.

The data structures for reification were described in Chapter 7. The basic structure is a bidirectional mapping with sensor/actuator specific representations on one side, and symbolic representations on the other. These symbolic representations are the same symbols as those used in the semantic memory. Thus, when the robot uses its sensors to perceive the world, these sensor specific data are used by the Reification Engine to determine the matching symbolic representations for the current state of the world.

It has been suggested that we do not live in the real world, rather that our conscious minds interact with a low fidelity representation of the real world. This virtual reality is constructed from the information provided by our senses, but is primarily a symbolic representation of the outside world. In our design this is literally true. The sensor data is interpreted by the Reification Engine, and a lower resolution, symbolic representation is generated. The inverse operation is invoked when the expected state of the world is presented to the Reification Engine to enable preafference. Recall that PerCepts have associated sensor tags, which capture the sensor specific indicators of the object that is perceived. These sensor tags are used by the Reification Engine to generate a sensor specific representation of what the world should look like. This can be envisioned as a virtual reality image of the representation of the expected state of the world.

This sensor specific representation is used as a presumptive test against the actual sensorium. If the actual sensorium matches the expectation to some degree of accuracy, the conscious mind may never become aware of any discrepancy.

8.5 Memory, What Was That Again?

From this brief outline (the last 20 pages or so...), it is clear that the mechanisms for memory are very complex, and that the choice of underlying representation has far reaching effects on the ability of the cybernetic system to behave in a manner that might be considered intelligent. This complexity must be balanced with the clear need for a simple underlying representation, since biological organisms seem to maximize reuse.

In this chapter we have explored three of the four independent memory structures: Episodic memory, Working Memory, and the representation of the internal state of the robotic system. These three types of memory have very different functions, and very different mechanisms; however, each of them is built up out of the same underlying data structures. These data structures have very different machinery attached to them. In the following chapter we explore the semantic memory.

Fig. 8.2 The equivalent scenes with Reality on the left, and a virtual-reality equivalent on the right.

Chapter 9
Semantic Memory and the Personal Rough Ontology

Much of the research into the representation of knowledge has been based on how we, as humans, think about things. The accessible portions of our reasoning are primarily symbolic. We think in words, in linguistic symbols, but is clear that not all reasoning creatures think in words. Anyone who has watched a dog 'figure out' how to get out of a fenced yard knows that animals can solve some problems that we would 'reason' about and it is a safe assumption that that dog did not solve the problem with a linguistic argument. However, when we try to watch ourselves think, we see symbolic manipulation. There have been linguists who have argued that it is not possible to *think* about something unless one has words (linguistic symbols) to describe the concepts[206]. So we will begin by looking at how we will represent symbolic knowledge in the persistent memory.

9.1 Semantic Memory

The question of how to represent knowledge in a computer has been a fundamental issue since the earliest research into artificial intelligence. While the underlying data structures are critical, the key question is more focused on how does one represent the incredibly rich set of concepts, relationships, and structures that make up our knowledge. In 1968, Quillian stated the question this way:

> The central question asked in this research has been: What constitutes a reasonable view of how semantic information is organized within a person's memory? In other words: What sort of representational format can permit the "meanings" of words to be stored, so that human like use of these meanings is possible?[163]

The primary representational mechanism for long term semantic memory will be a Personal Rough Ontology. Which begs the question:

9.1.1 What is a Personal Rough Ontology?

Perhaps the first question should be "What is an ontology?" An ontology is a way of defining the meanings of symbols. Unlike a dictionary, which defines one word by using sentences, an ontology attempts to capture the relationships between symbols. The term is primarily used in philosophy as the field of study relating to the precise utilization of words as descriptors of entities or realities. Any ontology must give an account of which words refer to entities, which do not, why, and what categories result. The use of the term has been adopted by researchers in computer science to focus on the data models that represent a set of concepts within a domain and the relationships between those concepts. The ontology is used to reason about the objects within that domain, and this is how we will use the term.

In the domain of computer science, research into ontologies has often focused on their use as a tool for sharing knowledge between distinct systems[83]. If computer system 'A' refers to a *tree*, how does computer system 'B' make sure that the symbol *tree* maps onto the same meaning? While this is of critical import when multiple heterogeneous knowledge systems must communicate, our focus is on representations within a single cybernetic system.

Typically, when an ontology is used to define concepts and the relationships between them, there are three characteristics that are desired: an ideal ontology should be complete, consistent, and accurate. These are necessary as a result of the logical operations that are used to manipulate and query the ontology. Using these logical operations, a computer can start from a collection of information, and derive additional statements that must be true, or the computer can demonstrate that a specific statement cannot be true. Truth in this context means that the statement does not contradict anything known to be true. The three criteria of completeness, consistency, and accuracy are all required if the ontology is to be reliable. If it is not complete, it may not be possible to invalidate (prove to be false) any given query, but if a statement cannot be proved false, it is assumed by the logical operations to be true - thus false things can be accepted as true. If the ontology is not accurate - that is to say that it includes statements as true, which are, in reality, false; then these logical operations will be able to prove false things which are, in fact true. Finally, if the ontology is inconsistent, if it contains statements as true, which are contradicted by other statements or derivations, then almost anything can be proved to be false or true. The logical operations are very literal, very 'narrow-minded' and so they require very carefully cleaned and maintained data sets on which to work.

When dealing with living systems however, the knowledge that they have is neither clean nor carefully maintained. It is not complete, consistent, or completely accurate; yet living systems seem to be able to perform effectively in the real world. Whatever representational scheme we use for our ontology must also be tolerant of these failings. The structure we utilize is a personal, rough ontology.

9.1.1.1 Why is it Personal?

An ontology captures the concepts and relationships with which we reason. For all the very precise definitions that exist in dictionaries, each one of us has our own, unique, understanding of each concept. As living systems, each of our ontologies have been built up over the years and decades of our experience, and this results in an individual collection of relationships and associations with each concept in our base of knowledge. Consider this quote from Oscar Wilde's *The Picture of Dorian Gray*:

> And so he would now study perfumes and the secrets of their manufacture, distilling heavily scented oils and burning odorous gums from the East. He saw that there was no mood of the mind that had not its counterpart in the sensuous life, and set himself to discover their true relations, wondering what there was in frankincense that made one mystical, and in ambergris that stirred one's passions, and in violets that woke the memory of dead romances, and in musk that troubled the brain, and in champak that stained the imagination. [207]

This captures the wealth of associations that are represented in human semantic memory, and the complex unfolding of these associations upon the activation of a memory or a concept. Where Wilde's narrator associated the scents with passions and romances, another person might have no deep reaction to the same scents, and would wonder what all the fuss was about. Clearly, each of us maintains our own personal ontology. While we do not expect that our robots will have the capacity to experience this depth of association, it is also clear that, if they are to function in a world populated by humans, they must have more depth that a simple dictionary style definition of *violets*.

9.1.1.2 Consistency versus Correspondence, or Why is it Rough?

An ontology is much more that just data. There are also numerous operations on these data that allow the computer to deduce information that is not explicitly represented in the ontology, operations that allow the computer to focus attention on a subset of the total data available, and operations that allow the computer to determine the 'meaning' of the otherwise meaningless symbols that make up the data itself.

Humans are not good at maintaining perfectly accurate or consistent bases of knowledge. This is important to remember when designing a representational structure and its associated reasoning mechanism, because it will not be possible to achieve a knowledge base that is perfect. We must be able to represent knowledge that is incomplete, inconsistent, and inaccurate. Hence, our use of a *rough* ontology. In this ontology there is not even an attempt at searching out inconsistencies. The focus is on maintaining correspondence with the world, and we accept error as a consequence of the probabilistic nature of reality.

Inconsistency is, in some ways, the most difficult aspect for a computer based reasoning system to handle. Since the most basic functions of computer based reasoning are dependent on logical inferences, inconsistency can result in the ability to prove everything true, or false, or both.

Correspondence is less of a problem for the reasoning system, since it can function with no relationship between the symbols and any external referent. However, if our robot is to achieve goals in the real world, the symbols that it uses must have correspondence with the things to which they refer. The PerCepts and the Reification engine allow us to maintain this correspondence without requiring consistency.

9.2 Building Semantic Memory

Once the decision to represent semantic memory as a personal rough ontology has been made, the question of how to build the data structures and mechanisms remains. There are a number of well designed and fairly mature software packages that have been developed to build ontologies. However, very few are designed for the rigors of deploying the ontology into a robotic platform. As we discussed above, embodied and embedded systems place hard requirements of size, speed, and power consumption on the processors and software. In addition, many of the existing ontological packages are designed for web based applications. Packages such as OWL and Jena are typical.

These web-based ontologies offer significant benefits to the researcher, and to the human user. Since it is a daunting task to attempt to compile the vast amounts of data needed to build a comprehensive ontology, the web-based ontologies use a divide and conquer approach. Rather than maintaining internal copies of all the possible sub-domains that might be needed, the ontologies reference other, external, ontologies. They do so using the web as a gigantic, distributed storage system. Unfortunately, our robots may not be able to depend on these external sources for day to day, and moment to moment operations. Fortunately, we also have somewhat simpler requirements for our robots, so there is a chance that they can achieve their goals without relying on terabytes of data stored on the web. In practice, most of the living systems that act as our exemplars are capable of storing locally the information they need to survive. So we need an ontology structure that is not designed around having constant access to the entire web.

We begin with the traditional approach of using an ordered triple to represent a relationship. The triple consists of a subject, a relationship, and an object, as in Equation 9.1.

$$(subject, relationship, object) \tag{9.1}$$

Using these triples, an ontology is designed to capture and represent the relationships between symbols, and capture the 'meaning' of the symbols. For example to represent that John is a child of Mary, one can specify:

$$(John, descendant\_of, Mary) \qquad\qquad (9.2)$$

These relationship statements are predicates, and the existence of a predicate in the data indicates that the predicate is true. This is consistent with the closed world assumption discussed earlier. In addition to the relationships, the ontology supports the definition of rules which can specify the properties of the relationships. For example, the *descendant_of* relationship is transitive – if A is a descendant of B and B is a descendant of C, then A is a descendant of C.

$$(rule : (X descendant\_of Y) \wedge (Y descendant\_of Z) \qquad\qquad (9.3)$$
$$then(X descendant\_of Z)) \qquad\qquad (9.4)$$

With the addition of this transitivity rule the reasoning engine in the ontology can prove the truth of new predicates from the data.

$$(Bob, descendant\_of, Shirley) \wedge \qquad\qquad (9.5)$$
$$(Alice, descendant\_of, Bob) \wedge \qquad\qquad (9.6)$$
$$(Shirley, descendant\_of, John) \Rightarrow \qquad\qquad (9.7)$$
$$(Alice, descendant\_of, John) \qquad\qquad (9.8)$$

In this example, the predicates in 9.5 through 9.7 are directly represented in the data, while the predicate in 9.8 is a derived predicate, based on the transitivity of the relationship *descendant_of*.

The ontology package supports the definition of arbitrary relationships and the creation of rules that are specific to the domain. These rules and relationships can be created and edited (the old rule removed and a new rule definition added) while the system is active. Specifically, it is not necessary to shut the ontology package down and reload it to have the new rules in effect.

The example above defines a single relationship and a single rule that applies to that relationship. In a more realistic example there are many types of relationships that a single entity might enter into, and there are complex sets of rules that might apply to any of those relationships. This complexity must be supported by the ontological underpinnings of the semantic memory.

In addition to the relationships between entities in the ontology, it is possible to define attributes (or properties) of the entity. For example, with Mary, Bob, and Shirley, we would include attributes such as height, weight, gender, hair color, and so on. More abstract properties would also be included, such as the fact that Shirley is laid-back, while Mary has more of a temper, and that Bob is touchy about his baldness. These properties are persistent knowledge, and are stored not as relationships but as properties associated with specific instances of people. When reasoning, these properties interact with knowledge about relationships and classes, enabling

Bob to reason that since Mary is female and Irish, and since Bob believes that Irish females are more likely to have anger management issues, this explains why Mary has a bit of a temper.

9.2.1 Structure of the Ontology

The basic structure of the ontology is a directed multi-graph:

$$Ontology \equiv (\mathbf{C}, \mathbf{E}) \tag{9.9}$$

where: $\mathbf{C}$ is a collection of nodes; and
$\mathbf{E}$ is a collection of directed Edges from one node to another.

9.2.1.1 A What??

If you are familiar with the concept of a directed multi-graph, feel free to jump ahead to the next section (Section 9.2.2), if you would like a quick review of graph structure, read on.

A graph, in the computer science / mathematical sense, is a structure that consists of nodes (or vertices) and edges. The nodes typically represent the objects and the edges represent some relationship between the objects. In a traditional graph, the there can be at most one edge between any two nodes, indicating that the relationship holds. Any two nodes that do not have an edge between them represent objects for which the relationship does not hold. In a traditional graph the relationship is assumed to be symmetric (for example, the equals relationship: if $a = b$ then $b = a$)

Since not all relationships are symmetric, a directed graph adds the capability of representing non-symmetric relationships such as the less-than relationship: if $a < b$ then it cannot be true that $b < a$. So there would be a 'less than' edge going from a to b, but not one going the other way. In the example above, the *descendant_of* relationship is not symmetric. With directed graphs, the idea that there is only one edge between any two nodes is a little more complex, it is still illegal to have two edges both running from Node A to Node B, but it is possible to have one edge going from Node A to Node B, and a second going from Node B to Node A. As an example think of a *likes* relationship. It is possible that person A *likes* person B and that person B *likes* person A: this would result in one edge going in each direction between the two nodes. However, just because person C *likes* person A, it does not mean that person A *likes* person C, and so only the edge from C to A would be present.

In this way a directed graph can capture complex structure with respect to the relationship that it represents, however, it is limited to representing a single relationship. With a multi-graph, that restriction is removed. A multigraph can have a number of different relationships represented by different types of edges. There can be multiple edges connecting any two nodes, with each type of edge representing the existence of a different relationship (See Figure 9.1).

9.2.2 The nodes in the multi-graph

Referring back to Equation 9.9, we see that the multigraph consists of a collection of nodes and a collection of directed edges. Each node C corresponds to a symbolic representation of an entity. The base class for these nodes is a Cept, hence the non-traditional use of **C** in equation 9.9. Each Cept may have a collection of properties that describe it. These properties are used in two ways. First, the ontological system can use these properties when applying rules, and second the deliberative system (described in Chapter 10) uses these properties to develop plans to achieve its goals. To facilitate these uses, the properties are represented as specific relationship arcs to other Cept.

$$\mathbf{Cept}(C) \equiv (symbol, \{P\}, \{R\}) \tag{9.10}$$

where: *symbol* is the symbolic representation of the concept (its name);

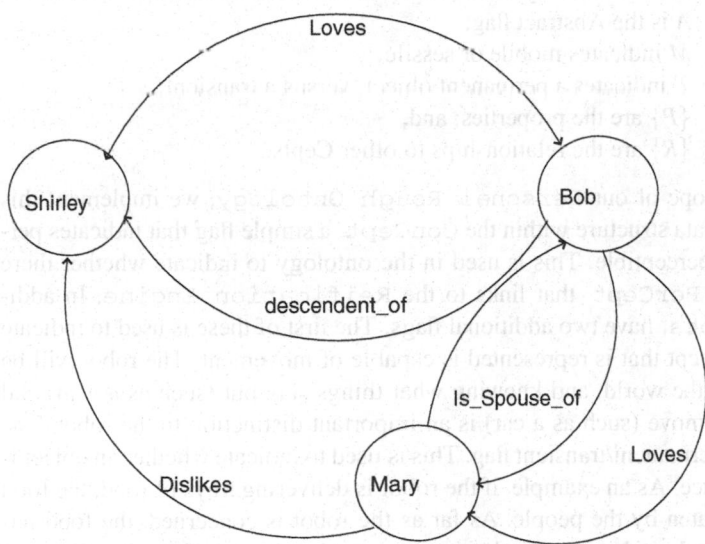

Fig. 9.1 In this example of a multi-graph, there are three nodes (Bob, Mary, and Shirley) and several types of edges (Loves, Is_Spouse_of, Dislikes, Descendant_of). The combination of nodes and edges capture a complex story.

$\{P\}$ are the properties; and

$\{R\}$ are the relationships to other Cepts.

The Cepts in our ontology represent the things about which we have knowledge. These things correspond to the subject and objects of the ordered triple shown in Equation 9.1. The common element of these things is the symbol and the list of properties. This base class is extended to represent specific types of knowledge in the ontology.

9.2.2.1 ConCepts

The simplest variant of a Cept is a ConCept. This is what is represented in a typical ontology, and makes up the bulk of the information in a semantic memory. The ConCept extends the basic Cept by adding the idea that a ConCept can represent either an abstract concept or something more concrete. As an example, the ConCept of a chair represents a perceptible thing that might exist in the world; however the ConCept of 'laid-back' is not something that is directly perceptible. Recall from earlier that one of the original purposes of an ontology was to formally distinguish between those things that are entities from those that are not.

$$\textbf{ConCept}(C) \equiv (symbol, A, M, T, \{P\}, \{R\}) \qquad (9.11)$$

where: *symbol* is the symbolic representation of the concept (its name);

A is the Abstract flag;

M indicates mobile or sessile;

T indicates a permanent object, versus a transient;

$\{P\}$ are the properties; and,

$\{R\}$ are the relationships to other Cepts.

Within the scope of our Personal Rough Ontology, we implement this distinction as a data structure within the ConCept, a simple flag that indicates perceptible or non-perceptible. This is used in the ontology to indicate whether there is an associated PerCept that links to the Reification Engine. In addition, all ConCepts have two additional flags. The first of these is used to indicate whether the concept that is represented is capable of movement. The robot will be moving through the world, and knowing what things stay put (such as a wall) and what things can move (such as a car) is an important distinction to the robot. The final flag is the permanent/transient flag. This is used to indicate whether an object is always in the space. As an example, if the robot is delivering trays of food, the food on the trays is eaten by the people. As far as the robot is concerned, the food has simply disappeared - it does not need to have a complete model of the digestion and assimilation of the food by the humans. It is convenient to tag certain objects with a flag that says "This ConCept can be deleted when it is no long of use." If a new person arrives at the party, the robot must instantiate a ConCept that corresponds to that person, in order to track her movements. However, once the person leaves, there is no need to continue to update that ConCept, and it can be deleted.

Using the example in equations 9.5 - 9.8, we can construct an example of a multi-graph. In Figure 9.1 we show the descendant_of relationship between Shirley and Bob (e.g., Bob is Shirley's son). We add the relationship between Mary and Bob - they are married, and so there are two directed spouse_of arcs, one from Bob to Mary, and one from Mary to Bob. Unfortunately, While Shirley loves Bob and Bob loves Mary, Mary does not get along with her mother-in-law, which undoubtedly causes stress between Shirley and her son. This simple multi-graph consisting of three nodes and six relationships captures a complex wealth of information in a clear and concise form.

As another example, consider a chair. The class of chairs has many specific instantiations, including the chair you are probably sitting in right now. This chair, in specific, has a number of properties including color, shape, softness, and so forth. However, there is also the more abstract concept of a *chair*. As a concept it has relationships with other concepts such as the notion of *sitting*, *support*, and *rest*. *Chair* has relationships to *legs*, *seats* and *backs*, and, in some cases, *wheels*. These relationships effectively define what makes the symbol *chair* have meaning, and are what enables us to thinks about, and reason about chairs. These more abstract ideas are represented by abstract ConCepts.

9.2.2.2 ActCepts

Much as the ConCepts correspond to nouns, the world is also full of verbs - the actions and events that cause change. We, as humans, have complex representations of the things that make changes to our world, and we reason about these continuously. Although knowledge about actions may seem to be fundamentally different than knowledge about things, they are still symbolic representations about the world. In the chair discussion above, it seemed natural that there would be a relationship between a chair and the concept of sitting, just as there seems to be a natural relationship between a bicycle and riding or a ladder and climbing. Note that the conceptual symbol associated with sitting differs from the mechanics of lowering ones body into a seated position - that is a function of the perception/action system, and more correctly corresponds to procedural memory.

To represent the conceptual model of an action, we modify the base Cept class by adding the necessary enabling conditions to undertake the action (e.g., to *drive_the_car* it is necessary to have a car), and the set of possible outcomes. The enabling conditions and outcomes can be directly mapped onto the corresponding components of the action representation used by the deliberative system, and so the semantic memory fulfills its design goal of being the repository of knowledge for the reasoning system.

The ActCept class is also extended with a category flag, much like the ConCept. In this case, we have ActCepts that are abstract, such as the general notion of movement. There are also concrete ActCepts which correspond to specific

actions that the robot might undertake to achieve a goal. Just as the concrete
ConCepts have corresponding sensor signatures stored in the Reification
Engine, procedural ActCepts have corresponding action sequences stored in
the Perception/Action system. These are the recipes for the execution of a specific
action.

$$\textbf{ActCept}(A) \equiv (symbol, A, \{P\}, \{E\}, \{O\}) \tag{9.12}$$

where: *symbol* is the symbolic representation of the node (its name);
         A is the Abstract flag;
         $\{P\}$ are the properties;
         $\{E\}$ are the enabling conditions; and
         $\{O\}$ are the defined outcomes.

The properties of an ActCept define specific aspects of the action it represents.
Two common properties are the Estimated Execution Time (EET) and the notion of
whether this specific action can be repeated if it fails the first time, or Retry on
Failure (ROF).

9.2.2.3 EventCepts

A specialized form of an action is an event. These are used to capture knowledge of
changes that occur to the world, for which the robot is not the initiator. The general
structure of the EventCept is the same as any action, there are necessary enabling
conditions, and an event has one or more possible outcomes. In general, there is no
equivalent to the unspecified outcome, since if the event caused no sensible changes
to the environment, the event did not really occur.

The most significant difference between an intentional action and an event is
how it is triggered. Where an ActCept is triggered by the robot undertaking the
action, an EventCept is triggered stochastically, if its enabling conditions are
satisfied. As an example, consider the case of a component failure, such as a light
bulb burning out. The enabling condition might be specified as the light bulb being
turned on. Given that the light bulb is on, there is a small, but significant chance
that it can burn out. We represent this probability as a Poisson distributed random
variable[158] with a probability of failing per unit of time.

$$\textbf{EventCept}(A) \equiv (symbol, \{P\}, \{E\}, \{O\}) \tag{9.13}$$

where: *symbol* is the symbolic representation of the node (its name);
         $\{P\}$ are the properties;
         $\{E\}$ are the enabling conditions; and
         $\{O\}$ are the defined outcomes.

These EventCepts are used in the deliberative process to evaluate possible outcomes of a complete plan. Specifically, there can be very good plans (e.g., they have high success rates when only the intentional actions are considered), however these plans can enable the possibility of very bad outcomes from the events in the domain. For example, A robot might decide to carry an object balanced on its end. If the robot does not get jostled, the plan is short and very successful. However, the outcome of being bumped by a person in the room (an event that is outside the control of the robot) must be considered when evaluating the quality of the proposed plan. The properties that are associated with an EventCept include the relative frequency of the event, given that it's enabling conditions are met. The EventCept provides a mechanism for the deliberative system to reason about these types of exogenous events. For more details about the exact mechanisms used see Section 10.4.

The four data structures defined above make up the classes that are the nodes in the semantic memory. Each corresponds to a key type of knowledge that is used when the system is reasoning about the current state of the world, the goals that need to be achieved, and the methods that can be used to achieve those goals. However, the reasoning process is not limited to isolated facts that can be juggled. In addition to these facts, are the relationships between them. These relationships make up the

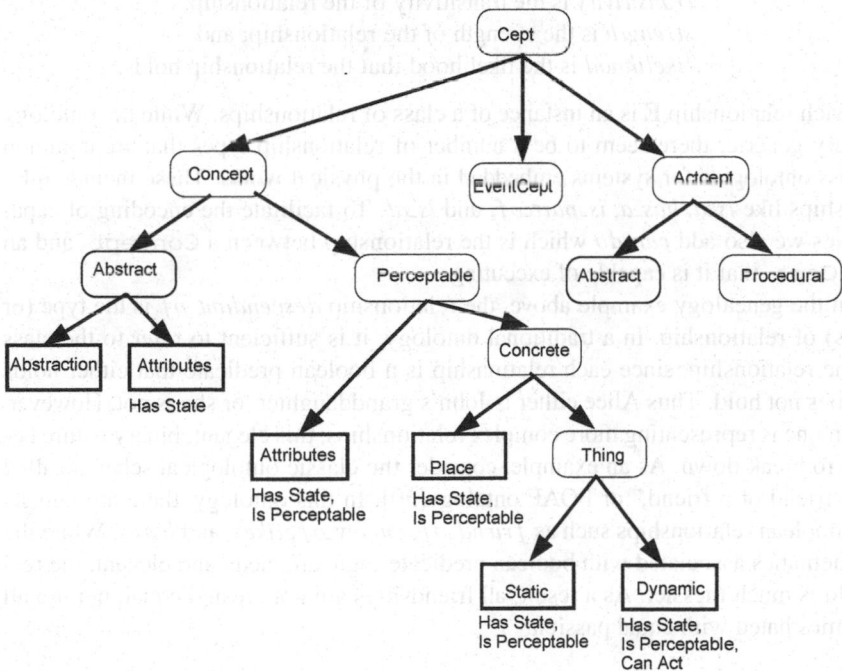

Fig. 9.2 The structural relationships between the types of nodes in the ontology.

bulk of the semantic memory, and, in essence, are what encode the meaning of the facts[40].

9.2.3 Relationships, the Edges of the Graph

Each edge in the multi-graph is a directed arc that leads from the subject node to the object node. Directed arcs are needed since not all relationships are symmetric, for example, if the type of the relationship is *part_of*, it makes sense to say that a leg is *part_of* a chair; however the reverse is not true. Each edge captures one specific type of relationship. In figure 9.1 there are two edges leading from Bob to Mary. One is the *loves* relationship, and the other is the *spouse_of* relationship. The representational schema for the arcs is:

$$\mathbf{Edge}(\mathbf{E}) \equiv (type, identifier, ToNode, transitivity, strength, likelihood) \quad (9.14)$$

where: *type* is the type of the relationship;
        identifier is the unique identifier of this relationship;
        ToNode is the identifier of the destination Node;
        transitivity is the transitivity of the relationship;
        strength is the strength of the relationship; and
        likelihood is the likelihood that the relationship holds.

Each relationship **E** is an instance of a class of relationships. While the ontology is very generic, there seem to be a number of relationship types that are common across ontologies for systems embedded in the physical world. These include relationships like *is_a*, *has_a*, *is_part_of*, and *is_at*. To facilitate the encoding of capabilities we also add *can_do* which is the relationship between a ConCept and an ActCept that it is capable of executing.

In the genealogy example above, the relationship *descendant_of* is the type (or class) of relationship. In a traditional ontology, it is sufficient to refer to the class of the relationship, since each relationship is a boolean predicate that either holds or does not hold. Thus Alice either is John's granddaughter, or she is not. However, when one is representing more complex relationships, this elegant, binary nature begins to break down. As an example, consider the classic ontological schema called the "friend of a friend," or FOAF ontology[50]. In this ontology, there are numerous boolean relationships such as *friend_of*, *enemy_of*, *likes*, and *hates*. While the mathematics associated with boolean predicate logic are clean and elegant, the real world is much messier. As a result, all friendships are not created equal, nor are all enemies hated with equal passion.

9.2.3.1 Strength

To be able to represent this complexity we replace the boolean predicates with a more flexible real valued weight term. Using this representation we can capture the idea that Bob likes Mary with a weighting term of 0.99, while he likes Bill with a weighting term of only 0.25 - Mary is his spouse and best friend, while Bill is more of an acquaintance. Thus each use of the *friend_of* relationship is an instance of the class *friend_of*.

9.2.3.2 Transitivity

The use of the transitivity term does not preclude the use of boolean predicates. By setting the weight to 1.0, each instance of a relationship behaves exactly the same as the existence of a boolean predicate. However, the machinery that applies rules and generated new, derived predicates from the explicit data must be more complex. As an example, a rule based on transitivity (such as the rule shown in Equation 9.4) must now examine the degree of transitivity. If the *friend_of* relationship were considered transitive, and if Mary is a friend of Bill, and Harry is a friend of Mary; by transitivity, Harry is a friend of Bill. If Mary is extremely gregarious, she may have hundreds of friends, and any friend of a friend is awarded all the rights and privileges of close friendship. For Mary, the *friend_of* relationship is highly transitive. Bill, on the other hand, has very few friends, and does not admit just anyone into that exclusive group. So his transitivity term for the *friend_of* relationship is low.

9.2.3.3 Likelihood

In addition to the strength term, there is a term for the likelihood of a relationship holding. In many cases, a relationship is definitional and thus it either holds or it does not. So our *descendant_of* relationship is either true or false - given complete knowledge. However, what is true, and what we *know* are not always the same. In the face of incomplete knowledge, many relationships must be quantified with a likelihood of truth. Using the *descendant_of* relationship as an example, recent studies using DNA have shown that descent down the male line is far less certain than might be supposed. The certainty of a relationship becomes even more problematic with more abstract relationships, and relationships that change over time. So we encode this lack of certainty in a likelihood term that can be reasoned about, and adapted as circumstances change.

9.2.4 A Note on Representing Probabilities

Probabilities are also used in the `ActCept` nodes, where an intended action has a probability of succeeding, and can have several possible failure modes. These likelihoods are used primarily by the deliberative system when it is evaluating the outcomes of possible actions that might achieve the system's goals. Since the universe is not a static place, and since our robot does not have complete knowledge, this likelihood will change as the robot gains in knowledge, and responds to changes in the universe. For example, when our autonomous ground vehicle is fresh from the factory, the robot might have extremely good tread on its tires. This tread enables it to accelerate more quickly, and stop very abruptly. So, the probability of a 'panic stop' resulting in a skid is low. However, over time, the tread wears down, and the stopping characteristics change. If the robot cannot alter its model of the stopping characteristics, it will be unable to adapt to the changes in the universe, and will begin to fail. So, especially with the action components (`ActCepts`), the likelihoods change. This can be thought of as asking the question "How likely is it that this relationship holds at the present moment?" To support this, the probabilities are not stored as simple real valued terms, but as pairs of counts: how many times has this been tried, how many times has it succeeded. These two values provide the necessary information to answer "What is the likelihood of success?", and to support a simple updating function as new knowledge is gained.

$$\textbf{Likelihood} \equiv (successes, attempts) \tag{9.15}$$

where: *successes* is the count of successful outcomes; and
         attempts is the total attempts of the actions

We can always reduce the counts to a simple likelihood, and provide a method to produce a real valued representation of the ration of success to the event count. In this way we can always project the count into a traditional probability value. This traditional representation contains less information however, and therefore fewer capabilities. By storing the actual counts associated with the likelihoods we gain several advantages.

To explore these capabilities, we will use the example of a gripper with rubber coated fingers. When fresh from the factory, the coefficients of friction are well known, and so it is a simple matter to estimate the probability of a gripper failing to hold onto an object, such as a glass. However, over several months of operation, the rubber coated fingers no longer have the same characteristics that they had when fresh from the factory. Portions of the gripper that habitually came in contact with the glasses have worn. In some spots the rubber has been polished and the coefficient of friction has decreased, in other spots there has been slight abrasion increasing the grip, in still other spots the rubber has worn away completely, exposing the underlying metal - with a radically different behavior.

If the likelihood of a failure were stored simply as a single real-valued number, it would be impossible to accurately update the information about how successful we can expect the grip operation to be. However, by maintaining both the number of attempts and the number of successes, we can update the values upon the completion of every attempt, either recording a successful attempt, or a failure. These incremental changes will result in a slowly changing likelihood of success, which corresponds to the actual success probabilities.

In addition, the use of the ordered pair representation allows the system to de-emphasize older data, in favor of more recent experience. After several years in service, the original factory specifications have little correlation to the present day experiences. Since both the number of successes and the total attempts are recorded, it is a simple matter to perform an exponential decay on the older data, by simply scaling the two values equally, and then continuing to record the actual successes and failures. So we support the following methods for the Likelihood class:

- double Likelihood.getProbability();
- void Likelihood.addSuccess();
- void Likelihood.addFailure();
- void Likelihood.decay(double scale)

9.3 Persistent Storage in the Personal Rough Ontology

Ontologies can get large, even for simple systems. As the range and scope of knowledge increases the size of the ontology can increase dramatically. As discussed above, in biological systems the storage mechanisms for semantic memory are not completely understood, however it is clear that the storage and retrieval mechanisms for the vast amounts of semantic information are different from that of short-term, working memory. In the ontology package, the large store of semantic memory is designed to be placed into a persistent database, and retrieved as necessary.

The format can be loaded at startup, and placed into RAM for faster access, provided the computer has sufficient RAM. Naturally this is an artifact of using a digital computer to emulate a biological system. There is no real equivalent to shutting the system down and reloading all the knowledge from off-line storage. In a biological system, shutting the system down may be far too easy, but bringing it back up again is trickier. as a result, whatever cybernetic mechanism we use, it must be capable of updating itself on the fly, and this encourages the used of a relational database for persistent storage, rather than a loadable file system.

9.4 Transient versus Persistent Knowledge

Knowledge changes over time. While many ontologies are designed to capture the relationships between permanent concepts such as what it means to be a mammal or what the definition of a prime number is; there is also a need to represent more transient information. This might include the properties associated with a person, such as their hair color, or that fact that Randi is allergic to seafood. This knowledge also includes the very fact that Randi is a person: that the ConCept that represents the Randi is a specific instance of the general concept of a *Person*.

There is a vast amount of relatively transient knowledge (Randi may change her hair color), far more than can be maintained in working memory at any point in time. So there must be a more permanent storage place. We include this transient knowledge in the form of properties attached to the ConCept, and use a specific relationship *instance_of* to link the individual ConCept to the framework of knowledge of more abstract concepts. In practice we have two specialized relationships for handling instance ConCepts: *thing_instance* and *location_instance*. These are used to provide the linkage from the specific instances to two corresponding nodes in the ontological frame work. These are labeled as *Place* and *Thing* (more specifically *StaticThing* and *DynamicThing* in figure 9.2.

In addition, there are instance ConCepts that appear and disappear from our knowledge base. We frequently encounter new people in our day to day interactions. While some of them may become friends or colleagues, many will be a single, short-term encounter. While we are interacting with them, we need to access the complex web of knowledge we have of people, and this can be done by instantiating an 'anonymous' person ConCept. This provides access to generic background information that allows us to reason about this person, but we do not need (or want) to clutter our ontology with references to every person we have ever encountered in our lives.

This is utilized in the interaction between the Personal Rough Ontology and the Reification Engine. When the robot encounters an object in the real world, it attempts to classify the object, so that a semantically tagged representation can be added to the current world state. The CWS includes knowledge about the permanent persistent features of the world, and it contains information about the current state of previously encountered transient objects. However, there is no pre-existing representation for an object that is encountered for the first time.

As an example, consider our robot serving drinks at a cocktail party. It knows about the general layout of the room - the walls, the big furniture, etc. This is permanent and persistent data. It also knows about the three smaller chairs, which are permanent, however, their current location may change as the chairs get moved around. However, it does not have instantiated representations for all the people who might arrive. Rather, when the robot encounters a new object, it will attempt to classify it. Using its sensor data, and the PerCepts that correspond to the currently instantiated objects, it fails to classify the object. It then uses the PerCepts associated with the more general concepts it might encounter. The PerCept for a generic Person has a high probability of a match, so the Reification Engine uses this to instantiate a new object in its current world state. This object is not permanent - rather it is transient. It comes into existence, and, after not being reinforced, it vanishes. In this way the size of the ontology is not ever-increasing with references to concepts, objects, and entities that will never be accessed again.

9.5 Extracting Problems for the Deliberative System

The Personal Rough Ontology acts as a repository for the complex knowledge base that represents the robot's representation of the world it inhabits. Much of this knowledge is necessary for modeling the relationships and interactions of the world. Other parts model the things that can be changed and the actions and events that can change them. When the robot needs to cause changes to the world to achieve its goals, it is these latter elements of the ontology that are required as inputs by the deliberative system. Thus a critical requirement of the ontology is the ability to extract a subset of itself, a problem description, and to provide that problem in a form that the deliberative system can manipulate.

The deliberative system is described in more detail in the following chapter, but it functions primarily as a problem solving engine. It is given the description of the world as it is, and a description of the world as we want it to be. It also needs a description of the actions and events that can change the state of the world. These components are packaged up into a problem description.

The Personal Rough Ontology has a single method that, when invoked, builds a complete problem description:

$$\mathbf{Problem} \equiv (CWS, Goal, Actions, Events) \qquad (9.16)$$

where: CWS is the Current World State;
         $Goal$ is the desired Goal State;
         $Actions$ is set of Actions that the robot can attempt; and
         $Events$ is the set of Events that can change the state of the world.

The Actions and Events are derived from the ActCepts and the EventCepts which are contained in the ontology, translated into a form that the deliberative system can use. This translation involves flattening the ontological structure. Recall that in the ontology, any given ActCept may be an instance of another, more general, ActCept. For example, *Roll* is an action that is a specialized form of *Locomotion* which is a specialized form of *Move*. The deliberative system does not need to know all of the complexities of the hierarchy of movement, it simply needs to know that the robot can Roll from the library into the office, provided that the intervening door is open.

9.6 Focusing Attention by Finding Sub-Ontologies

A second result of having a large ontology, is that typically only a small subset of any ontology will be relevant to any given situation. The ontology must be complete enough to have information about the many types of situations that the robot might encounter, so, unless the robot is a very special purpose unit, the ontology will need to be fairly comprehensive. If the robot is designed to be a general purpose house-hold unit, the range of situations that it might encounter is immense, and the detail required for any given situation is significant. One attempt at a general purpose on-tology is the Cyc project, spearheaded by Doug Lenat. As of 2005, the Cyc database included over three million assertions, and over 26,000 relationships[127].

Unfortunately this demand for a complex and comprehensive knowledge base is directly at odds with the computational complexity of problem solving. As the size of the knowledge base grows, the complexity of solving a traditional planning problem grows exponentially. So the deliberative system needs to have a tightly filtered, focused subset of the problem at hand, not the complete ontology. Thus, we need the ability to produce a salient subset of all the knowledge in the ontology, a subset that is significant to the task at hand. Without this ability, the deliberative system will be drowning in the social dynamics of office politics while attempting to determine how best to pick up the dog before the pet groomers close.

9.6.1 Weighted Transitivity

When the ontology is used to extract a problem, the general method is to begin with the differences between the CWS and the goal state. The Current World State has information about the state of everything the robot knows about. This can be compared with the state that the robot needs to achieve, as defined by the system goals. The salient differences in these states are the things that must be changed to achieve the goal. Note, they may not be the only things that have to change, but at the very least these features have to be changed from the way they are now to the way we want them to be. These features are part of a complex hierarchy of features linked by relationships. So in the process of expanding these sub-ontologies to include these features, additional related features will be also included in our sub-ontology.

We then can look at those actions that might change the state of the features and include them in the sub-ontology. These actions are also part of a hierarchy of ac-tions, and so we expand the subset to include related actions. These actions have spe-cific enabling conditions which are dependent on other features of the world being in a given state. So we can add these features and their relations to our sub-ontology, and then look at the actions that might be able to affect these features. This process continues alternately adding new features to the sub-ontology, and then adding new actions that can influence the state of the features. At some point, no new features will be added to the sub-ontology, and therefore no new actions will be added. At this point, if it is possible to achieve the goal by the application of intentional ac-tions, we have the necessary subset. Unfortunately, there is no guarantee that the subset is any smaller than the original ontology, let alone significantly smaller. This is due to the nature of ontologies and the graphs that represent them.

In general, the directed multi-graph that makes up the Personal Rough Ontology is connected. This means that there exists a path (or sequence of edges) the can be traversed from any node in the graph to any other node. The number of edges that must be traversed may be large, but, in general, the path exists. If that path exists, then eventually, every node on the graph will be included in our sub-ontology. Yes, it is very unlikely that the fact that the technician at the dog groomer's is married to the receptionist at your wife's dentist will be useful in figuring out how to pickup the dog before the groomer's close for the night. However, it is still possible that a quick phone call might get them to stay open late. So all these relationships might be useful to the deliberative system when it is trying to solve the problem. If some kind of a cut-off could be used to stop the propagation through the ontology, it would result in smaller and more tractable ontologies. This comes at a cost however. The cost is that the solution may require one of the actions, or relationships that have been cut off; and therefore the deliberative system will be unable to solve a problem which has a theoretic solution.

In spite of this potential problem, we implement this approach in the Personal Rough Ontology for two reasons. First, even though the hypothetical theoretic solution may exist, in the real world, no computational system has infinite resources. As a result, the target is not the theoretic solution, rather it is the solution available to a limited system. This is the idea of 'bounded rationality' developed by Newell and Simon in the 1970's[140], and expanded by others[16, 75, 209]. The second reason that we use this approach is that we can relax the constraint in response to the result that the deliberative system gets. If a simple, 'quick and dirty' sub-ontology does not produce a solution, we can produce a larger, more complete sub-ontology and try again. Eventually, this could expand to include attempts that allow solutions that are more *outside the box* than the simpler sub-ontologies permit.

The methodology for this adjustable extraction is dependent of the transitivity term that is part of every relationship. Since every directed edge in the ontology graph has a transitivity term, every path from one node to another has a value that is determined by the intervening relationships. If we have a relationship edge from node A to Node B, with a transitivity of 0.9, and a relationship edge from node B to node C with a transitivity of 0.8, we can use a simple multiplicative model to calculate the connection between node A and Node C. This multiplicative model results in a non-increasing weight as more edges are added to the path. Furthermore, if the transitivity terms are strictly less than 1.0, the path values steadily decrease with each additional edge. By setting an path transitivity threshold, eventually the propagation of new nodes stops, and therefore the addition of new features is controlled by this threshold term.

This gives us the ability to generate a sub-ontology that is focused to a greater or lesser degree, and thus is controlled in size. Smaller sub-ontologies produce smaller problem specifications, which produce either faster solutions, or they fail to produce a solution. If no solution is produced, the deliberative system can progressively widen the scope of the problem until a solution is produced, the world has changed in such a way that a new goal is more important, or the system terminates.

Chapter 10
Deliberative System

Since the beginnings of computer science the concept of an 'intelligent' robot has been identified with the idea of deliberate actions intended to achieve goals. While there has been significant research into more reactive systems[9, 14, 22, 68, 74, 107], these have not produced behaviors with the intelligence that we expected. Rather, we have seen more and more development of teleoperated systems where the deliberative aspects are performed by one or more humans in the loop. Over the same sixty years we have seen significant advances in 'intelligent' software, such as chess playing programs, complex scheduling systems, and other programs. These software systems work in a purely symbolic domain which is ideal for deliberation. Unfortunately, the domain that we wish our robots to work in is not a clean, deterministic domain. We need them to function in our world, constantly changing, uncertain, and probabilistic. In the first half of the 20th century, it was well understood that the world was a messy place, and that living systems had to make the best of it. Writing in 1950, Egon Brunswik was presenting material on the manner in which living systems dealt with the complex and ever changing world they survived in. In talking about the mechanisms used to maintain stability in the rapidly changing world, he suggested that:

> [This] injects an element of reasoning into stabilization mechanisms. Implicit reasoning of this kind may readily be made explicit by modern "cybernetics," or by "mathematical biophysics."[28]

Unfortunately, rather than incorporating techniques for dealing with the uncertain world into cybernetics research, the approach was to reduce living systems to computers.

In the middle of the last century there was a significant change in the way scientists envisioned human cognition. The model of cognition as 'information processing' took advantage of new understanding of biological systems, as well as new insights into the mathematical representation of problem solving. Newell and Simon[140] writing in the 1970's state that thinking (cognition) can be explained by information processing theory, and that such a system is comprised of four elements:

1. an environment;

2. a collection of sensors and effectors that interact with the environment;
3. a set of symbols and the relationships between the symbols; and,
4. a processor that can manipulate these symbols and interact with the environment through the sensors and effectors.

Implicit in this description in the idea that there is something in the background that is responsible for mapping from the sensors onto the symbols, and back again. The deliberative system - that part of cognition that did the 'thinking' - worked in an isolated abstract world of symbols, but in this abstract world it is possible to deliberate, to reason, to think.

10.1 Deliberation

Deliberation can be defined in many ways, but a key component is the idea of thinking about the current state and exploring possible outcomes. It is frequently associated with the idea of planning, and intelligence in general. We use the following definition:

> A deliberative system is one that models the world in a symbolic form, and can predict the future state that will result from the application of intentional actions. These predicted future states can be used to choose between different possible courses of actions in an attempt to achieve system goals.

In this chapter we are going to focus on the deliberative system in our robot, see figure 10.1. One key question that we will ask is "What does the reification system have to provide to enable our robot to reason about the world?"

The general model we will present is based on work done on Probability–Aware Planning and Execution Systems[87] (ProPLAN). This system was developed to provide fast and effective planning for mobile robots. The planning and execution system is based on a simple observe – orient – decide – act loop[15]. The deliberative system accesses the Current World State to assess the current situation. It relies on the Personal Rough Ontology to provide context for the goals and to orient itself. It then develops a number of possible courses of action which might achieve the current goals. The deliberative system then selects one of these courses of action and sends it to the execution system to be implemented. This execution includes information about the expected outcomes of each step in the plan, and the execution system monitors the actual outcomes to see if the action succeeded or failed. If the action succeeded, the next step in the plan is executed, otherwise the process is restarted from the failed state, and tries once again to achieve its goals.

Recall that there are many different ways that deliberation can be undertaken, and we have chosen one of these ways to develop our deliberative system. Any system that can provide the necessary functionality is equally valid, however to fully explore the deliberative process we need to delve into the details of some system, and so we have chosen the ProPLAN implementation.

There are three key aspects to the process of machine deliberation:

1. How does the machine represent and reason about the present state and the system's goals;
2. How does it model the future, and choose between alternative solutions; and
3. How does the system reason about and respond to failures.

Unless our robotic systems can address each of these issues successfully, it will not be able to function effectively in the dynamic and uncertain world that it will share with the humans.

The general control flow of the deliberative system is shown in Figure 10.2. The deliberative system begins with a set of prioritized goals, and examines the current world state to determine if any goals are unmet. The details of how this is done are presented in Chapter 11. Once a goal (or goals) have been selected for achievement, the deliberative system relies on the `Personal Rough Ontology` to extract a subset of the current world state and the salient information. This is used in combination with the goals as input to the planning process. The planner first generates a number of candidate plans, any one of which will achieve the goals with varying probabilities of success. These plans are then further evaluated for internal conflicts that might change the success probability. Finally, the plan that is most likely to succeed is selected for execution.

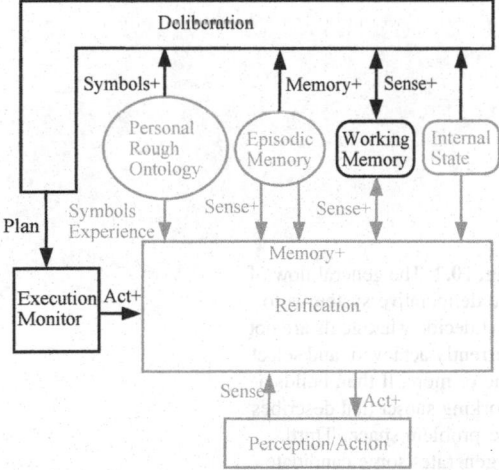

Fig. 10.1 The Deliberation Module evaluates the current state of the world, and the current goals of the intelligent system. From these it must produce a plan of actions that can achieve the goals. These actions are based on the model of the world and the changes that can be effected by the system.

10.2 Reasoning About the Present

The world is a complex place. Every object in the world, and every action that can be taken exists in a complex web of relationships. Reasoning about these relationships is a key requirement for being able to model the world, and to achieve the goals of the system, the robot must be able to model both the present state of the world and the desired state of the world. It is not sufficient for our robot to know that a door is a rectangular surface, it must also know that doors can be opened and closed, locked and unlocked, and that they can be blocks to travel, or can facilitate movement from one place to another.

When you look across a room, you don't see a roughly rectilinear object with a surface (A) roughly normal to the gravitational gradient, approximately 0.75 m above the floor, and with a perpendicular surface extending upwards at the rear of surface A. You see a chair. With that knowledge comes a host of relationships, actions, and behaviors that allow you to reason about the chair. You know that it is a seat, that it was engineered to hold the mass of an adult human, that you can stand on it to reach something on a high shelf (but that is not its designed purpose). You are reminded of other chairs, some soft, some hard; you recall an accident where the chair collapsed, or went over backwards. You might remember sitting in a chair while talking with a loved one, or recall a blistering dressing down that you received

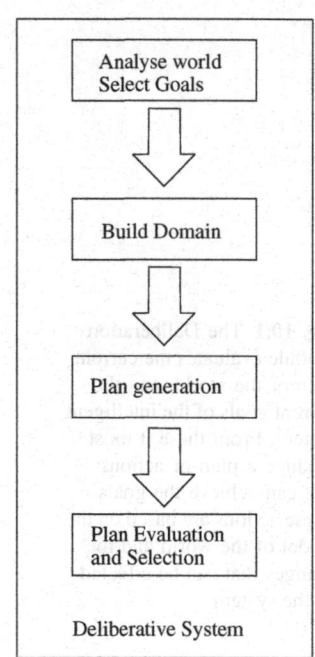

Fig. 10.2 The general flow of the deliberative system is to first decide what goals are not currently achieved, and select one or more. It then builds a working subset that describes the problem space. Third, it generates some candidate plans. Finally, it evaluates those plans and selects one for execution.

from a boss. Any, or all, of these might flash through your mind in the instant that your deliberative system becomes aware of the *symbolic* 'chair' across the room.

These relationships, memories, and feelings all contribute to the model that you form of the world, and they also affect the deliberation that you undertake to solve the problem of getting a book that you need off the top of the bookcase. If a robotic system is going to reason about the present, it needs to have similar sort of symbolic representation of the world in which it exists. Perhaps not as complex, or as broad, but unless it, too, can evaluate the possibility of climbing up onto the chair to reach the top of the bookcase, it will be unable to deliberate about possible courses of actions. Reification can provide the symbols that represent the state of the world, but our robot needs far more than simple symbols to reason about achieving its goals.

10.2.1 Sense-Symbols from the Reification Engine

One of the primary functions of the Reification Engine is to provide the deliberative system with the symbols that correspond to the objects in the world that have been recognized. Thus in the description above, the Reification Engine would process the sensory data that correspond to the chair and would pass the sense symbol chair to the deliberative system. This sense-symbol acts as a key to access the complex relationships stored in the ontological database. Along with this sense symbol, additional information is passed along which captures the ephemeral details of the current situation, information such as scale (how big a chair?), location (where is the chair?), orientation (is it upright?, has it fallen over?, is it turned toward the robot or is it facing away?), associations (is there anything on the seat?) and so forth. This information is situational, it is not a permanent feature or aspect of chair.

10.2.2 Symbols from the Ontology

Another collection of inputs into the ProPLAN system are the symbols from the ontological database. These contain the long term knowledge about the world and the things that make it up. This is the database of what things mean, the semantic memory of our robot. Stored in an ontology, each symbol is linked to a web of other symbols and the entire set of relationships define what the symbol means.

There are two events that cause the retrieval of ontological symbols, one is the existence of a sense symbol in the feed from the Reification Engine. If the robot has sensed a chair, the Reification Engine will pass chair on to the deliberative system. In addition, if there were other sense symbols from previous iterations of the loop, these will still exist in the world model of the deliberative system. For example, if the robot had previously been sensing the bookcase, even though the robot has turned, and the bookcase is no longer directly sensed, the `bookcase` does not disappear from the world model of the robot. This collection of things in the world along with the relationships that define them are the raw materials that the Deliberation Module uses to reason about the world.

10.2.3 Internal State

A third primary component derived from biological systems is the internal state of the entity. This has a significant impact on the outcome of the deliberative process. Just as with a biological entity, if the robot has large amounts of energy available, it may choose a course of action that expends that energy. However, if the batteries are nearly drained, that course of action may not be possible to execute, and another, less energy intensive, course of action would be selected.

Without all three of these sources of information, the internal state, the semantic memory, and the external state of the world, the robot would be hard pressed to even begin the process of figuring out how to achieve its goals. With these sources of input, the robot (via the `ProPLAN` system) can begin to reason about what it can do to change the world from the current state toward one that meets its goals.

10.2.4 Reasoning with `WorldSets`

In order to begin the process of deliberation, it is necessary to have tools that allow the system to compare the state of the world as it is perceived with the state of the world as it is desired to be. Unless the system can detect that the goals are not met, there is no way for the system to even begin the process of planning. Unless the system can contrast the impact that one action might achieve with the effects of a different action, there can be no real basis for choosing one action over another. In the act of deliberation is the act of comparing multiple possible future states and choosing between them, it is necessary to be able to contrast these possible states. To that end, a number of comparison operators are needed to operate on `WorldSets`. The deliberative system we are using has three comparison operators:

1. Equality: is one `WorldSet` equal to another, $WS \times WS \rightarrow Boolean$
2. Containment: is one `WorldSet` contained within another, $WS \times WS \rightarrow Boolean$
3. Consistency: is one `WorldSet` consistent with another, $WS \times WS \rightarrow Boolean$

In addition there are two transforms that can be applied to `WorldSets` to support deliberation. These take two `WorldSets` and produce a new `WorldSet` as a return. The transforms are:

1. Fusion: a merging of two `WorldSets`, $WS \times WS \rightarrow WS$
2. Difference: what changes need to be made to one `WorldSet` to make it consistent with another, $WS \times WS \rightarrow WS$

Equality takes two WorldSets and produces a boolean value indicating if the two are equal. This is the most strict of the three comparison operators. Equality is defined as two WorldSets describing exactly the same configuration of the world. For each feature i $WS_1[i]$ must have the same value as $WS_2[i]$. If the feature is specified in one, it must be specified with the same value in the other. If the feature is unspecified in one WorldSet it must also be unspecified in the other:

$$Equals(WS_1, WS_2) \equiv \bigwedge_{i \in F} WS_1[i] = WS_2[i] \qquad (10.1)$$

Containment is less strict than equality, it has the sense of a subset/superset relationship in the multi–valued logic used by the deliberative system. If one WorldSet, WS_2, is contained by another, WS_1, every feature that is specified in the container WorldSet must have an identically specified value in the contained WorldSet. Any feature that is unspecified in the container can have any value, or may be unspecified, in the contained WorldSet. The formal definition is:

$$Contains(WS_1, WS_2) \equiv \bigwedge_{i \in F} \begin{cases} true, & WS_1[i] = DontKnow \\ WS_1[i] = WS_2[i], & otherwise \end{cases} \qquad (10.2)$$

The semantics of containment allow the deliberative system to assess whether a goal has been achieved, since whenever a forecast WorldSet contains the WorldSet that defines the goal, all of the conditions required by the goal state have been met. Any conditions which are unspecified in the goal state can have any values in the forecast. This allows the deliberative system to make the minimum number of changes to the world to meet the goal.

The final comparison operator supported by the ProPLAN system is the consistency operator. Consistency is less strict than containment, and has the semantics of *not contradictory*. The key difference lies in the treatment of unspecified features. In the consistency test if a feature is unspecified in either of the two WorldSets, those features are consistent. This contrasts with containment, where the contained WorldSet must be no less specific than the containing WorldSet:

$$Consistent(WS_1, WS_2) \equiv \bigwedge_{i \in F} \begin{cases} true, & WS_1[i] = DontKnow \\ true, & WS_2[i] = DontKnow \\ WS_1[i] = WS_2[i], & otherwise \end{cases} \qquad (10.3)$$

The two transform operators, fusion and difference, allow the deliberative system to reason about the impacts of changes to the forecast WorldSet. Since the core of deliberate action is to change the world from one state to another, more desired, state, deliberative systems must be able to reason about the effects of changes before selecting a course of action. These two operators provide the system with that reasoning ability.

The fusion operator provides a mechanism for applying the expected effects of an action to a WorldSet that describes the world in which the action was taken.

While the fusion operator takes two WorldSets as its parameters, these two WorldSets have very different semantics. The first term is a representation of the initial state of the world, while the second parameter represents the changes that will be applied to the initial state to produce the result of applying the action:

$$Fusion(WS_{old}, WS_{new})[i] \equiv \begin{cases} WS_{old}[i], & WS_{new}[i] = DontChange \\ WS_{new}[i], & \text{otherwise} \end{cases} \quad (10.4)$$

The final operator we will discuss here is the difference operator. The difference operator is used to answer the question "Given the current state of the world and the goal state, what features have to change to transform the current state into the desired state?" This transform provides the deliberative system with the ability to extract the salient changes needed to achieve the goal, which can significantly reduce the computational burden. The difference operator allows a guided search through all the possible actions that *might* be undertaken.

$$Difference(WS_1, WS_2)[i] \equiv \begin{cases} DontCare, & WS_1[i] = WS_2[i] \\ WS_2[i], & \text{otherwise} \end{cases} \quad (10.5)$$

These five operators provide the ProPLAN system with a collections of primitive functions that can be used to reason about the the current state of the world, the systems goals, the range of possible actions that might be used to achieve these goals, and to deliberate about alternative methods of attempting to achieve its goals. The question still remains how is the ProPLAN system going to use the tools to generate and choose a specific path to the future?

10.3 Choosing the Future

In the Library example, our robot is confronted with an unsatisfied goal. It has been told to go get the book from the library, and needs to come up with a plan to achieve that goal. Solving problems like this have been identified by many researchers as the core of intelligence. As Donald Norman put it in "Things that Make Us Smart"[143]

> Complex planning is another mental activity at which humans excel. To plan is to consider several alternative courses of action, weigh the implications of each of those alternatives, compare then select. Although animals can form simple plans, such as to stack several objects on top of one another to form a platform that will enable them to reach objects hanging in the air, chess is beyond their abilities (pg. 126).

In this section we look at how our deliberative system reasons about the current state of the world, finds possible ways to achieve its goals, and evaluates those possible courses of action, finally selecting one to attempt. The word 'attempt' is important. If our robot is going to function in the real world, it cannot assume that any course of action will succeed. Rather, every plan has a probability of failing, and the likelihood of failure of one course of action versus that of an alternative course affects the selection process.

Beginning in the early 1960's the process of planning was described as a search problem[139]. The general idea is that the world is in a specific state. We have a set of actions available to us, and many of these will change the state of the world into a new, slightly different, state. From that new state there will be another set of actions that can be taken, any of which will change the world a little more. If we can find a sequence of these actions that results in the world being in the state we want, we can execute these one after another and achieve our goal.

During the last half of the twentieth century numerous planning systems were based on this concept. A partial list was compiled by Tate *et al* [193] which included systems ranging from the Voyager Spacecraft Mission Sequencer[202] to a Mechanical Engineers Apprentice Supervisor[175]. For our example, we might envision the robot looking at the current state as "I'm in the office; the book is in the library; I don't have the book." The goal is "I'm in the office; the book is in the office; I gave you the book ". Now it needs to look at the many things it might do to change the current world state into the goal state. It might reason as follows:

1. To give you the book, I need to have the book.
2. To have the book, I need to pick up the book.
3. To pick up the book, I need to reach for the book, so I need to go to the book.
4. The book is in the Library, so I need to go to the Library.
5. To go from the Office to the Library, I need to go through the doorway.
6. Once I have the book, I will be in the Library, to give you the book, I need to go to the Office.
7. To go from the Library to the Office, I need to go through the doorway.

Reading this from the bottom to the top, we have the makings of a plan to achieve our goals. Of course, as humans we barely had to consciously think about any of this. The entire plan most likely appeared in your conscious mind without any thought. Unfortunately, the computer that is our robot's brain does not work like that. We need to be able to specify every step that the program will follow to produce this plan. Instead, it will follow all sorts of blind alleys that do not lead to getting the book, and it will do these step by step by step until it finds a good plan. Fortunately, computers are good at this mind numbing kind of task, and they are exceedingly fast. Figure 10.3 reproduces the example we presented earlier.

10.3.1 Planning as Search

The brute force approach to planning is to build a list of everything the robot could possibly do in the current situation. Then it must build the representation of the world that results for every one of those actions. Then for every one of those world states, it must build the list of every action that could take place in *that* world, and then build another set of worlds that result. Just keep repeating this process over and over until either 1) you find yourself int the desired world state, 2) the problem gets so large that the computer can't continue, 3) you get tired of waiting or 4) you have explored every possible world state that can be reached by any possible sequence of actions, and none of them achieve the goal. An alternative approach is to start from the goal state and work backwards (sometimes called backward–chaining or backward reasoning, see Rich and Knight[167]).

The `ProPLAN` deliberative system is a forward chaining planner. It begins from the current state of the world, and examines the `WorldSets` that can be reached by applying actions which are valid (i.e., the current `WorldSet` satisfies the enabling conditions of the action) in this state. From each of these resulting `WorldSets`, it examines the actions that can be applied, and the resulting `WorldSets`. These are represented in a directed graph, where each node is a `WorldSet`, and each arc is an Action that results in a change to the world. In each iteration, a node is selected for expansion, the applicable actions are determined, and new nodes are added to the frontier of the graph for each resulting `WorldSet`.

The System begins with a planning problem defined as:

Definition 10.1. Planning Problem

A **Planning Problem** Υ is a 4-tuple:

$\Upsilon \equiv (\mathbf{F}, \mathbf{A}, i, g)$

where: $\mathbf{F}$ is a set of features of the planning domain;
$\mathbf{A}$ is a set of Actions that can be taken;
i is the initial WorldSet; and

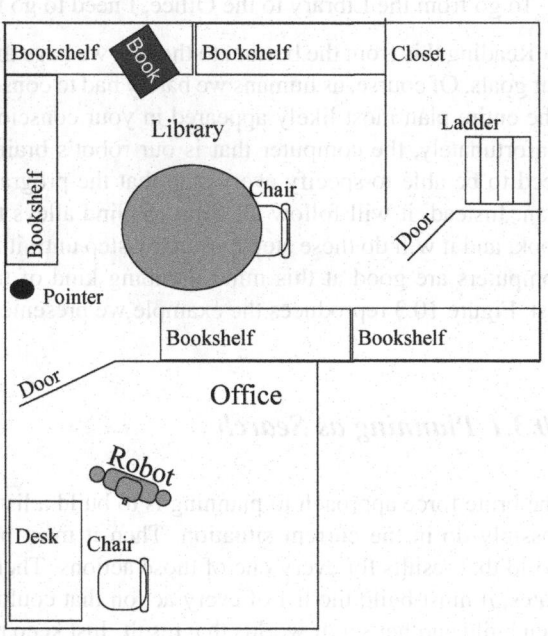

Fig. 10.3 The robot is given the task "Get me the book from the top of the bookcase." The book is out of reach, so the deliberative system must formulate a plan to reach the book. While this is beyond the capabilities of most autonomous robotics systems, the deliberative systems necessary to solve this kind of problem have been available for over half a century.

g is the goal WorldSet.

A Planning Problem defines the domain of the problem, the initial state of the world, the desired state of the world, and the actions that the system can apply to attempt to achieve the goal state. Since this is a probability aware planning system, the natural uncertainty of the world will be reflected in the problem specification. For example, one or more of the features may be unknown at the time the problem is specified (in our Library example, the actual state of the closet door in the library may not be known). The goal state will very likely have many unspecified terms, if they are of no consequence to defining the goal (whether the pointer is still in the same position or orientation may not matter). Finally, every action will have possibilities of failure which will mean that some possible outcomes will not be specified. We want our planner to solve the planning problem by producing a plan, a sequence of actions which start from the world-as-it-is, and ends in the world-as-we-want-it. The desired solution to a planning problem is a plan. A Plan is defined as:

Definition 10.2. Plan
A **Plan** for planning problem is a sequence of actions A_1^n that, if executed in the absence of exogenous events from the initial state, and the most probable outcome occurs, will achieve the goal state.

$$A_1^n \equiv \{A_1, A_2, A_3, ..., A_{n-1}, A_n\} \tag{10.6}$$

But we want more than this. We want an intelligent robot. In the "Go get me the book" plan described above, our robot knew that it was unnecessary to open and close the door several times before going through it. It knew that having picked up the book once, it did not need to put the book back down, exit the Library and then re-enter and pick the book up again. Either of these alternatives would have (eventually) ended with the book being delivered, but they would not be particularly effective plans.

Definition 10.3. Effective Plan
An Effective Plan is a plan that achieves the goal state, and that contains no subsequence of actions which will achieve the goal state.

From this point forward whenever we discuss plans, we will mean effective plans. The plan is defined as a sequence of actions, which represent the trajectory through the state space of the domain. This perspective is very natural in that many humans envision a solution to a problem as the things one must *do* to achieve the goal. We think of transforming the world by our actions. In this view, if the initial conditions specify a valid precondition for A_1 and all actions succeed, the world state after the execution of A_n will meet the goal requirements.

However, it is also possible to view the dual of the action-based view. Since each action begins in an initial world state, and terminates in a second world state, the trajectory can be interpreted as a sequence of world states, beginning in the initial state i and ending in g. If an action is successful, the end state of action A_{n-1} must satisfy the preconditions of action A_n. So the equivalent definition would be represented as:

$$A_1^n \equiv \{i = WS_0, WS_1, WS_2, ..., WS_{n-1}, WS_n = g\}, \qquad (10.7)$$

Thus, a plan can also be viewed as a sequence of WorldSets (equation (10.7)), where WS_0 must be the initial state i, and the final state WS_n is the goal state g. Since all Action Outcomes are uncertain, in this latter view each step in the plan represents a WorldSet with a specific Probability of Occurrence (POC).

Formally:

Definition 10.4. Probability of Occurrence (POC)
Given the Action Sequence A_1^n from the initial WS_0 to WS_n, the Probability of Occurrence of a WorldSet WS_τ, $0 \le \tau \le n$, is defined as:

$$POC(WS_\tau) = \begin{cases} 1.0, & \text{if } \tau = 0 \\ \prod_{i=1}^{\tau} \underset{j=1}{\overset{m}{\text{Max}}}(P(A_i.Outcome_j)), & \text{otherwise} \end{cases} \qquad (10.8)$$

where: m is the number of possible outcomes of Action A_i
τ is the step in the plan for which the POC is being calculated

The planning process begins with a planning problem Υ. The pseudo-code for the algorithm is shown in Figure 10.4, the description will refer the the line numbers in parentheses on the left.

From the initial state, a single node is created representing the world-as-it-is (Line 1). This node is assigned a POC of 1.0. The algorithm expands this graph by selecting the node with the highest POC and testing to see if the goal has been reached. The initial selection is trivial, since there is only one node in the graph. The expansion (Lines 4–15) consists of finding every action that can be applied to the selected node and determining what the resulting world state would be, if that action were taken and the most probable outcome were to occur (See Definition 10.2).

There are two classes of outcomes, either the outcome is a new world state, one that has not been added to the graph previously, or the result of this action may return to a world state that has already been generated. In the case of a new world state, the state is added as a leaf node into the graph, and the POC is determined by taking the origination node POC and multiplying it by the likelihood of the most probable outcome of the action (Eqn. 10.8). This case is handled in Lines 7–9. In the case of an outcome that returns to a state already included in the graph, it is possible that the existing node has a lower POC than the new result. If this is so, we update the graph with the new path to this world state, and use the new, higher, POC as the likelihood (Lines 11-14). If the new result has a lower POC than the existing node, the algorithm simple discards the edge and result. As each new node is added to the

```
(1)    Initialize graph G with current world state
(2)    Loop Select node N_MAX with highest POC
(3)         Add all Actions applicable to Node N_MAX to ActionSet Cas
(4)         For each Action A_i in Cas:
(5)              Determine Node N_Outcome(A_i)
(6)              Calculate P(N_Outcome(A_i))
(7)              If N_Outcome(A_i) ∉ G then
(8)                   Add N_Outcome(A_i) to G
(9)                   Add Edge E to graph from N_MAX to N_Outcome(A_i)
(10)             Else
(11)                  If P(N_Outcome(A_i)) > P(ExistingNode) then
(12)                       Update N_Existing with P(N_Outcome(A_i))
(13)                       Update N_Existing.Source with N_MAX
(14)                  End If
(15)             End If
(16)             If Goal.Contains(N_Outcome(A_i)) then
(17)                  Extract Plan
(18)             End if
(19)        Next Action
(20)        Mark N_MAX as expanded
(20)   End Loop
```

Fig. 10.4 Plan Graph Expansion Algorithm.

plan graph, it is compared to the goal state, and if it contains the goal, the sequence of actions is extracted from the graph (the path from the root to the leaf node that contains the goal) and saved as a candidate plan (Lines 16–18).

After all applicable actions have been expanded, the node is marked as expanded (Line 20). The algorithm continues, selecting the unexpanded node with the highest POC, and expanding it. The algorithm is similar to Dijkstra's shortest weighted path algorithm, and can be implemented using a similar dynamic programming technique. Since the selection criterion is the POC of the frontier nodes, plans are generated in rough decreasing probability order. As a result, the algorithm can be terminated any time after the first plans are generated. It is not quite an anytime algorithm[56, 66], since there is no bound on the length of time needed to produce the initial plan. This planning algorithm has the following properties:

1. It is decidable - If there exists a plan that achieves the goals, the planner will return it;
2. It is complete - All effective plans that achieve the goal will eventually be found; and
3. It is correct - All plans returned by the planner are effective.

The forward chaining search, coupled with the fact that plans are generated in a highest probability first order, enables the planner to have flexible termination conditions. Depending on the nature of the planning domain, and the needs of the robotics system, the planner can terminate under one of several conditions:

1. A sufficient number of candidate plans have been found;

2. A sufficient number of expansions have been completed; or
3. The POC of the best remaining possible solutions fall below a threshold.

In the last two cases, it is possible that the planner has failed to find any candidate plans. While it has been shown that the planner will eventually find a plan if one exists, there is no guarantee how quickly such plans will be found, hence the second and third termination conditions, can be used to re-frame the planning problem as part of the deliberative system's response to not finding a feasible plan.

At this stage of the deliberative process, the planning system has produced a collection of candidate plans, each one will, if executed correctly, achieve the goals defined in the planning problem with some likelihood. This likelihood has been calculated, and the plans have been ordered such that the highest likelihood plan is easily accessible. One might think that, at this point, the deliberative process is over. However, we must recall that in the interests of producing a plan quickly, we evaluated the plans based on the most likely outcomes occurring, what if some other outcome occurs? What if the plan fails?

10.3.2 Adapting to Failure

In a static, deterministic domain it would be sufficient for the deliberative system to simply return one or more effective plans. If the planning domain were static, there would be no changes to the state of the world, unless they are made by our robot. If the world were deterministic, the model of the world that our robot used for planning would be accurate, and every action our robot took would succeed. This would mean that the world would undergo the step-by-step transformation outlined by our plan, and the goals would be achieved. As we know, the real world is not like this. Our robot's model of the world depends on limited, inaccurate sensors, and so is inherently inaccurate. Our robot's actions can fail, and there are other events in the world that can change its state into ones that interfere with our robot's plan. Any of these failures can interact, causing a compounding of the deviation for our robot's idealized vision of the future. So, if our system is to be effecting in this dynamic, uncertain world, it must be capable of adapting to failure.

Some types of failures are explicitly represented in the ActCepts. The deliberative system can reason about these failures before selected a plan to execute. Suppose there are two candidate plans which are identical in every except one. The first plan has a failure mode that leaves the robot broken, while the other has no such disastrous outcome. It would not be intelligent to select between these two plans at random. So the deliberative system needs a way to evaluate the candidate plans.

10.4 Plan Evaluation and Selection

The ProPLAN system is aware of the probabilities associated with the outcomes of each action, however, to reduce the computational burden, it only explores the worlds that result if the action results in the most likely outcome. This is considered to be optimistic planning. The algorithm described above does not use resources to keep track of what might go wrong. Modeling the many ways that things can go wrong, and producing contingent plans has been shown to have hyper-exponential complexity[46, 78, 122, 123], which makes it a poor candidate for our robot, which must deal with a complex and changing world. Rather than increase the complexity of the planning process, the ProPLAN system takes a different approach. Once the plans are generated, they are simulated using a Monte Carlo simulation technique. This allows the deliberative system to assess two things at once. First, it assesses the negative aspects of the less likely outcomes of each action. Second, by simulating the execution of the entire plan, if there are interactions between individual actions in the plan, the Monte Carlo simulation will catch these as well.

Markov Chain Monte Carlo (MCMC) simulation is a technique for evaluating the outcomes of stochastic processes. In brief, the stochastic process has one or more well defined random variables, and, for each of these, an independent draw is made during each simulation. The overall results of the simulation run are recorded, and the simulation is re-run with new random draws for each variable. This process is repeated until sufficient results are obtained to be statistically significant. The results of each simulation run are treated as a distribution, and are analyzed statistically, producing an aggregate assessment of the processes behavior. For more information of MCMC simulation see Gilks *et al*[76]. The biggest difficulties with MCMC simulation are:

1. Acquiring accurate distributions for the random variables in the process; and
2. Building simulator with sufficient fidelity to make the aggregate statistics meaningful.

10.4.1 Acquiring Distributions

The ProPLAN system requires the existence of accurate probability distributions for each of the actions that the planner can use to achieve its goals, so the first need is met. The second requirement is a high-fidelity simulator for the domain. Since the planner is projecting forward the results of the actions it is evaluating, it has an internal simulator. During the planning process this forecaster is making very optimistic predictions, however the machinery is present to forecast the results of any of the outcomes of an action. So very little additional machinery is needed to create a Monte Carlo simulator. However, the Monte Carlo Simulator provides a significant benefit to the deliberative system. The simulator does not look only at the most likely outcomes of the actions, it evaluates the range of possible outcomes.

When our robot is planning to get the book from the Library, one plan might include standing on the chair to reach the book, while another requires using the pointer to push the book off the top of the shelf onto the floor, and bending over to pick it up. The most likely result of both of these action sequences is that the book is in the hand of our robot. However, some of the lower probability outcomes might include the book being pushed off the back of bookcase, to a point where the robot cannot reach it. This would mean that no plan the robot could generate would achieve its goals. A low probability outcome of standing on the chair, and reaching for the book, might be the robot falling and damaging itself. Either of these outcomes significantly affect the suitability of the corresponding plan in as much as neither plan would then achieve the goals.

Since the Markov Chain Monte Carlo simulator utilizes the lower probability outcomes of the actions in the plan, and produces statistical analysis of the overall plan results, the outcomes that result in plan failure can result in slightly different value for the overall POC of the plan. This arises from the interaction of different actions in the plan. Recall that the planner looks at each step in the plan independently and only looks at the most likely outcome. The MCMC simulation looks at the distribution of outcomes that each action can produce, and uses those resulting world states as inputs to the succeeding action. This can, and does, result in complex interaction terms that materially affect the plan success, and therefore the plan success rates as calculated by the MCMC simulation. It is these success rates that are used in the final analysis to select the plan most likely to succeed.

10.4.2 Simulator Fidelity

The question remains "Is the simulator of sufficient fidelity?" Based on the definitions of the actions that part of the planning problem, we know that each action has a set of mutually exclusive outcomes, with the associated likelihoods. However, it is also clear that these are not necessarily and exhaustive set of outcomes. There may be a (possibly large) number of outcomes that are not modeled. From the biological evidence, it is clear that living systems do not maintain a complete model of the world, and all the possible events that might occur. It is clear that humans, while they do some modeling of what might go wrong, do not evaluate every possible outcome, regardless of its likelihood. When one thinks about going into the kitchen to grab something to drink, do you plan for events such as meteorites crashing through the roof, or discovering a snake on the kitchen floor? We, as humans, are considered to be very effective planners and problem solvers, but there are limits to the computational burden we can neurologically and psychologically undertake. So, our robot will have similar limitations, in particular, the fidelity of the simulation will be based on the fidelity of the world model itself. If our robot can produce a higher fidelity representation of the world, it will use that improved representation both for planning how to achieve its goals, and to evaluate what might go wrong when executing that plan.

10.5 Summary

This chapter presents the details of the deliberative system, the machinery that allows a robot to reason about the world and to select intentional changes to that world in the pursuit of its goals. Deliberative systems have been part of the artificial intelligence arena since the earliest days of computer science, although they have tended to focus on purely symbolic manipulation. Using the data provided by the `Reification Engine`, it is possible to maintain an effective symbolic representation of the state of the world as it is. Combining this with the rough ontology's representation of semantic memory, the deliberative system can place its goals into an appropriate context, which allows the symbolic planner to produce effective plans for goal satisfaction.

The deliberative system has the responsibility of determining the appropriate behavior for the robot to achieve its goals. This responsibility is met by performing a sequence of actions:

1. Select which goals are to be achieved;
2. Extract from the semantic memory a subset of the world state to use as a planning domain;
3. Use the probability aware planning system to produce a set of feasible plans;
4. Use the MCMC Plan evaluator to assess the overall POC of each plan; finally
5. Select the plan with the highest POC.

The deliberative system brings together a number of the components that necessary to act intentionally in a dynamic world. Several were discussed earlier, and the focus of this chapter was to present, in perhaps painful detail, the mechanisms that our autonomous, intelligent robot must have to reason about the world and its complexity. We have shown how the robot can observe the world, not directly, but mediated through the reification process; how the robot can focus attention on the salient features of the world, to establish a context in which to reason; how it can model the world, and model the changes that it might make in an attempt to achieve its goals; and finally, how it can evaluate candidate solutions to its problems, test them against experience and look at what might go wrong to finally produce a course of action that might achieve the systems goals.

Chapter 11
Putting it All Together

11.1 How it Fits Together

In this chapter we look at an example that brings all of the elements together. It would be nice if we could implement the "Go get me the Book" example, but the huge amount of data required, and the complex interactions between the systems would take many hundreds of pages to detail. Instead we will use a simple example with Basil as a stand-in. Basil's primary purpose is very similar to the humanoid robot, but the hardware is significantly less advanced. While Basil can approximate the reasoning of our ideal robot, Basil is quite incapable of opening doors (let alone unlocking them), cannot carry a ladder (or climb it), nor can Basil knock books off of the top of a book case using a pointer. Basil can (provided someone puts a book on the tray) deliver it to a destination in spite of obstacles. Of course, once at the destination, Basil must wait, with cybernetic patience, until someone takes the book from the tray.

In spite of these failings, Basil's cybernetic brain is up to the task of achieving fairly complex goals in the dynamic and uncertain environment. In this chapter we will focus on the interactions between the components that have been described throughout the book, and examine how these components work together to enable a robot to model the current state of the world, select goals to achieve, develop plans to achieve those goals, and execute those plans in the real world, while monitoring the environment to assure that the plan is succeeding.

The four major components that we will look at are:

1. The Perception/Action System;
2. The Reification Engine;
3. The Execution Monitor; and
4. The deliberative system.

As we have said before, these components are tightly coupled. This coupling occurs in two ways, there is control coupling, shown by the descending arrows in Figure 11.1; and there is tight coupling in information. Based on the robot's goals, the deliberative system generates a plan (a sequence of actions) that can

139

achieve the goal. This plan is passed to the Execution Monitor, which extracts the individual actions, and verifies that they can be executed using the Reification Engine. These actions are converted into specific commands and are passed, in turn to the Perception/Action system, where they are finally implemented. The Reification Engine generates a new symbolic representation of the world, which is used by the Execution Monitor to confirm that the world is as it is expected to be. This coupling requires that each component have data representations that corresponds to the representations that are used by the others - if the Execution Monitor is testing the viability of an action (such as "Move to the kitchen"), its model of what this action means must match the model used by the Reification Engine when it is testing the heading and obstacles along the path.

At the same time, the components are also coupled in the information that they use. The upward arrows show the increasing complexity of the representations as additional meaning is incorporated at each stage. When the sensors report a set of objects at a given position, there is little information beyond the position of obstacles in space. When these are reified into a chair, the meaning encoded increases, and the Execution Monitor can evaluate the question of whether a chair (versus a table or a person) was expected to be there rather than somewhere else. As the symbolic information is placed into the framework provided by the Personal Rough

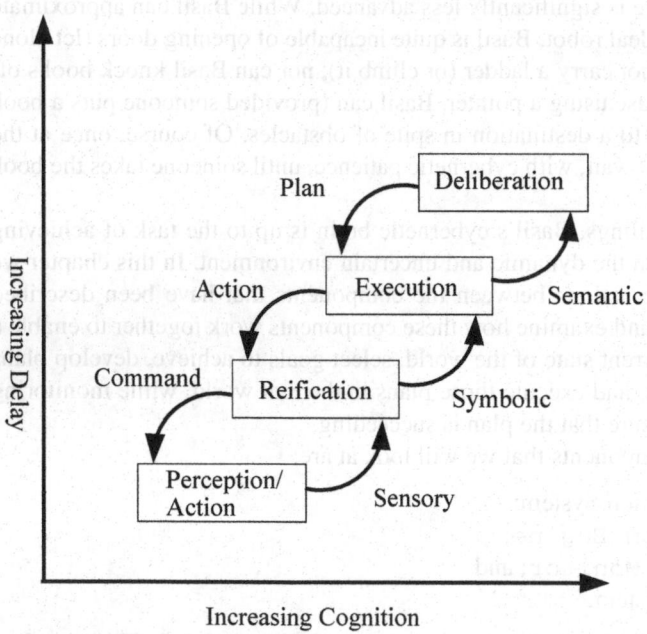

Fig. 11.1 This is the general interaction pattern of the major components of the cybernetic brain. The rough scale shows the increasing 'cognitive' capability increasing to the right, and a corresponding increase in the time required for cognition vertically.

Ontology, the deliberative system can reason that, since the chair is movable, the robot's plan should be modified to include pushing the chair out of the way, whereas if the obstacles reported by the Perception/Action System were a table, the deliberative system would 'know' that the robot cannot move the table, and so it must plan to go to the kitchen by a different path. At each stage of this upward process, the information manipulated depends on shared knowledge with the surrounding components.

It is well known in computer science and software engineering that excessive coupling of these two types is bad[120, 161]; it seems, however, that biological organisms disagree. Brains are incredibly tightly coupled structures, and since our design is driven by this biology, the cybernetic brain is also tightly coupled. However, as Fred Brooks said in "No Silver Bullet:"

> The complexity of software is an essential property, not an accidental one. Hence, descriptions of a software entity that abstract away its complexity often abstract away its essence. For three centuries, mathematics and the physical sciences made great strides by constructing simplified models of complex phenomena, deriving properties from the models, and verifying those properties by experiment. This paradigm worked because the complexities ignored in the models were not the essential properties of the phenomena. It does not work when the complexities are the essence[19].

It may be that this level of coupling between these four components is simply the essential complexity of intelligent software. In Figure 11.1 we place these four components into a two dimensional continuum. The horizontal axis indicated the amount of 'cognitive' representation that the components utilize. For our purposes, this corresponds to the amount of meaning (semantics) that the data objects contain. The vertical axis captures a loose notion of the complexity of the processing in each component. The speed is inversely proportional to the complexity, and so the delay increases as the cognitive level increases. This layout is similar to continua proposed by other researchers in many fields[14, 90, 133]. We will follow the interactions between these components in two examples: building a semantically tagged map, and the delivery of food and drink in a complex, dynamic environment.

11.2 Goals and Environment

Up to this point we have been deep down in the nuts and bolts of the system, and, while we have alluded to system goals, we have not spent much time on describing them. The goals drive the cybernetic brain. If the brain has no goals, it has no need to make any changes to the world. Without the need to make changes, there is no need for a plan, no actions to execute, no commands to issue to the Perception/Action system. The robot is static, unmoving, and fundamentally uninteresting. So let us give the robot some goals.

We focus on two classes of goals: symbolic and non-symbolic. It is clear that many biological systems have goals that are not symbolic such as stay alive and reproduce. On a lower level there are many goals that biological subsystems 'achieve':

keep the blood oxygenated, maintain temperature , and fight infections. These are clearly not symbolic goals, we do not wake up each morning and say "I really need to keep breathing." In the chapter on Perception/Action systems we discussed these non-symbolic goals obliquely by putting homeostasis tasks in the same category as procedural memory. In Figure 11.2, we add the goal structure to the deliberative system. We will focus on symbolic goals in this chapter, and follow the flow of control and the flow of information as the robot attempts to achieve its goals.

There is one other point to make about this diagram. The goals are internal to the cybernetic brain. It is common in artificial intelligence research to speak of the goals being 'given' to the system from the outside. Indeed, we have spoken that way in this work on several occasions. However, we take the view that while the goals may be suggested from the outside, until they are internalized they do not have the force of law, they're more like guidelines than actual rules. In addition, note that there is not **a goal**, there are **goals**. The deliberative system has the task of both achieving goals, and of managing the relative priority of the goals[86, 85]. In order to reason about the goals they must be internal to the deliberative system.

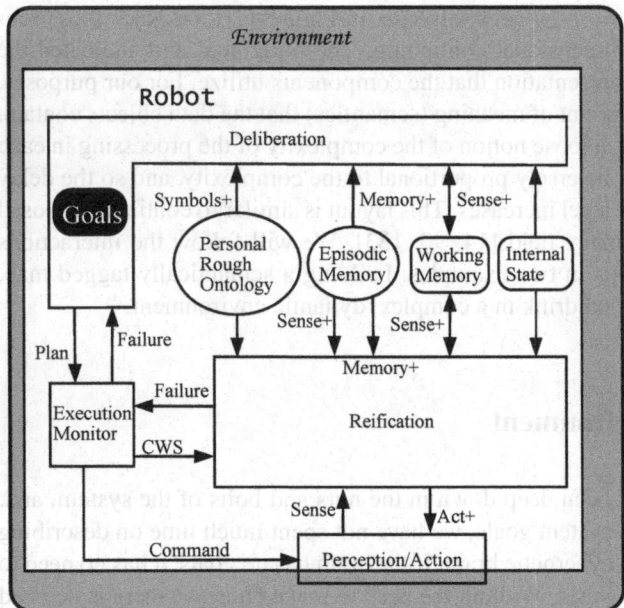

Fig. 11.2 In this completed image of the Cybernetic brain we add the system goals to the deliberative system and place the robot into an environment. These goals are symbolic in nature, and can be of two types: maintenance goals and achievement goals. The environment is the arena in which the robot functions, it is here that the goals have a context, and here that the changes that the robot attempts to achieve must be realized. The Perception/Action system crosses the boundary into the environment to signify that the robot is a part of the world.

Just as the goals are internal to the robot, the robot is not the extent of the system. The robot exists in an environment, and that environment impacts the robot. In this chapter we will examine the robot in the environment of the Gamma Two lab. The general layout of the lab is shown in Figure 11.3. It is a fairly simple space, but it is relatively cluttered with tables, chairs and people. Since many of these objects are moved frequently, the robot must continually update the model of the lab as it moves around. So we have the basics of a dynamic and uncertain environment, with changing demands on the robot. This environment approximates the environment in which the robot will need to function in the real world.

With the example we will first look at how the knowledge of this environment is encoded so that the robot can reason about it goals.

11.3 Knowledge Sources

The task we will examine is a simple delivery task: take the tea from the kitchen to the conference table. We will look at the setup for this task, specifically what information is in the ontology. We will then follow the interaction of the various systems as we walk the robot through this task. Before the robot can even begin the process of achieving a goal, it must have enough knowledge to be able to put the goal into a context (the ConCepts and relationships between them), it must have enough knowledge to reason about what needs to change to achieve the goal (instantiated PThings), and what actions or behaviors can be used to make those changes (the ActCepts and their effects), it must also have enough knowledge to understand what to look for in the world to both find the things and to confirm

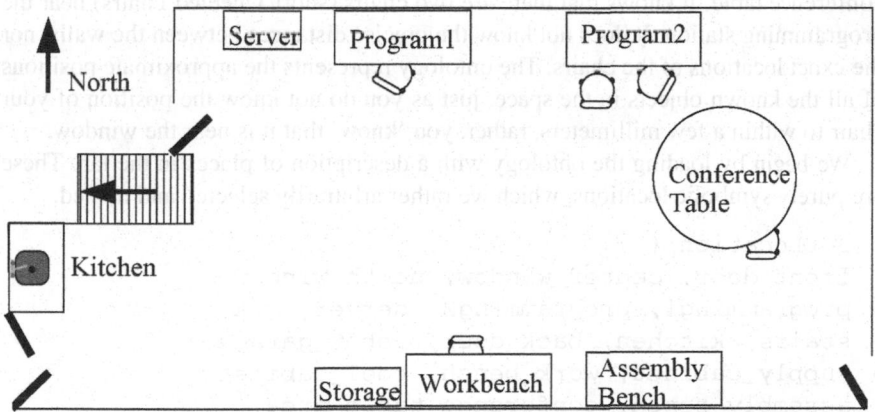

Fig. 11.3 The general layout of the lab.

the changes that have been made (PerCepts). The knowledge that is used by the robot, ultimately derives from three sources as shown in Table 11.1.

Table 11.1 Information sources within the Cybernetic Brain

System	Knowledge	Level
Ontology	ConCepts and ActCepts	Semantic
Reification	PerCepts	Symbolic
Perception/Action	Procedural	Sensory

Each of these three systems must be loaded with the data that will be used by the robot to model the world. So in the next few sections we will look at the specific information that is needed by the robot to undertake tasks in our lab.

11.3.1 Ontological Knowledge

The ontology for this task must consist of basic knowledge about the kinds of things that the robot might encounter. We will run this test in our lab, so the robot must have representations for the types of chairs, tables, people, and walls that might exist. In addition, since the robot is familiar with the lab, it has specific knowledge about instances of these things. It has a frame of reference that includes a zero point, which is in the south-west corner of the lab. It knows that there is an East Wall that marks the eastern boundary of the lab. It knows that the conference table is near the east wall, and that there is an area known as Program2 that is adjacent to the conference table. It knows that there are two chairs (short_wheeled_chairs) near the programming station. It does not know the precise distances between the walls, nor the exact locations of the chairs. The ontology represents the approximate positions of all the known objects in the space, just as you do not know the position of your chair to within a few millimeters, rather, you 'know' that it is near the window.

We begin by loading the ontology with a description of places in the lab. These are purely symbolic locations, which we rather arbitrarily selected and named.

```
BotLocation {
front_door, center_window, north_window,
programming1, programming2, server_rack,
stairs, kitchen, back_door, robot_garage,
supply_cabinet, work_bench, tool_cabinet,
assembly_bench, conference_table_area,
room_center}
```

These place names correspond (roughly) to the features in the lab that we, as humans, care about. They are not uniform in size, placement, or arrangement. Rather they refer to the semantic aspects of the lab. The robot is expected to function in the lab, on our terms. When we talk to other people, we do not say "Take this over to X=9000, Y=750," we say "Take this over to the assembly bench." The robot is in an environment that it shares with humans, it must model the world the same way that humans model the world.

The ontology also contains a high level topology of the lab layout. The area is tessellated into regions, and there is an equivalent to an adjacency graph in the ontology that captures the layout. The rough topology is shown visually in Figure 11.4. The topology is significant because is defines how the robot can move through the space. In fact, the only way that the topology is encoded is as the actions that it enables. If two areas are adjacent, there is an action encoded that captures the fact that the robot can move between them. This is a sample of an encoding of the ActCept that corresponds to the movement from the workbench to the center of the room:

```
[A24|GoWorkBenchToRoomCenter|P|[]]
GoWorkBenchToRoomCenter
ROF 1 EET 4000
Enablers 1
Enable 1 (BotLocation, work_bench)
Outcomes 1 0.90 Result 1 (BotLocation, room_center)
```

As we discussed in Chapter9, this encodes the preconditions for the action: the robot must be at the workbench, and it encodes the outcomes: with 90% likelihood, the robot will end up in the center of the room. It also encodes an estimate of how long the action should take to complete. In this case the the estimated execution time (EET) is 4000 ms. It also includes an indicator of whether the robot should attempt the action over again if it fails the first time. The Retry on Failure (ROF) is set to 1, you can try it once again, but if that also fails the robot must give up. The existence of this action is the indication that the two areas are connected in the topology, and if the robot needs to get to the room center, one place that can be used to reach it is the workbench.

The ontology consists of objects and the relationships between them. For our robot, the types of relationships are limited, and fairly simple. We begin with seven basic relationships:

```
RELATIONSHIPS
[is_a|0]
[has_a|1]
[is_at|2]
[allowed_in|3]
[can_do|4]
[place_inst|5]
[thing_inst|6]
```

Each relationship has a name (like is_a), and an index number. The first three relationships (is_a, has_a, and is_at) are common to almost any ontological structure that involves physical things in an environment. They allow the ontology to represent ideas like a wheeled chair is a type of chair, and a chair is a type of thing, or that the wheeled chair is at the conference table, and the tea tray is at the kitchen. The next two relationships are useful in our ontology to address the issues that there are limitations to the robots mobility that are not shared by all the entities in the world. For instance, the people are allowed to go up the stairs, and Basil's model of the world must include this; however, Basil's drive system does not allow the robot to climb stairs so Basil cannot go up them. In addition, there are many actions that Basil can undertake, such as loading the tea tray, but there are actions that the robot is incapable of doing, such as opening a door. The ontology uses the can_do and allowed_in relationships to capture the knowledge of Basil's capabilities.

The last two relationships are used to provide a link between the purely symbolic representation of the world to the sensory based representations. It is one thing to know that there is a location called Kitchen, it is another thing to be able to recognize it when you see it. The relationship thing_inst stands for the idea that one symbol is a physically instantiated instance of a more abstract class of thing. This enables the ontology to capture the knowledge that there may be many instances of the same type of thing. The ontology represents that the specific chair that I am currently sitting in as an instance of *short wheeled chair*, which is a type of *chair*, which is a type of *thing*. The place_inst relationship is used to reflect that the programming station that I am working at is instantiated in the world model. This knowledge is used to link the ontology information to the perceptual information stored in the Reification Engine.

The other half of the ontology is composed of the things in the world. Basil's world is fairly limited. Between the places that he knows about, and the things in his world, the entire knowledge base is less than a few kilobytes. There are twenty ConCepts that basil needs to be aware of for simple tasks:

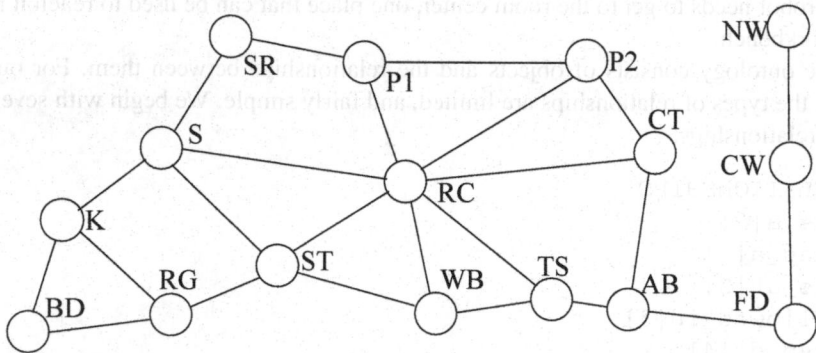

Fig. 11.4 The lab topology. This is not stored directly, rather it is stored as the locations and the ActCepts that indicate that travel is possible for the robot between locations. Each arc corresponds to a single action, with an associated set of preconditions, outcomes, and a likelihood of success.

```
CONCEPTS
[C0|location|N|S|P|[]]
[C1|thing|N|?|?|[1,C0,1.0,1.0]]
[C2|robot|P|?|?|[0,C1,1.0,1.0]]
[C3|Basil|P|M|P|[1,C0,1.0,1.0],[0,C1,1.0,1.0],
   [0,C2,1.0,1.0],
   [4,A0,1.0,1.0],[4,A1,1.0,1.0],[4,A2,1.0,1.0],
   [4,A3,1.0,1.0],[4,A4,1.0,1.0],
   ...
   [4,A38,1.0,1.0],[4,A39,1.0,1.0],[4,A40,1.0,1.0]]
[C4|conference_table|P|M|P|[6,C7,1.0,1.0]]
[C5|tea_tray|P|M|P|[0,C1,1.0,1.0],[2,C0,1.0,1.0]]
[C6|tray_holds|P|?|P|[]]
[C7|table|P|S|P|[0,C1,1.0,1.0]]
[C8|wall|P|S|P|[0,C1,1.0,1.0]]
[C9|short_wheeled_chair|P|S|P|[0,C1,1.0,1.0]]
[C10|east_wall|P|S|P|[6,C8,1.0,1.0]]
[C11|north_wall|P|S|P|[6,C8,1.0,1.0]]
...
[C18|stool|P|M|P|[0,C1,1.0,1.0]]
[C19|toy_stool|P|M|P|[6,C18,1.0,1.0]]
```

Each ConCept has an index number, a name, a few flags, and then the list of relationships it has with other ConCepts. The flags indicate three things:

1. Is this ConCept perceivable (P), or is it not (N)?
2. Is this ConCept something that can move (M) or is it sessile (S)?
3. Is this ConCept a permanent feature of my world (P) or is it transient (T)?

These flags are used to manage the state of the concepts in the ontology, and are linked to the Current World State.

The last component of the ConCept is the collection of relationships that it has with the others. These relationships are the directed arcs in the ontology, and they lead away from the ConCept. So, in the sample above, we see the concept of thing:

```
[C1|thing|N|?|?|[1,C0,1.0,1.0]]
```

It has an index of C1, and the symbolic name *thing*. It is not perceptible (e.g., there is no generic thing detector that the robot knows about), it may move, and it may come and go. Finally, it has one relationship. It is a type 1 relationship, which is a has_a relationship with ConCept C0 (location), this relationship always holds, and should always be propagated through the ontology.

Contrast this *thing* concept with that of the Basil concept. *Basil* is a *robot* (Concept C2), which is a type of *thing*, and has_a *location*. *Basil* also has 40 or so can_do relationships with ActCepts A0 through A40. These actions are what enable the deliberative system to find plans to achieve goals, such as "Bring Tea to The Conference Table"

In a traditional ontology this knowledge of the things and concepts in the world is frequently the largest, after all, this knowledge of categories and their relationships is what ontologies are intended to capture. For our robot, we have a fairly thin ontology. However, Basil needs very little knowledge about abstract concepts to function in the real world - however, without sufficient knowledge, the robot cannot maintain the semantic models that enable it to function. So what is necessary must be there.

11.3.2 Reification Knowledge

The second major class of knowledge that the robot must have is the knowledge used by the Reification Engine. For every concept that corresponds to a perceivable thing or location, the robot must know how that thing appears to the robot's sensors. The basis of this knowledge is encoded in the PerCepts. Each perceptible thing has a PerCept, which can be used to identify it, and to build an expectation of how it would appear in the world. The details of the PerCept were explored in Chapter 6. In Basil's simple world, there are PerCepts for the fixed structure of the lab: the walls, the workbenches and programming stations. There are also ones for the movable items, the chairs, the tables, the people. These PerCepts are linked to the corresponding entries in the ontology.

The knowledge that is required for reification is far less complex than that needed by the deliberative system. This is exactly what we would expect since our design is biologically driven. While the machinery associated with reification is complex, the basic data upon which it works is straight forward. Not necessarily small, but simpler in structure. Referring back to Table 7.1, we see that the size of the data ranges between 2 and 7 kilobyte for each thing that can be recognized, where the entire ontology is loaded from a text file that is only 10K.

11.3.3 Perception/Action Knowledge

The final class of knowledge is the low level information in the Perception/Action system. This primarily consists of implicit memory, and specifically procedural memory. This is the knowledge the robot used to know how to turn, to move, to use its sensors, etc. We have spent very little time on these components since they are very specific to the precise implementation of the robotic chassis. However, this type of knowledge is the foundation upon which the performance of the robot is built. If the representations of sensor data and internal and external state are not consistent with the corresponding representations used during reification, the coupling between the Perception/Action system and the Reification Engine will break down, and the robot will be unable to function in the world.

11.4 The process

Now that we have discussed the knowledge that Basil needs for this simple task, we can (finally) begin following the process. We will begin at the bottom of the cognitive continuum, since Basil is a robot, and robots are grounded in the physical world. We will follow the upward chain in Figure 11.1 until we reach the semantic level, then follow (in greater detail) the downward path to see how the pieces fit together.

11.4.1 Perception/Action

Basil begins by sensing the world. Like a biological entity, the process of sensing the environment is continuous, and unceasing. The sonars ping, the returns are detected, and the Perception/Action system builds a sonar image. This image, along with proprioceptic and enteroceptic data is provided to the Reification Engine on demand, and (in our example) the data indicate that Basil's batteries are topped off, the robot is facing east, and has a velocity of zero. There were no returns from the sonars, so the image is empty. All is right with the world.

11.4.2 Reification

The data are received, and the Reification Engine compares the results with the expected state of the world. The Current World State indicates that The Robot is near the work bench (actual robot position X = 6498, Y=1834, θ = 64), and that there should be nothing on sonar. The raw data and an symbolic summary are combined into a record for the Episodic Memory and logged, and the Reification Engine informs the Execution Monitor that everything is as expected. The complete Current World State is updated.

11.4.3 Execution

The Execution Monitor examines the Plan that was last sent down from the deliberative system, and finds that it has nothing to do, so it returns control to the deliberative system. In the process it provides a semantically tagged response that indicates that all is according to plan.

11.4.4 Deliberation

The deliberative system (in this case the ProPLAN Probability–aware planner, with dynamic goal reprioritization) receives the response from the Execution Monitor and turns to its goal stack to re-evaluate the goals. Here it detects that a new request has been added to the goal stack: "Bring tea to the Conference table."

Bingo, after hundreds of thousands of milliseconds with nothing to do, there is work to be done!

The goal is parsed into a description of the desired WorldSet:

```
(TrayLocation, conference_table_area)
(tray_state, unloaded)
```

This is passed to the Personal Rough Ontology, along with the Current World State, and the salient differences are added to a list of salient features. The ontology uses this information to begin compiling a list of actions that might change the salient differences between the current state and the goal state. These actions have necessary enabling conditions, which are added to the salient features. This, in turn, generates more actions that might be needed, which, in turn, generate more features. Using the strength of the transitivity relationships, this process slowly winds down, until a final set of actions are produced. Using the Goal, the Current World State, and the list of salient actions and features, the ontology builds a problem description which is returned to the deliberative system.

The deliberative system now begins exploring the space of reachable states and presses out the boundaries of the possible outcomes until it finds a sequence of actions that result in a world that meets the goals state. This plan is stored, and the search continues until a number of candidate plans have been produced. These are passed to the MCMC simulator for final ranking and the best plan is selected. The plan looks something like:

```
GoWorkBenchToRoomCenter
GoWorkBenchToStairs
GoStairsToKitchen
LoadTeaOnTray
GoKitchenToStairs
GoStairsToCenter
GoCenterToConfArea
UnLoadTrayAtConfArea
```

Each of these actions has a set of necessary enabling condition and the symbolic representation of what the world should look like associated with it. The overall plan has an assessment of the probability of success. The deliberative system determines that the plan is sufficiently likely to succeed, and emits it to the Execution Monitor for execution. Here we begin the downward path.

11.4.5 Execution, Reification and Action

Now that the Execution Monitor has a plan to work with, it begins. The first action is to go from the workbench to the room center. Keep in mind that the deliberative system was working in an abstract world of ideas and concepts, but the execution must occur in the real world. So the Execution Monitor works closely with the Reification Engine to translate the rarefied symbolic plan into more a pragmatic format.

The first step is to confirm that the world is sufficiently close to the necessary starting point to allow execution, the enabling conditions are passed to the Reification Engine and the expected state of the world is used to generate a preafference image, which is quickly compared to the actual data. It is close enough (e.g., no necessary preconditions are violated) so the action can be undertaken. This first action is to move from the workbench to the center of the room. This action is devoid of any real details, all the planner cared about was that the robot was somewhere over by the work bench, it had no knowledge of which way the robot was facing, or its precise location. It is up to the execution system to deal with the details. Using procedural memory stored in the Perception/Action system, the robot determines that to get from its precise location to the room center it must rotate 64 brads counter-clockwise, set the speed to 9, and travel 2000mm. This muscle memory is invoked and the robot trundles off.

This time everything goes smoothly, there are no unexpected obstacles (the process is monitored by the Perception/Action system, and constant updates are requested by the Reification Engine to maintain the current world state. After about 3 seconds the robot position is within tolerance of the room center, and the Execution Monitor is given a success response.

This enables the execution system to get the next step in the plan, confirm the necessary preconditions, and execute the next step. This tight loop of get the next step, confirm, and execute is followed without any intervention by the deliberative system, it is completely devoid of higher thought. This is the same basic process that living systems go through on a moment by moment basis. When you reach for a coffee cup, the actions are non-conscious, unless you focus on them. Even more startling is the experience of driving home after a long day, when you suddenly realize that you are in your driveway, and you don't really remember the drive. As long as things were going the way that they were expected to go, there is very little need for conscious involvement.

But, what happens if things do not go so well?

Let us imagine that we are well into the plan, the tea tray is loaded, and the robot is on its way to the conference table. The next step is to travel from the room center to the conference table areas. The preconditions are met, and the procedural memory is fired. The robot begins to trundle along, and someone steps in front of it.

11.4.6 Perception/Action - Reflex

The sonars are constantly firing, and as the person steps in front the sonars detect the obstacle. The short range returns from the sonars are intercepted directly on the low level motor controller board. This causes a reflex behavior to fire, and Basil slows to a halt. Since the person is walking past, the sonars clear and Basil begins moving again. No intervention was required in this case, however, during then event, the Reification Engine was querying the state of the world on a continuous basis, and logging the events to episodic memory. This information was also used to update the Current World State, so it is available to the higher level systems.

Suppose however, that the person refused to move from in front of the robot. What would have happened then? Recall that each action has additional information attached to it, specifically an estimated execution time, and a retry on failure count. If the interruption was long enough, the Execution Monitor would detect the failure of the action, due to excessive time. This would cause the monitor to query the ROF counter, to assess whether it should try again. Assuming the action was allowed a retry, the Execution Monitor would query the Reification Engine to see if the enabling conditions were still met, and (if so) it would re-attempt the action. If (by now) the person had moved out of the way, the action would be restarted (relying on the procedural memory to adapt the specifics for the new state of the world), and with luck it would complete successfully. Once again, there would be no involvement of the deliberative system.

11.4.7 Execution Failure

But what if the person did not move, or something else went wrong? If the ROF counter runs out, or the person does not move, or any of a thousand other things go wrong, the Execution Monitor reaches a point where it cannot take the next action in the plan. Let us assume that it was not a person that stepped in front of the robot, but that there was a chair that had been pushed into the middle of the room, and it was blocking the robots path.

Since the precondition for moving from the room center to the conference table included no obstacle in the way, the Reification Engine would report that the preconditions were not met. The Execution Monitor would respond by passing the failure message up to the deliberative system, indicating that it had no way to proceed.

11.4.8 Back Up to Deliberation

Once again control reaches the deliberative system, The system checks the goals, and the Current World State, and realizes that the deliver the tea goal is still unsatisfied. So, it treats the situation as a brand new problem, and passes the relevant information down to the ontology. The ontology works through the same process, but a much simpler problem description is generated (recall that the tea is already loaded on the robot). This new problem description is passed to the planner, and a new (shorter) plan is generated. This plan takes into account that the path from the room center directly to the conference table is blocked, and a new plan is generated:

```
GoCenterToProgramming2
GoProgramming2ToConfArea
UnLoadTrayAtConfArea
```

This plan is completely independent of the previous deliberation, no copy of the old plan was kept, no intermediate results were stored. While this may seem wasteful on the surface, it has been shown that the computational complexity of trying to repair a plan is just as great as the complexity of solving a new problem, and can be greater[137]. So we simply start from scratch.

With the new plan the process continues (without a mishap) and after dodging moving people, and routing around obstacles, the robot successfully navigates to the general area of the -conference table. But, the high level plan does not know precisely where the table is, it only knows that it is over by the windows. How will this abstract action of `GoProgramming2ToConfArea` be executed? How will the robot find the table, and position itself in space?

11.4.9 Procedural Memory and Localization

When the `Execution Monitor` encounters the action to go to the conference table area, it uses the preafference service provided by the `Reification Engine` to get a sensor-based representation of what the world should look like. This representation is built from the detailed knowledge maintained in the `Reification Engine`. This detailed knowledge includes the last known position and orientation of the conference table, not in abstract terms, but in the detailed coordinate system of the lab. The precise position of the robot (to the accuracy that is available) is also known. This enables the generation of a preafferent sonar image, that places the exact view of the table, from the robot's present position.

In addition, these data can be used by the procedural memory in the Perception/Action system to execute the movement. Given the known position of the table and the position of the robot, the procedural memory for movement executes two steps: point and shoot. The point operation simply determines in what direction and how far the robot needs to turn to be pointing at the estimated position of the table. The shoot operation executes the necessary command to move the robot the estimated distance to the table, and then stop. Of course, since the conference table is about 1.5m in diameter, we do not want to aim at the centroid of the table. Rather we want to aim at the point that is just short of the closest edge of the table. This is done by using the preafference image that was generated, since this models the sensible surface of the table - the closest point that will create a sonar return. By using this preafference image, generated by the `Reification Engine` from data supplied by the `Execution Monitor`, the procedural memory aims the robot at precisely the point we need to achieve. Once this command is executed, the preafference images are used to monitor the action. By repeatedly comparing the expected state of the sensorium with the actual data, the system can both confirm the progress, and localize the robot.

The localization is a critical step. Robots are notorious for getting lost in their own backyards[1]. Biological systems localize by sensing the things in the world, and adjusting their positions, as does the cybernetic brain in Basil. Any time Basil moves, the estimate of the robot's position drifts from the actual position. This is due to errors in the sensors that are used to track position. In general, the further the travel, and the more turns, the worse the estimate. So what is a robot to do?

As Basil gets closer to the table, the preafference image is based on Basil's estimated robot position. The actual sensor data is grounded in the actual robot position. Encoded in Basil's procedural memory is a simple idea: the robot is usually wrong. So, if the two images differ, it is more likely that Basin has a bad position estimate, than that the table has moved. When the edge of the table gets into sensor range, the two images are compared, and Basil's position is updated, on the basis that the robot's estimate is wrong. With each new sonar image, the position gets progressively closer to the actual position as reported by the real world data. In this way the mental model that Basil maintains is kept in correspondence with the real world.

Basil has a target position to arrive next to the table, and the robot uses reification based localization to arrive at that point. When the final position is reached, the Perception/Action system returns an action succeeded response to the `Reification Engine`, which, in turn, responds with a success message to the `Execution Monitor`. This is passed up to the deliberative system, which determines form the Current World State that the goal has, in fact, been satisfied. The deliberative system now re-evaluates the goals and, perhaps it selects a new goal to pursue, or it simply waits with near infinite cybernetic patience for the next task, the next problem to solve.

11.5 A Few Notes About the General Flow

In this chapter we have put all the parts together and walked our way through a simple example. We based this example on Basil since this robot is a functional instantiation of the cybernetic brain embodied in a robot. The focus was on the flow of control and information between the four main components: the deliberative, execution, reification and perception/action systems that make up the robot. These

---

[1] Well, the availability of cheap GPS receivers has enabled robots to know where they are when outdoors. However, the installation of external beacons for localization in indoor environments lags behind, and is significantly more expensive, since both the beacons and the receivers must be installed and maintained.

components are tightly intertwined, sharing details, and passing responsibility back and forth as needed. However, this tight coupling may be the minimum needed to get the kind of intelligent behavior that we want from robots, but of which we have few examples.

The general flow is a set of nested loops, and the level of cognition drops as we descend from the deliberative to the perception/action system. At the same time the speed at which changes occur, and at which decisions must be made increases as we get closer to the hardware. The trade off is that the lower level systems are generally using less complete data to make simpler decisions, and that they depend on the correct context being maintained by the systems above them.

One of the reasons that this kind of tight coupling is discouraged in software is the difficulty that it causes when one is trying to test the code. This is exacerbated when there are non-deterministic aspects to the execution paths, and given the need for the cybernetic brain to react quickly to a dynamic environment, there are many such aspects to the software that makes up the cybernetic brain. Even in the deliberative system, the selection of one possible plan over another might favor one plan on one run, and another plan on the next. So we have the question "If one time on the tea delivery task it goes by way of the workbench, and the next time it goes through the center of the room: is one a failure?" In the next chapter we discuss the issues surrounding the testing of embodied systems, and present the results of some of the testing on the reification portion of the system to support our original hypothesis that the addition of reification would improve the ability of the robot to make sense out of the world.

Chapter 12
Testing

There are two critical aspects of an autonomous intelligent robot that must be tested: the robot, and the autonomous intelligent aspect. These two aspects require very different test strategies, and both aspects are difficult to test. We will address them separately, focusing primarily on the testing methodology in Sections 12.1 - 12.5, and focusing primarily on the tests themselves in Section 12.6.

Let us set the stage[1]. It is late on Sunday and your robot is scheduled for a demo tomorrow. Your team has been tweaking the code to get a new behavior to work properly. You call a halt to a process and start a final test of the robot, and it fails. What do you do now? If you are like most of us, you have a large set of possible error sources, a hardware component could have failed, the new software components could have failed, or the new software could be causing a communications error between the hardware components. If you start on the hardware and it turns out to be the software, you have wasted valuable time, and vice versa. It looks like it is going to be a long night. This chapter was inspired by that frustration.

12.1 Testing the Robot, or How Does One Test an Embedded System?

In this chapter we discuss ways to implement eXtreme Programming (XP) methodologies on embedded systems. We will start with a brief discussion of XP, and the advantages that it brings to software development. Then, we will discuss the unique challenges posed by embedded/robotic systems and propose some solutions. We will discuss an XP methodology that we have implemented in the development of robotic code. Finally we demonstrate the final tests that demonstrate the improvement that adding reification gives to the robot's performance. These final tests are only possible because we have tested all of the underlying code. Because of this we

---

[1] The first part of this chapter is an extension of work presented at the IROS 2007 Workshop on Performance Evaluation and Benchmarking for Intelligent Robots and Systems.

have confidence that the behaviors that we are seeing are not just an artifact of an undiscovered bug in the code.

12.2 eXtreme Programming

In the last decade many methodologies have been proposed to improve the quality and reduce the cost of developing software. Among these tools, eXtreme Programming (XP) is becoming widely accepted as a methodology that supports the development of highly reliable software. For an overview see Kent Beck's work[8]. This is due, in part, to four specific practices: continuous testing, continuous code review (pair programming), continuous integration, and pragmatic coding standards. Most of the practices required by XP are the same whether they are applied to a pure software development project, or to an embodied system. However, the introduction of co-development of hardware, firmware, and software requires significant adjustment of some traditional XP practices. In specific, the application of continuous integration, and continuous testing require some re-evaluation in the hardware/firmware domain. According to the National Institutes of Standards and Technology (NIST), inadequate testing infrastructures result in tens of billions of dollars in additional costs, and significant over-runs in development time[142]. As mentioned above, one of the core practices of XP is continuous integration and testing. XP relies on the use of automated test tools such as the xUnit family (JUnit for Java, CppUnit for C++, etc.) of programs. These tools allow the developer to produce detailed unit tests (tests at the function or method level) which can be automatically run, and the results evaluated, summarized, and displayed to the developer. It is not uncommon to have several hundred test cases, covering every method and execution path, run in a few seconds at the press of a button. This allows the developers to make significant changes to the code (re-factoring) while remaining confident that no unanticipated side effects have broken the code base. This capability also supports the nearly continuous integration of the new code into the build process. While these techniques have been well developed for traditional software projects, their integration into embodied systems lags behind[187, 114, 84, 52, 18]. In the current model of hardware/software co-development, this has frequently resulted in software being developed well in advance of the hardware that it is designed to control. As a result, the high-level software is often tested in isolation, and integration testing becomes a significant factor in total development cost and time to deployment. It would be extremely powerful to have the benefits of continuous testing when dealing with hardware and firmware, but in practice, the notion of unit testing needs to be extended to handle the new domains.

12.3 Methodology for Testing Embodied Systems

In this section we discuss a methodology that we have developed for testing embedded systems. In the interests of clarity, the following definitions are used in this Chapter:

- Software is the high level code, for example the planning and reification system.
- Firmware is the lower level code that controls the hardware.
- The interface allows the passing of information and control between firmware and software modules.
- The system is the combination of the software, the firmware, the interfaces, and the hardware.
- A scenario is a preplanned sequence of inputs, for which the preferred output is known.
- A simulation is an unplanned or random sequence of inputs for which the preferred output is only known in a probabilistic way.

In traditional software deployment, every effort is made to abstract away from the specific hardware underlying the virtual machine. This is possible because, for the most part, the hardware is completely substitutable. One can look at the continual wars between Apple, Windows, and Linux as an indirect result of a lack of substitutability. In embodied systems, the hardware is an integral part of the system, and the substitutability assumption can not be made. This lack of a (more or less) uniform platform causes the developers to be responsible for the production and testing of not only high level code but also lower level interface and firmware control code as shown in Figure 12.1. The fact that the developers may be responsible all of these components leads to a complex process of co-development. The high level software must interact with the firmware, which must be written to interact with the high level software. This tight coupling significantly increases the chances of software failure. The potential of software failure can be mitigated by automated testing, but this requires testing both the high level software and the firmware[1]. We have developed a different way of thinking about testing in embodied systems.

Fig. 12.1 Three level structure of an embodied system. Frequently, the developers are responsible for coding and testing the firmware, in addition to the high level software.

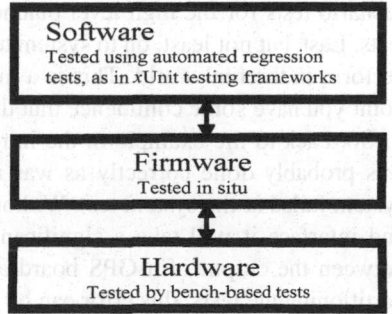

The first improvement is the splitting of testing into static testing and dynamic testing. For software only systems, this would be the difference between regression testing (static) and full simulation testing (dynamic). The second improvement is a split between the testing of hardware, firmware, software, interfaces, and system as a whole. This framework is shown in the table below.

Table 12.1 Breakout of testing levels and classes

Level	Static tests	Dynamic Tests
Hardware	A. Bench Testing	-
Firmware	B. Static firmware testing (using mocked components)	E. Scenario Testing of the firmware (using mocked components)
Software	C. Regression Testing	F. Scenario or Simulation Testing
Interface	D. Static Interface testing	G. Scenario Interface Testing
System	-	H. Full System testing

The first test that happens is bench testing, when the individual components are tested for input and output parameters, often on the robotic chassis. Once the behavior of the component is known, then the component can be "mocked up" in software (see Rainsberger[14] for more details on mock objects). This allows the programmer to create and run regression tests on that component in a software environment such as jUnit. The next set of static testing will be done on the higher level software (but as a good XP programmer, you already have a set of regression tests on your high level software). Once the firmware and software have been tested, then the interfaces between them can be tested. So far so good, but thus far only the behavior in a static environment has been tested. Now, we need to test the system in the presence of chaos, dropped messages, moving targets, moving obstacles, and other hazards. Dynamic testing comes in four different flavors. We assume that the high level planning software has been run through simulation testing. However, in order to make the firmware and interface testing fit the XP framework, the tests take the form of pre-scripted scenarios, for which the appropriate behavior is known. This allows the programmer to have the same confidence in the system's dynamic behavior that the regression tests give in the static behavior. It also would be a good idea to write scenario tests for the high level planner in addition to the probabilistic simulation tests. Last, but not least, on to system tests, where the robot is taken out and allowed perform in the real world. This is a much less frustrating experience, since at this point you have some confidence that the software is working correctly.

So, back to the example in the introduction, what went wrong? The bench test was probably done correctly as was a static test of the high level software. The system failed at the system test. Without the static and dynamic test of the firmware and interface it will take a significant amount of time to discover the mismatch between the output of a GPS board and the input of the high level software. By partitioning the tests, this error can be detected before the expensive field testing.

12.3.1 Benefits of Partitioning the Tests

So, what lift do we get from this partitioning? Ever since the introduction of functional decomposition, it has been clear that neatly decomposed software is easier to develop. One key reason for this is that software that has been decomposed into (relatively) independent modules has lower levels of coupling[118]. In this chapter we are presenting a methodology for decomposing tests into roughly independent classes, and addressing cross product terms explicitly. This is driven by the need to effectively cover a large, complex space of test cases, in a domain that is not easy to exhaustively cover. From the test decomposition shown in Table 1, we can extract six classes of 'software only' tests. High level software has been extensively researched with respect to testing, and it is not uncommon to have two to three test cases for every function or method in the code. While the automated testing of firmware is not as well researched, it is expected that approximately the same test-to-function ratio will hold. Without any type of decomposition, the number of tests needed to cover the combination of software, firmware, and interfaces would be:

$$TestCount = Test_f \times Test_s \qquad (12.1)$$

where: $Test_f$ is the number of firmware tests, and
$Test_s$ is the number of high-level software tests.

This results from the need to test each function with each combination of tests for the other classes. This is significant since it in not uncommon to encounter test libraries with thousands of individual automated tests. This can easily result in millions of test cases to assure coverage. It is, of course, possible to reduce the rather large number of test cases by effectively partitioning the space. If partitioned perfectly, the total number of test cases reduces to the sum of the test cases in each class, a significant reduction. It is rarely possible to partition the test space perfectly, since there are interactions between the various software components. As a result, we test the firmware and hardware classes as though they were partitioned perfectly, and then test the interface between the layers as a separate class of tests. The key condition for the interface testing is the ability to rely on the successful testing of the components on either side of the interface. In effect, given that the firmware is correct, and that the software is correct, it becomes possible to test the interface as an independent class of tests. Given the validity of this assumption, the total number of tests becomes:

$$TestCount = Test_f + Test_i + Test_s \qquad (12.2)$$

where: $Test_f$ is the number of firmware tests,
$Test_i$ is the number of interface tests, and
$Test_s$ is the number of high-level software tests.

For the case where we have approximately 700 firmware tests, 1100 high-level software tests, and 200 interface tests; we go from 770,000 unpartitioned tests to 2000 partitioned tests.

12.4 General Testing Guidelines

As mentioned above, the structural decomposition is into three layers: high-level software, firmware, and hardware. Each of these has characteristics that affect the way in which testing is done. In order to reduce the costs and delays associated with systems integration, we have developed several guidelines for the design of auto-mated tests for the firmware layers in embodied systems. This code is written in a requirements driven development environment. Practitioners of test driven develop-ment will notice that the following code guidelines will violate some of their rules. We have found that for embedded systems the constraints imposed by the combina-tion of the requirements and the physical environment are limiting enough that the addition of test driven development may make the coding task impossible. So, the following are our "in house" testing rules.

- Some things cannot be tested
- Do NOT change the code to make testing easier
- Use public accessors for setting and testing variables
- Test physical constants
- Mock hardware components and interfaces. Note: this often requires duplicating hardware performance in testable software modules
- The static tests are unit tests, test unit level functions.

12.4.1 General Partitioning Guidelines

Another possible source of confusion is the line between static and dynamic testing, so here are our rules for that partitioning. Static unit tests are traditional automated tests, in which the required behavior of a method or function is verified. These tests typically involve setting up a test harness for a method, invoking the methods with a specific input set, and confirming that the return data are the expected value(s). These tests are the staple of all unit testing frameworks. Dynamic unit tests are used to test the performance of a module under changing conditions. These tests are critical for embodied systems, such as autonomous robots, since they will almost always be deployed into dynamic and uncertain domains. Dynamic testing is done using a scenario generator. This software is built out of traditional unit testing com-ponents, which have been extended to allow the specification of a sequence of tests, which correspond to a requirement of dynamic behavior. For example, consider an autonomous ground vehicle that is expected to detect a dead-end, and avoid getting 'trapped.' This required behavior can best be tested by creating a scenario which consists of mocking the sensory data that would correspond to the robot entering the dead-end and detecting the blockage. This scenario would have an expected behavior that corresponds to reversing course, extricating the robot from the dead-end, and proceeding in a manner that would avoid the dead-end.

12.5 Testing in the lab

As a case study, we will use an autonomous ground vehicle that is currently under development. In Figure 12.2, the autonomous ground vehicle (Kitty) is shown undergoing unconstrained environment testing at a recent robotics exposition. (Please note that the robot was moving toward the people when the photo was taken) While there is an emergency stop control system, during these tests the E-Stop was unnecessary.

12.5.1 Hardware

Kitty has an architecture that is biologically inspired. Based on research into neurophysiology, the core structure uses a model based on the brain stem and functional units of simple terrestrial vertebrate nervous system. In Figure 12.3, the UML de-

Fig. 12.2 The autonomous ground vehicle 'Kitty' during unconstrained field tests. Note: Kitty is driving toward the people at about 4 m/s, and has just adjusted the steering for a hard right turn. Kitty will clear the woman (and her child) with about 15 cm to spare.

ployment diagram for the brain stem of the vehicle is shown. Each of the major nodes (the cubes in the figure) is an independent processor module. These are real-time modules which are programmed in a subset of the Java Programming language, and which emulate the parallel processing capability of living systems. For the entire system for to perform reliably, each of these modules and their components must function correctly and the interactions between each module must perform correctly. The XP methodology relies on continuous testing to assure the developers that any new code that has been integrated is performing correctly, and to assure that the most recent changes have not caused any previous software to fail.

12.5.2 Static Tests

The static tests focus on the behavior of the structure of the system. It looks at each component in isolation, and determines that these components do what they are

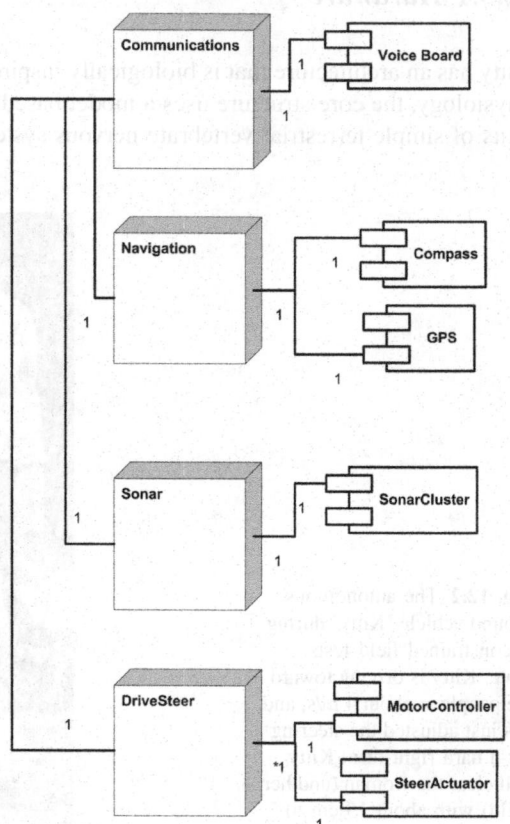

Fig. 12.3 The UML deployment diagram for an autonomous ground vehicle.

expected to do. Usually, this is done by providing specific inputs to the component, and confirming that then output matches the expected result. As an example, if one were testing a square root function, the tests would include a few known squares, a test of zero, and a test of a negative number.

12.5.2.1 Hardware Bench tests

The first stage of testing is making sure that the hardware is doing what it is supposed to be doing. Without this foundation, it is extremely difficult to debug software failures. In traditional software-only development, this step is typically skipped, since the underlying hardware is assumed to be tested and functional. If the development is being embodied into a commercial, off-the-shelf robotic platform, this step is often provided by the platform manufacturer. However, if the embodied system is a custom, or in-house developed, platform some level of assurance must be provided that the hardware is functioning correctly. The second benefit of this bench testing is that it provides the 'gold-standard' data needed to successfully build software mock objects to use in the firmware testing.

12.5.2.2 Static Firmware Tests

The firmware acts as an abstraction layer between the hardware and the high-level software. In the past, firmware was frequently developed in hardware specific application languages, which generated obstacles to automated testing. Recently, there has been growing acceptance of higher level languages as the primary development tools for embedded micro-controllers, and low-level hardware interfaces. The use of a high-level language such as Java or C++ allows significant flexibility in testing firmware. For example, Kitty's brain stem is running on five independent Parallax Javelin[39] chips, microcontrollers which are programmed in a subset of the Java programming language. These chips provide Java wrappers for hardware components such as Universal Asynchronous Receiver/Transmitters (UARTs), timers, and motor control systems. When the embedded code is running on the actual chip, these hardware components are instantiated, and connected to the Java code. During static testing, it is necessary to test on mocked components, enabling the embedded code to compile and execute. By building the mock components, we have the ability to verify the function of the firmware, without having to run the actual hardware[80]. This means that automated static test libraries can be developed and archived. They can then provide full regression tests at the firmware level. As an example we have mocked the UART wrapper used by the Javelin chip. A UART is used to provide serial communications between independent devices. The firmware can instantiate a UART and assign it to any input/output (I/O) pin on the chip. The mocked UART has the ability to accept data from the firmware and store it into a transmission buffer, which is visible to the verification tests. This allows the static test to automatically verify that the order in which the data are transmitted is correct, and that each datum has the correct value. If, during development, a change is made that results in a software error affecting this information packet (perhaps the order of data is altered, or a data item is skipped) the automated tests will detect and flag the error. It is important to note that the mocked hardware components should only have enough fidelity to enable testing the firmware. The focus is not on testing the hardware itself, that step was completed by the bench testing in the previous step. The question under consideration is: "If the hardware is working correctly, will the current firmware code meet the requirements?"

12.5.2.3 Static Software Tests

The static software tests are traditional unit tests. Many of the resources previously cited provide coverage of the process of testing traditional software. However, it is important to note that by previously testing the firmware, the testing of the high-level software can be separated from the testing of the underlying firmware. As mentioned above, this partitioning significantly reduces both the number of tests needed to cover the high-level software, and reduces the complexity of those tests.

12.5.2.4 Static Interface Tests

The final leg of the static testing is to test the interfaces between the different components. It is entirely possible for two software components to each pass all their individual tests, yet fail to function as a complete system. In embodied systems this can become a major problem, since there are typically numerous independent microcontrollers, processors, and discrete hardware components that must all interact to meet the system's requirements. As an example, consider the navigation and communications modules as shown in Figure 12.3. The individual tests on the firmware code running on each of these modules shows that the navigation board is correctly reading and packaging the GPS and compass data, and loading that data into the UART for transmission. In the same manner, the static tests on the communications board show that it is correctly receiving the data packet, and unpacking it into local storage for dissemination. However, even though all the tests are passing, the system fails in the field tests. This comes about because the navigation board and the communications board (developed by different teams) have an incompatibility. This was the cause of the failure of the Mars Climate Orbiter[136]. The use of automated interface testing can detect and flag these types of errors. In the case of the interface between the communication board and the navigation board, the tests would instantiate a copy of the navigation firmware, and load known values, mock the transmission of the data to the communications board, and then verify that the correct data is stored on the communications board. This could be caught during the test writing process as a developer writes:

AssertEquals(COMM.HeightInFeet(),NAV.HeightInMeters());

In addition, during dynamic testing, the behavioral requirements would detect and flag the error.

12.5.3 Dynamic tests

The static tests on the firmware focused on the fixed behavior of the methods and functions. The dynamic tests address issues that occur during continued operations. These tests include verifying correct behavior in cases such as buffer over-runs, loss of communication, updating rapidly changing data, and run-time performance. These types of tests require extending the model of unit tests. In keeping with the notion of building firm foundations, dynamic tests of the firmware are the logical starting point.

12.5.3.1 Dynamic Firmware Tests

In the static testing of the firmware, it was necessary to create mock objects that corresponded to the structure of the hardware components that the firmware utilized. These objects must be extended to provide some of the dynamic behavior that the hardware objects display. As an example, in the case of the UART provided by the Javelin chip, there is a fixed size transmit/receive buffer. During static testing it was sufficient to mock the capacity of the buffer, however to support testing of buffer over-run behavior, it is necessary to mock a certain amount of the run-time behavior. The description of this run-time behavior may be described in the technical documentation of the hardware, or it may be necessary to discover the behavior by running additional bench tests. However, not knowing how the hardware performs under dynamic load means that the developers have a large class of errors that will only occur at run-time. A case in point was the behavior of the Pathfinder Mars Rover, which underwent system level resets (unfortunately, on Mars[59]) when a hardware priority inversion fault occurred. The dynamic firmware tests for the navigation board include building a scenario which will continuously generate and export compass heading data, to confirm that the firmware does not get overwhelmed. Additional tests include updating the mocked data registers on the GPS module during the read by the firmware to verify that the data are consistent. In addition, general performance tests are run on the firmware loops, to verify that requirements of update rates are being met.

12.5.3.2 Dynamic Software Tests

The dynamic software tests are a natural extension of the firmware tests. Since the hardware has been mocked up to provide realistic dynamic behavior, and the firmware has been tested to verify that its dynamic behavior meets the requirements

of the system, it is possible to develop similar tests of the dynamic behavior of
the high-level software. In many embodied systems there are additional requirements for the high level software. These requirements may include adaptive behaviors, learning, and autonomous behaviors. These requirements are aspects of the
high-level software that require dynamic testing of a slightly different nature than
the lower level firmware. For example, if the system is supposed to function au-
tonomously, it may not do the same thing, in the same way, time after time. This may
require dynamic tests which setup the same situation time after time, and record the
behavior of the embodied system. No single test can necessarily answer the question "Is the system performing correctly?" Rather, it may require statistical analysis
of the aggregated result before the automated test can be verified. If the system is
supposed to learn from its actions in the environment, then we compound this verification problem. It is necessary to run a series of aggregate tests to establish the
current behavior, allow the system to experience failures and learn from them, and
then rerun the aggregate test to establish that the learning has occurred. Now the test
harnesses must provide a complex and dynamic set of test cases, and measure the
change in aggregate response distribution. While it is certain that designing, developing, and, ironically, testing these test scenarios is a major undertaking; it is clear
that attempting to do this in the field is far more time consuming, and physically
challenging. (Consider setting up a physical test to introduce reliable, repeatable
noise into a sonar sensor, versus pumping 'noise' into the software mock of the
sonar sensor. See the recent report by Tse et. al.[198] for an example in the manu-
facturing domain.)

12.5.3.3 Dynamic Interface Tests

The dynamic interface tests are extensions of the previous tests. They are more
complex since they are testing the interactions between multiple components in the
system. But the same types of tests that were run to verify the dynamic behavior of
the individual components can be extended with the static interface tests to establish
correct dynamic behavior.

12.5.3.4 System Level Testing

Systems level testing is actually composed of two phases. The first is a general systems test which is run every time the robot turned on. The second is more interactive
formal systems test protocol.

1) The Robot dance (systems self-test): The first phase is the something we call
"the robot dance," which is run every time that the system is started. In the "robot
dance" the hardware is self-tested by the machine and the success or failure of that
hardware is announced in a way that the human can understand. So Kitty, on startup,
uses a voice output to say her name and software revision numbers, turns the steering to the left and right, activates the sonar sensors and announces the results, runs

backwards and forwards, activates the compass and announces the result, and activates the GPS and announces the results. The steering and drive train tests explain the "robot dance" label. This sequence becomes a hardware regression test, although the complexity of the test is limited by the need for a human to observe and interpret the results. As we add new hardware, new tests are added to the dance. This test perhaps the most tedious of the set, because it happens just as you are ready to test all the new cool behaviors that have just been added and tested since you had the robot out last. However, this test is also essential. If you have completed all of the tests, you have an assurance that any anomalous results you may see in the final test sequence are the result of unexpected interactions and not testable software or hardware bugs.

2) Formal Systems tests: Finally, we come to the last tests. At this point, you are probably saying "Enough already, we have tested this to oblivion, what else could go wrong?" What we have not yet built is trust. This is an autonomous machine that we are proposing to send into real environments, we need to learn to trust that it will behave "well" even in situations for which we have not programmed it explicitly (See Gunderson and Gunderson[144]). This final testing takes the longest, but is also the most fun. However, if all of the previous testing has been done, we can be assured that what we are testing is the intended behaviors and not an artifact of errors in the software or hardware. That is a way to build trust in the system that you are about to send out into the real world.

12.6 Formal System Tests - Testing In The Real World

In this section we discuss the final (and most fun) type of testing. This is when we get to watch the robot actually perform. This is also the most time consuming part of the testing sequence. The automated tests that we ran in the previous section are *fast*. Just how fast, you suddenly realize when you take notes on the robot trundling around for a few days, and realize that the testing is only half done. But it is also a very rewarding time, because you actually get to watch the robots move in the real world (not in simulation). So below you will find the tests that mark the transition from theory to practice.

12.6.1 Testing Recognition

The first set of tests were to determine that the robot could correctly identify objects for which it has PerCepts. For this test, we exposed the robot to an object, and record the object that it identifies. This test is required to determine that the recognition system is working correctly. It should be noted that was not a test that can be used to measure the system with reification against either a reactive system or a deliberative system.

12.6.1.1 Recognition Testing Protocol

In this test we showed the robot a set of different objects. They were:

- A short wheeled chair
- A wooden chair
- A toy box
- A round table
- A person

The robot was pointed directly at each of the objects for 10 times/object, each time with the object at a different pose and distance. The response of the robot was recorded. This is a traditionally difficult test, since it relies only on the identification of objects without any context. In a living system, this is equivalent to being knocked unconscious, and waking up in a totally unfamiliar location. The organism has nothing to go on but direct sensory information, and that is limited to a single glimpse of the surroundings.

The robot is activated, and allowed to use its sensors to take three independent sonar images of what is in front of it. These sensor images are processed by the pattern recognition portion of the `Reification Engine` and any `PerCepts`

Fig. 12.4 These are the 4 common objects that the robot must recognize. They include two types of chairs (a wheeled desk chair, and a legged wooden chair), a small storage box on wheels, and a large (1.5m diameter) round table. In addition, the robot must be able to recognize a person (not shown).

which match above a 90% threshold are listed as possible candidates. A typical return might look like:

Bird Brain starting
x = 0, y = 0, h = 0
Creating Episodic Memory
Creating Reification Engine
Scanning [(-200:200,1184:1584,165:165,1384,1215259809853,1000)]
        [short_wheeled_chair::(0,1521,0)@0, short_wood_chair::(0,1309,0)@0]
Scanning [(-200:200,1184:1584,165:165,1384,1215259810967,1000)]
        [short_wheeled_chair::(0,1521,0)@0, short_wood_chair::(0,1309,0)@0]
Scanning [(-200:200,1184:1584,165:165,1384,1215259812077,1000)]
        [short_wheeled_chair::(0,1521,0)@0, short_wood_chair::(0,1309,0)@0]
Shutting down
System terminated

In this example, there was a wheeled chair (See Figure 12.4) approximately 1.5m in front of the robot. The robot returned two possibilities for the sonar images that it perceived, either a wheeled chair or a wooden chair. Going through the output in more detail, the first four lines are reporting on the initialization of the cybernetic brain. This particular brain model is called "Bird Brain" since it has the deliberative system removed. The robot takes three sonar snapshots, each of which is reported in two line couplets. The line that begins with "Scanning" shows the observed obstacles that the Perception/Action system generates. The next line of the couplet shows the symbolic objects that correspond to these observations, along with their estimated position in global coordinates, and orientation. In all cases there were two possibilities.

This is a typical result, since the two chairs are almost impossible to distinguish except in specific poses. One of the most difficult aspects of context-free recognition is disambiguating the data. As we discussed earlier, one of the major benefits of reification coupled with memory is that this disambiguation becomes much easier if the system can rely on previously generated models of the world. However, in this sequence of tests, that model is intentionally removed from the robot's memory.

Given that the robot returns a number of possible symbolic returns, the question of how to measure the results becomes more complex than the simple approach of counting up the right versus wrong answers. If the robot only knows about six objects, how does one score the result if the robot suggests that a particular object might be one of several different types? We use a metric called the Jaccard index[102], also known as the Jaccard Similarity Index. The value ranges from 1.0 - indicating perfect agreement, to 0.0, indicating a complete miss. The Jaccard Index reduces the 'value' of the agreement as the wideness of the guess increases. We use the following equation to calculate the Jaccard Index:

$$JaccardIndex = \frac{M_{11}}{M_{11} + M_{10} + M_{01}} \tag{12.3}$$

where: M_{11}: count(A and B both have a value of true)
M_{01}: count(A is false and B is true)
M_{10}: count(A is true and B is false)
M_{00}: count(A and B both have a value of false)
subject to $M_{11} + M_{01} + M_{10} + M_{00} = total samples$

In the examples given above, the Jaccard Index is 0.5, since one possibility was correct, while the other was not.

12.6.1.2 Recognition Testing Results

In this section we will look at the recognition test results. We will show one example of the raw testing data, and then present summary data for the rest of the testing.

We ran each test series with gradually increasing distances between the robot and the object to be recognized. This is due, in part, to the rather myopic nature of Basil's sonar imagery. As with any sensor there is a maximum range beyond which the sensor is ineffective. The technical data sheets for Basil's sonars give a value of approximately 3m for the maximum range. As with most sensors, the maximum effective range is frequently less that the rated value. The maximum effective range is also a function of the specific objects that are being sensed, some objects provide much clearer sensor images than others, and we found that the lab furniture was no exception.

For each of the objects, at each of the ranges, the protocol was the same. The object was initially placed with its center directly in front of the robot at the test distance. The robot was asked to report what object was in front of it. It took two to three snapshots of the scene, and then reported what object, or objects, it could recognize. The object was then moved slightly. This move included rotating the object and displacing it a small amount both radially (either closer or further away from the robot) and either closer to or further from the robots centerline. This process was repeated nine times, to generate ten data points at the distance. The object was then repositioned at the next test distance, and the process was repeated. We took readings at three different ranges, separated by 0.5m. A typical run would be at 0.75m, 1.25m, and 1.75m, the maximum effective range of the sonars.

From the data in Table 12.2 it is clear that the individual Jaccard Indices are larger the more precise the robot's estimate of the object (provided that it is accurate), and that the result is penalized if the robot includes additional possibilities in its estimate of the type of object. The Mean Jaccard Index is calculated as a simple arithmetic mean of the individual results.

The mean results, displayed by object type and distance are summarized in Table 12.3. Several things are very clear from the results. First, even at short ranges the ability to recognize objects varies widely, from a low of 0.38 to a high of 0.83. Much of this confusion comes from the fact that it is very difficult to tell the difference between the chairs from the back. To sonar, they present a nearly identical image of a short, nearly vertical surface. This is also true of the storage box, which presents the same short, vertical surface regardless of its orientation (See Figure 12.5).

Table 12.2 Recognition of Wheeled Chair At 0.75m. The 'Y' indicates that the robot indicatied the actual object might belong to this class of objects.

Wheel	Wood	Box	Table	Person	JI
Y	Y	-	-	Y	0.33
Y	Y	-	-	-	0.50
Y	-	-	-	-	1.00
Y	-	-	-	-	1.00
Y	-	-	-	-	1.00
Y	-	-	-	-	1.00
Y	Y	-	-	-	0.5
Y	-	-	-	-	1.00
Y	-	-	-	-	1.00
Y	-	-	-	-	1.00

Average Jaccard Index = 0.83

Table 12.3 Mean Jaccard Indices of context-free recognition

Range	Wheel	Wood	Box	Table	Person
Short	0.83	0.38	0.35	0.67	0.79
Mid	0.35	0.30	0.20	0.15	0.80
Long	0.43	0.42	0.12	-[a]	0.45

[a] Due to the size of the table, only two ranges are used

A second clear result is that as the object gets further away from the robot, its ability to distinguish one object from another decreases. This is common with most sensors. Consider your own ability to tell one person from another if they are a few feet away, compared to the case where they are several blocks away. You can

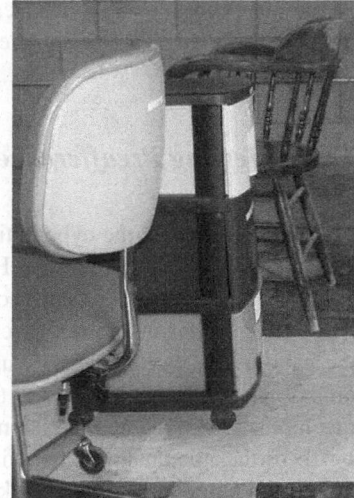

Fig. 12.5 This is the side view of the three most commonly confused objects: the wooden chair, the storage box, and the wheeled chair. Notice that in all cases the surface presented to the robot is a short vertical surface. These three objects generate almost identical sonar images, making them almost impossible to distinguish.

probably (depending on your eyesight) tell that it is a person, not a dog, from 500 meters, but identifying the exact person may be problematic. The sonar image that we are using is quite poor, and has very low resolution, hence Basil, like many people, is quite myopic.

So here we have Basil, activated in an unknown location, allowed one quick blink, and asked to identify the object at some location in the field of view. In spite of these handicaps the overall performance averages a Jaccard Index of 0.45, and was wrong less than 25% of the time. These data were generated with only the recognition side of the Reification Engine active. This context-free recognition task is quite common in robotics, and the issue of disambiguation is an active research area. However, living organisms rarely wake-up with no context for their environment. In general, they have a mental model of what they expect to see when they open their eyes, and the reification process takes advantage of this mental model to both simplify the recognition process, and to increase its reliability. In the next section we look at the results of using reification in the recognition of objects.

12.6.1.3 Disambiguation

Since it is almost impossible for Basil's sonar to distinguish between the two types of chairs, it is perhaps unfair to score his performance on both types of chairs. This is analogous to asking a visitor to a convention of identical twins to tell the twins apart after a brief meeting. If we accept this limitation and analyze Basil's performance on the basis of four categories Chair, Box, Table, and Person, we get a better idea of the true accuracy. Replicating the raw data in with a single chair category gives the results shown in table 12.4.

The impact on identifying the wheeled chair as 'chair' is negligible, this is due to the relatively high rate at which if either chair was identified, both would be reported. However, when we look at the overall accuracy of the system the grouping of the chairs into a single chair category, increases the overall Jaccard Index from the 0.45 reported above to an index of 0.62.

12.6.2 Testing Preafference

The performance of the cybernetic brain in a pure recognition mode is reasonable given the low resolution sensors. However, as we discussed above, this is like asking someone to identify objects in a completely unexpected scene, given a single glance. Biological organisms do not function in this way, rather, they maintain a model of the state of the world, and they use this model to modulate their perception of the outside world. The next series of tests looks at the effects of having a full reification mechanism available to the system.

To further the analogy of waking up in an unfamiliar room in a strange country, the preafference tests are more like waking up in your own room. You are still only

Table 12.4 Recognition of Wheeled Chair At 0.75m

Wood	Box	Table	Person	JI
Y	-	-	Y	0.50
Y	-	-	-	1.00
Y	-	-	-	1.00
Y	-	-	-	1.00
Y	-	-	-	1.00
Y	-	-	-	1.00
Y	-	-	-	1.00
Y	-	-	-	1.00
Y	-	-	-	1.00
-	-	-	Y	0.00
Y	-	-	-	1.00
Y	Y	-	-	0.50
-	-	-	-	0.00
Y	-	-	-	1.00
Y	-	-	-	1.00
-	-	-	-	0.50
Y	-	-	-	1.00
Y	-	-	-	1.00
Y	-	-	-	1.00

Average Jaccard Index = 0.83

given a quick glance at the scene, but you know your room. You know what kind of tables and chairs are there, and you know their approximate location within the room. Given that one quick glance you could probably tell with high accuracy what was there, if it had been moved very far, etc. This increase in accuracy is due to your ability to make use of both aspects of a complete reification system. You simplify the task of building a symbolic representation of the environment by using preafference to load your sensory cortices, and then using recognition to fill in the rest. You take advantage of your mental model to confirm what you expect to see, so that you can focus your cognitive ability on the parts that are unexpected.

In these tests, the robot is given a mental model of the world. This mental model includes the PerCepts that correspond to the things it has knowledge about - these are the same five objects: Person, Wheeled Chair, Wooden Chair, Toy Box, and Round Table. In addition to these PerCepts, the Mental Model includes the memory of the last known state of the world. Specifically, it includes information on the robot's position and orientation, and the position and orientation of objects in the room. Figure 12.6 is a photo taken from above the test area. The detailed Current World State is shown in Table 12.5.

Since the robot has this mental model available to it, the cybernetic brain first generates a preafference expectation of the view, given what it knows about the world and its own position and orientation. This preafference is used to confirm that the world is approximately in the configuration that is expected. For example, if the robot has the CWS described above, and it knows that it is facing toward the round table (a global heading of 192 Binary radians), it does not expect to see the person in the field of view of its sensors. Nor does it expect to see the chair or the storage box. So the `Reification Engine` performs a presumptive test - does the sensor image match the table in its expected position and orientation. If this match is acceptable, no general recognition is performed. The robot sees what it 'expects' to see, and it goes on. Only if the preafference image is not confirmed by the sensor image does the system bringing the recognition system into the process to attempt to resolve the conflicts.

12.6.2.1 Preafference Testing Protocol

In these test we focus on the ability of the robot to correctly classify objects using a combination of recognition and preafference.

The test protocol was as follows:

1. Place the objects and the robot into their assigned positions;
2. Load the robot with the Current World State;

Fig. 12.6 This is the setup for the Preafference tests. The objects to be classified are groups around the robot with about 1m between their centroids (except the table which is at 1.5m). The objects are at 90 degree separation around the robot. One of the authors is the example of a person. Note the cable connected to the Robot. This is to enable the capture and analysis of the data generated by the test, the robot is running all software on its onboard processor.

Table 12.5 Preafference Test Setup

Object	X^a	Y^a	θ^b
Robot	10500	2900	varies
Round Table	9000	2900	64
Wooden Chair	10500	3900	128
Person	11500	2900	192
Box	10500	3900	0
Wheeled Chair[c]	11500	2900	192

[a] mm from origin in Global Coordinates for the lab.
[b] in Binary Radians compass coordinates.
[c] replaced the person for latter tests.

3. Orient the robot toward the first object;
4. Allow the robot to report on its classification two to three times;
5. Change the position of the object slightly in X and Y;
6. Repeat 4 and 5 until 30 observations have been recorded;
7. Physically rotate the robot to the next test position; and
8. Repeat 4 - 7, until all objects have been examined.

As in the previous test, we recorded the results of the classification as the set of objects that the robot returned as possible candidates. Since the preafference process is a presumptive test, it only returns at most one result. It either fails to classify anything and returns null, or it does classify something, and returns that single value. However, if the preafference test fails, the `Reification Engine` invokes the general recognition process, as described in the previous tests. Therefore we record a more complex result than the earlier tests (see Table 12.6).

Table 12.6 Preafference of Wheeled Chair At 1.0m Note this is a subset of a full run. P indicates that the object was classified by Preafference. R indicates that preafference failed, and the classification was generated by the Recognition system.

Wheel	Wood	Box	Table	Person	JI
P	-	-	-	-	1.00
-	R	-	-	R	0.00
P	-	-	-	-	1.00
-	-	-	-	-	0.00
R	R	-	-	-	0.50

Since these tests are rather extensive, and there is little to be gained by presenting several pages of tables, we will focus on the summary data from the tests.

12.6.2.2 Preafference Testing Results

We ran tests on six different objects, the five described above in table 12.6, as well as pointing the robot at nothing to make sure that it did not return a classification. Each object was classified 30 times, and over the run we altered the position of the object 10 times. These changes were restricted to relatively small alterations, since the preafference expects the object to be in a known location and orientation. In the summary below, we capture the overall performance of the combined preafference and recognition classification. Later we discuss the comparison between the two mechanisms.

Table 12.7 Preafference of all objects at mid range. The range was 1m for all objects except the table, which was at 1.5m. The results are shown as the Jaccard Index.

Object	Combined	Preafference	Recognition
Wheeled Chair	0.75	0.77	0.18
Wood Chair	0.74	0.81	0.33
Storage Box	0.86	1.00	0.00
Round Table	0.60	0.63	0.33
Person	0.94	0.97	0.00
Nothing	1.00	1.00	1.00

There are a couple of notes about the results presented in Table 12.7. The combined column refers to the overall performance of the overall reification process. Recall that this means the system first attempted to use the presumptive preafference test, and only if that failed to confirm the data was the general recognition algorithm invoked. The following columns show the individual components of the process. The preafference system provided the classification approximately 75% of the time, and the recognition system provided the classification approximately 11% of the time. The remaining cases neither system provided any classification. Overall, the complete reification system has a Jaccard index of 0.78 at the mid range, compared to the recognition only value of 0.36.

In Figure 12.7 we show the relative improvement provided by complete reification over simple pattern recognition alone. These comparison tests were done using exactly the same PerCepts, so there was no additional structural information available to the cybernetic brain. The only additional information was that the brain had a model that included the last position of the objects it knew about. Since it knew where they were the last time it looked, it was able to generate a preafference image - the way the world was expected to look. Using this expectation, the robot could quickly and accurately assess whether the world was generally as it was expected to be. These results was generated with small perturbations of the actual position of the objects away from their last known position. In spite of these perturbations, the preafference image enabled the Reification Engine to increase its ability to both model the world, and to maintain that model. This clearly shows the benefits provided by reification in robotic systems.

12.6.3 Testing Self-Localization

The next test is based on the fact that the robot's motor and wheel assembly are prone to slippage. Since the robot estimates its position and heading by measuring the amount of time that the motors are running, its estimated position suffers form this slippage. Because of accumulated error, this estimate of pose becomes more inaccurate over time. One way to correct this is to use preafference and object constancy. As the robot moves through space, it creates an image of the expected pose of the objects in its view. By comparing the observed position of the object with the actual position of the object, the robot can correct its pose.

12.6.3.1 Localization Protocol

The testing protocol for the localization tests is simple. The robot is placed at a known location, in a known orientation. The robot is given a mental model that includes the position and orientation of an object, roughly in front of the robot. The robot is given an incorrect estimate of its starting position. Without reification, the robots estimate of its position would have a fixed error, ranging between 100mm and 250mm.

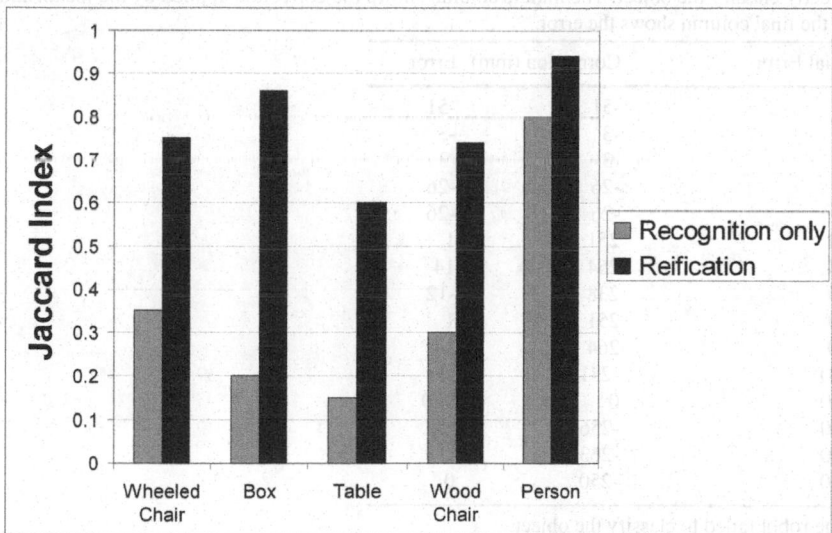

Fig. 12.7 This chart compares the ability of the robot to classify objects using simple recognition versus a complete reification process. The full reification process first attempts to do a presumptive classification, based on the last known position and orientation of the object. If that fails, the recognition process is invoked. The quality of the classification is shown as the Jaccard Index between the classification set and the actual state.

In the reification based tests, the robot maintains the same mental model of its position, however, if the sensor data from the sonar images indicate that the internally derived estimate is incorrect, it uses the sensor data to adjust its estimate. This uses the idea that the things in the world do not (in general) spontaneously move around, or appear or disappear (object constancy).

For the test, the robot is given the opportunity to take a number of sonar images and generate a final estimate of its actual position. The error is the difference between the actual position, and the corrected estimate. The tests were run with three different distances between the robot and the reference object. Since the ability of the robot to classify objects varies with distance, the distance should affect the ability to localize.

12.6.3.2 Localization Results

Each test was run multiple times, and the robot could fail to classify the object, and therefor be unable to localize or the robot would classify the object and make an adjustment to its position. In Table 12.8 the raw data from a run are reported.

Table 12.8 Raw localization data for a typical test. The reference object is a toy box, and it is located 1500mm in front of the robot. This is close to the maximum range at which the robot can correctly classify the object. The middle column shows the correction applied by the localization, and the final column shows the error.

Initial Error	Correction (mm)	Error
0	-51	-51
0	-3	-3
0	-3	-3
0	-26	-26
0	-26	-26
250	251	1
250	264	14
250	238	-12
250	251	1
250	264	14
-250	-251	-1
-250	0^a	250
-250	-256	-6
-250	-263	-13
-250	-250	0

^{a} The robot failed to classify the object.
The mean squared error over the run was 24.3mm.

In this test sequence, the reference object was the same small toy box used in many of the previous tests. It was placed approximately 1500mm in front of the robot. The RMS error was approximately 24mm, however the average error was a little over a centimeter (13mm) This is important because during actual operations the correction terms are applied sequentially, if one correction factor is over, the next correction is applied to the new estimated position, so the errors tend to cancel out.

Looking at the results at different distances we get table 12.9.

Table 12.9 This table shows the results for localization tests using the tox box at 1500mm. The RMS error and the Mean Error are in mm.

Distance	RMS error	Std. Dev.	Mean Error
1000	15.8	12.8	15.7
1500	28.6	36.1	12.0

With the additional information provided by the Reification Engine the robot can localize itself to within a few centimeters of its actual position. This is independent of any inertial sensors, odometry, or other navigational aids. Just as a biological organism (like a human) knows where they are, not by taking readings off satellites, but by knowing where things are in the world, and sensing where they stand relative to those reference objects.

12.7 Summary

The deployment of embodied systems such as robots into 'real world' environments is risky. Once a robot is removed from the tightly controlled environment of a laboratory or a factory floor, the range of situations and events that the system must handle increases dramatically. The experience of successfully 'testing' the robot in the lab, or in a controlled test environment, only to have it fail (sometimes dramatically) in the field is the norm. This unpleasantness has been experienced by teams from universities, commercial labs, and national governments. These failures can be avoided by incorporating a more formal test methodology, which takes advantage of both the recent advances in testing software, and new development methodologies such as agile development and XP. We present an extension of the XP methodology that has been designed to assist developers in producing reliable, well tested embodied systems. The methodology is based on three core concepts:

1. Partitioning the space of tests into nearly independent classes;
2. Adding a separate class of tests for the cross product terms that result from the partitioning; and,
3. Extending the testing methodology to include both (traditional) static tests and dynamic tests.

These expanded tests make extensive use of the concept of 'mocking,' producing lightweight software components to replace either hardware components or heavyweight components that interfere with testing. The result of applying these techniques enables the developers to test, in software, aspects of embodied systems that previously were tested in the field. This results in far more tests being run, and the tests being run far more frequently. This combination results is a much higher level of confidence in the ability of the embodied system to meet its design requirements when it is deployed. In the last section of this chapter, we show the results of the system level tests. These demonstrate that the robot with the `Reification Engine`enabled performs better than the system with the reactive component only enabled.

Chapter 13
Where do we go from here

Normally this section would be called "Conclusions," but this is just the first step on a long road. This is a stopping point, where we can catch our breath, before starting back to work. In the next section, we will outline the next steps on the road. But now, to recap the book. At this point in time, one can not buy a general purpose useful robot. Robots like Rosie, from the Jetsons, or R2D2 and 3CPO, from Star Wars, are simply not available. This is despite the fact that many intelligent people have spent many years trying to make this happen. So where is my robot?

13.1 A Stopping Point

In order to answer this, we looked at natural intelligent systems, and formed a hypothesis that there was a gap in the theory. Most researchers were working either from symbolic reasoning down or from reactive systems up. We hypothesise that there is a gap in the middle. By examination of the exemplars in natural intelligence, we concluded that there was a missing piece.

This critical piece translates sensor data into symbols and translates symbols into a sensor based representation. This bidirectional mapping is what bridges the gab between the symbolic domain and the sensor domain. The two directions are called recognition and preafference. This capability appears to be a necessary part of a cybernetic brain that is embodied in the real world. This led to the task of designing and building a reification Engine.

Since a key aspect of reification is the mental model of perceived objects, we drew from current research into how living organisms build mental representations of what they perceive. These structures are called percepts by cognitive scientists. We used the lens model from Egon Brunswik's work to build an analog to the natural percept, and used these percepts to build a reification engine. But reification by itself is not terribly useful, so we build a cybernetic brain to go with it. This brain consists of

- A perception/action system that can affect and perceive the world;
- A reification mechanism that can translate the sensor data into symbols and translate the symbols into sensor data;
- A deliberative system that can manipulate the symbols;
- An execution monitor that can sequence the actions coming out of the Deliberation module;
- A semantic memory (`Personal Rough Ontology`) to hold general knowledge about the world;
- An episodic memory for storage of personal experiences;
- Working memory for temporary storage; and,
- Internal state storage - for temporary items like hunger, pain, and fear.

These are shown in Figure13.1. The biologic principle for each of these components is described in Chapter 3. The implementation details are described in the rest of the book.

Then, using the full cybernetic brain, we were able to test to see if reification improved the performance of a robot. In Chapter 12, we were able to show that adding preafference to recognition significantly improved the ability of the robot to semantically tag normal objects in the real world (or at least in our lab). This semantic tagging allow the robot to use its deliberative system to reason about objects in the

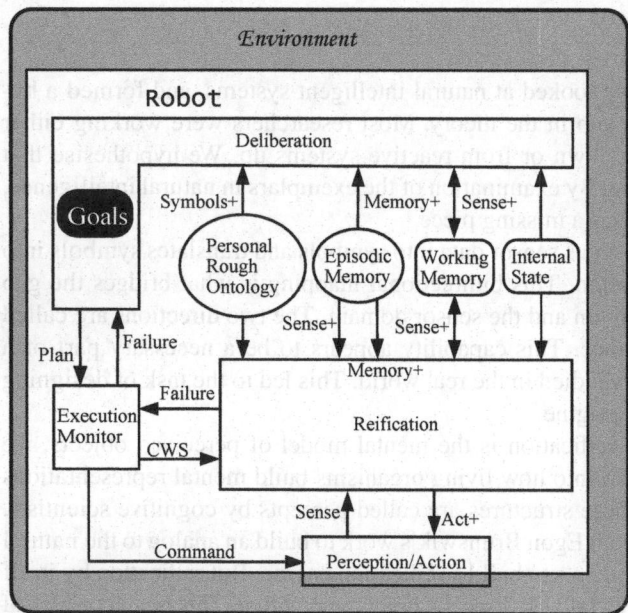

Fig. 13.1 The cybernetic brain, as currently built

perceptible world. Reification also allows the robot to know where it is in relation to the objects that it can identify. This in turn allows it to localize itself, without specific fiducial marks or other aids.

13.2 Next Steps

13.2.1 Adding Learning to the Model

One of the obvious deficits of this model, is that the robot can not learn. To start with the simplest type of learning, it must learn to construct its own percepts. For this book, we have constructed all of the percepts from the sonar data provided by the robot. Since the percepts are data structures, this is a task that the robot can do much more effectively that we can [1]. The robot also must be able to learn the appropriate weights for the lens models. The theory of judgment analysis suggests methods by which the robot can learn these weights by experimentation. It will be interesting to see what type of models the robot develops with less human intervention.

One form of learning that also needs to be created is the building of new semantic memory (our `Personal Rough Ontology`) from episodic memory. As we mentioned previously, it is clear that in living system, there is a way to create new semantic memory from episodic memory. In the current robots, we have instantiated episodic memory and semantic memory. But, the `Personal Rough Ontology` used in the current cybernetic brain was created by humans. This means that connection between these two types of memory still needs to be created, if the robot is to build its own ontology. Another related form of learning that still needs to be created is the formation of the emotional tags in the episodic memory. If the previously mentioned episodic to semantic link has been created, then once the emotional tags are created, they can be moved from the episodic memory into semantic memory.

13.2.2 Adding Additional Data Sources

An advantage of the model is that it allows for the merging of different types of data. Since the current robot is only using sonar data, it is not taking advantage of the strength of the lens model. However, given the difficulty of developing even the simple sonar models, this data fusion will need to wait until the robot is capable of building its own percepts. One of the next steps will be merging visual and infrared information into the existing percepts. This will allow for more flexibility in the ability of the robots to perform useful tasks.

---

[1] Robots don't get bored, don't get frustrated, and they rarely make transposition errors

13.2.3 Porting the Brain into New Bodies

The astute reader will have noticed that we reference robots other than the two described in Chapter 5. We have some outdoor robots, that need the cybernetic brains to perform their intended tasks. One of these tasks will be security patrols. If a robot can semantically tag its environment, then it can learn what is supposed to be in that environment. This, in turn, means that it can call for help if it identifies something that is not supposed to be there, a backpack or bag for example. Another task that semantic tagging makes possible is mapping. This will depend both on the ability of the robot to semantically tag objects, but also on its ability to localize itself with respect to those objects. Closely related to the two previous tasks is the task of monitoring an environmental feature. If the robot can localize itself, then it could be sent out with monitoring equipment, such as hazardous gas or radioactivity monitors. This would allow the robot to free up a human in an emergency response situation (and the robot does not need a 'moon suit'.

All of these tasks depend on the ability of the robots to learn their own percepts. So, the next step will be teaching robots to learn. After that, who knows what comes next.

Glossary

Many of the definitions provided here are based on those provided by WikiPedia.

Affordances Affordances are the qualities of an object, or an environment, that allow an individual to perform an action with that object or in that environment.

Attention To quote William James, "Everyone knows what attention is. It is the taking possession by the mind, in clear and vivid form, of one out of what seem several simultaneously possible objects or trains of thought. Focalization, concentration, of consciousness are of its essence. It implies withdrawal from some things in order to deal effectively with others, and is a condition which has a real opposite in the confused, dazed, scatterbrained state which in French is called distraction, and Zerstreutheit in German[104]."

Cladistic analysis The starting point of cladistic analysis is a group of species and molecular, morphological, or other data characterizing those species. The end result is a tree-like relationship diagram called a cladogram. The cladogram graphically represents a hypothetical evolutionary process. Cladograms are subject to revision as additional data become available.

Deliberative System A system that models the world in a symbolic form, and can predict the future state that will result from the application of intentional actions. These predicted future states can be used to choose between different possible courses of actions in an attempt to achieve system goals.

Distal Located far from a point of reference, such as an origin, a point of attachment, or the point of perception. Contrast with Proximal.

Engram Engrams are a hypothetical means by which memory traces are stored as biophysical or biochemical change in the brain (and other neural tissue) in response to external stimuli. They are also sometimes thought of as a neural network or fragment of memory. The existence of engrams is posited by some scientific theories to explain the persistence of memory and how memories are stored in the brain. The existence of neurologically defined engrams is not significantly disputed, though its exact mechanism and location has been a persistent focus of research for many decades.

Enteroception The sensitivity to stimuli originating inside of the body, such as pain, hunger, etc. Technically enteroception is only the sensing of the internal state of hollow organs, but we include most of the sensations corresponding to the body state of the robot. For a robot, this would include battery charge state, the power applied to drive systems and effectors, damage sensors, etc.

Feature A characteristic of the domain, represented as an enumerated list of allowed values or ranges. In addition to the enumerated values, a Feature can be assigned an unspecified state.

Genotype The genotype of an organism is the specific genetic code of that organism.

Heuristic A heuristic is a trial-and-error method of problem solving often used when an algorithmic approach is impractical. A heuristic does not guarantee an optimal solution.

Markov Chain Monte Carlo simulation A technique for evaluating stochastic processes. It generates multiple simulations, each performing independent stochastic evaluation of the random variables in the process. These simulation runs are aggregated, and overall statistical analysis is performed to assess the behavior of the stochastic process.

Ontology A structural representation of terms and symbols which encodes the semantic relationships between the symbols. This allows a deliberative system to reason about the symbols. From Wikipedia: In both computer science and information science, an ontology is a data model that represents a set of concepts within a domain and the relationships between those concepts. It is used to reason about the objects within that domain. An ideal ontology is accurate, complete, and consistent, contrast this with the rough ontology.

Percept The mental image formed from the stimulation of sensory systems.

Phenotype The phenotype of an organism is the physical manifestation of that organism. The phenotype is the result of interactions between the genotype of the organism and the environment in which that organism lives.

Preafference The mapping of the expectation derived from the symbolic representations onto the expected sensory results. It is one of the two components of reification.

Probability Of Occurrence (POC) The likelihood associated with a forecast state of the world.

Proprioception The sense of relative positions of neighboring parts of the body. In the case of a robot it is derived from the position and orientation sensors at the joints and the effectors.

Proximal Nearer to a point of reference such as an origin, a point of attachment, or the midline of the body: *the proximal end of a bone*. Contrast with Distal.

Pulse width Modulation A power control technique used to control the speed of direct current motors by applying short (millisecond) bursts of full voltage separated by periods of no voltage. The ratio of time spend at full power to the total time of an 'ON/OFF' cycle is called the duty cycle.

Recognition The mapping of sensory data onto symbolic representations. It is one of the two components of reification.

Reification The bidirectional mapping of sensory data onto symbolic representations (recognition), and the mapping of the expectation derived from the symbolic representations onto the expected sensory results (preafference).

Rough Ontology An ontology that is lacking one of the criteria of an ideal ontology. A rough ontology may be inaccurate, incomplete, or internally inconsistent. The semantic memory of all living systems suffer from one, or more, of these failings.

Stereotypy The expression of is a repetitive or ritualistic movement, such as feeding behavior in amphibians, or (in the case of humans) a repetitive or ritualistic movement, posture, or utterance, found in patients with mental retardation, autism spectrum disorders, tardive dyskinesia and stereotypic movement disorder.

Unspecified In the representation schema of the deliberative system, unspecified applies to any feature for which the current value is not drawn from the enumerated range of legal values. It can have three related semantics either *unknown* (DONTKNOW), *unimportant* (DONTCARE), or *unchanged* (DONTCHANGE).

WorldSet A WorldSet is a collection of one or more WorldStates. These can be contiguous WorldStates, defined as having one or more features in the unspecified state, or can be a collection of noncontiguous WorldStates defined by enumerating a disjunction of WorldSets.

WorldState The collection of Feature — Value pairs that are salient to the current deliberation. The WorldState is a unique configuration of the Features that describe the domain.

References

1. Albus, J., Lacaze, A., Meystel, A.: Multiresolutional intelligent controller for baby-robot. In: Proc. of the 10th IEEE Int'l Symposium on Intelligent Control. Monterey, CA (1995)
2. Alighanbari, M., Kuwata, Y., How, J.: Coordination and control of multiple uavs with timing constraints and loitering. In: Proceedings of the 2003 American Control Conference, vol. 6, pp. 5311–5316 (2003)
3. Arkin, R.: Behavior–Based Robotics, chap. 3, pp. 65–121. MIT Press (1998)
4. Atkinson, R.C., Shiffrin, R.M.: Human memory: a proposed system and its control processes. In: K.W. Spence, S.J. T. (eds.) The Psychology of Learning and Motivation: Advances in Research and Theory, pp. 89–195. Academic Press (1968)
5. Ayers, J., Witting, J.: Biomimetic approach to the control of underwater walking machines. Philosophical Transactions of the Royal Society A **365**, 273–295 (2007)
6. Baddeley, A., Della Sala, S.: Working memory and executive control. Philosophical Transactions: Biological Sciences **351**(1346, Executive and Cognitive Functions of the Prefrontal Cortex), 1397–1404 (1996)
7. Bardack, D.: First fossil hagfish (myxinoidea): A record from the pennsylvanian of illinois. Science **254**, 701–703 (1991)
8. Beck, K.: Extreme Programming Explained: Embrace Change. Addison Wesley, Boston, MA (1999)
9. Beetz, M.: Structured reactive controllers – controlling robots that perform everyday activity. In: Agents '99 (1999)
10. Beetz, M., Bennewitz, M.: Planning, scheduling, and plan execution for autonomous robot office couriers. Tech. Rep. WS-98-02, American Association for Artificial Intelligence (1998)
11. Bellingham, J.G., Rajan, K.: Robotics in remote and hostile environments. Science **318**(5853), 1098–1102 (2007)
12. Biro, D., Matsuzawa, T.: Use of numerical symbols by the chimpanzee (*pan* troglodytes): Cardinals, ordinals, and the introduction of zero. Animal Cognition **4**, 193–199 (2001)
13. Bonasso, R.P., Firby, R., Gat, E., Kortenkamp, D., Miller, D., Slack, M.: Experiences with an architecture for intelligent, reactive agents. Journal of Experimental and Theoretical Artificial Intelligence **9**(2), 237–256 (1997)
14. Bonasso, R.P., Kortenkamp, D.: Characterizing an architecture for intelligent, reactive systems. In: AAAI-95 Spring Symposium (1995)
15. Boyd, J.R.: Organic design for command and control. Briefing Notes (1987)
16. Bratman, M.E., Israel, D.J., Pollack, M.E.: Plans and resource bounded practical reasoning. Computational Intelligence **4**(4), 349–355 (1988)
17. Brill, F., Wasson, G., Ferrer, G., Martin, W.: The effective field of view paradigm: Adding representation to a reactive system. Engineering Applications of of Artificial Intelligence **11**(2) (1998)
18. Broekman, B.M.: Testing Embedded Software. Addison-Wesley (2002)
19. Brooks, F.P.: No silver bullet - essence and accident in software engineering. Computer **20**(4), 10–19 (1987)
20. Brooks, R.A.: A robust layered control system for a mobile robot. IEEE Journal of Robotics and Automation **RA-2**(1), 14 – 23 (1986)
21. Brooks, R.A.: Intelligence without reason. In: J. Myopoulos, R. Reiter (eds.) Proceedings of the 12th International Joint Conference on Artificial Intelligence (IJCAI-91), pp. 569–595. Morgan Kaufmann publishers Inc.: San Mateo, CA, USA, Sydney, Australia (1991). URL citeseer.ist.psu.edu/article/brooks91intelligence.html
22. Brooks, R.A.: Intelligence without representation (revised). In: Mind Design II. The MIT Press, Cambridge, MA (2000)
23. Brown, F.M. (ed.): The Frame Problem in Artificial Intelligence: Proceedings of the 1987 Workshop. Morgan Kaufmann, Los Altos, USA (1987)

24. Brunswik, E.: Probability as a determiner of rat behavior. Journal of Experimental Psychology **25**, 175–197 (1939)
25. Brunswik, E.: Perception and the Representative Design of Psychological Experiments. University of California Press, Berkeley, CA (1947)
26. Brunswik, E.: Perception and the Representative Design of Psychological Experiments. University of California Press, Berkeley, CA (1947)
27. Brunswik, E.: The Conceptual Framework of Psychology. University of Chicago Press, Chicago, IL (1950)
28. Brunswik, E.: The Conceptual Framework of Psychology. University of Chicago Press, Chicago, IL (1950)
29. Brunswik, E.: Representative design and probabilistic theory in a functional psychology. Psychological Review **62**, 192–217 (1955)
30. Burnham, K.P., Anderson, D.A.: Model Selection and Multimodel Inference: A Practical Information-Theoretic Approach, 2nd edn. Springer-Verlag, New York (2002)
31. Butters, M., Glisky, E., Schacter, D.: Transfer of new learning in memory impaired patients. Journal of Experimental and Clinical Neuropsychology **15**, 219–230 (1993)
32. Campbell, N.A., Reece, J.B.: Biology, eighth edn. Benjamin Cummings (2007)
33. Carter, L.S.: Scrambled sound. Dartmouth Medicine pp. 32–37 (2000)
34. Churchland, P.M., Churchland, P.S.: The Computer and the Brain, chap. Foreword. Yale University Press (2000)
35. Clapardéde, E.: Recognition and 'me'ness. In: D. Rapaport (ed.) Organization and pathology of thought, pp. 58–75. Columbia University Press, New York (1951)
36. Cohen, B.J., Taylor, J.J.: Memmler's The Human Body in Health and Disease, 10 edn., chap. 9, pp. 178–199. Lippincott Williams and Wilkins (2005)
37. Cooksey, R.W.: Judgment Analysis. Academic Press (1996)
38. Coradeschi, S., Saffiotti, A.: An introduction to the anchoring problem. Robotics and Autonomous Systems **43**(2–3), 85–96 (2003)
39. Corp., P.: Javelin stamp user's manual. Tech. rep., Parallax Corporation, Rocklin, CA, USA (2002)
40. Craven, M., DiPasquo, D., Freitag, D., McCallum, A.K., Mitchell, T.M., Nigam, K., Slattery, S.: Learning to extract symbolic knowledge from the World Wide Web. In: Proceedings of AAAI-98, 15th Conference of the American Association for Artificial Intelligence, pp. 509–516. AAAI Press, Menlo Park, US, Madison, US (1998). URL cite seer.ist.psu.edu/article/craven98learning.html
41. Damasio, A.: The Feeling of What Happens. Harcourt, Inc., New York (1999)
42. Damasio, A.: The Feeling of What Happens. Harcourt, Inc., New York (1999)
43. Darwin, C.: On the Origin of Species by Means of Natural Selection, or the Preservation of Favoured Races in the Struggle for Life. John Murray, Albemarle Street, London (1859)
44. Darwin, C.: The Variation of Animals and Plants Under Domestication, second edn. D. Appleton and Co., New York (1883)
45. Davelaar, E.J., Goshen-Gottstein, Y., Ashkenazi, A., Haarman, H.J., Usher, M.: The demise of short-term memory revisited: Empirical and computational investigations of recency effects. Psychological Review **112**(1), 3–42 (2005)
46. Dearden, R., Boutilier, C.: Abstraction and approximate decision-theoretic planning. Artificial Intelligence **89**(1–2), 219–283 (1997)
47. Deban, S.M., O'Reilly, J.C., Nishikawa, K.C.: The evolution and motor control of feeding in amphibians. Amer. Zool. **41**, 1280–1298 (2001)
48. Dellaert, F.: Toward a biologically defensible model of development. Master's thesis, Case Western Reserve University; Dept. of Computer Engineering and Science, Cleveland; OH 44106 (1995). URL http://www.cc.gatech.edu/ dellaert/pubs/Dellaert95msc.ps.gz
49. Dennett, D.C.: BrainChildren, chap. 11, Cognitive Wheels, pp. 181–205. MIT Press, Cambridge, MA, USA (1998)
50. Ding, L., Zhou, L., Finin, T., Joshi, A.: How the semantic web is being used: An analysis of foaf documents. In: Proceedings of the 38th Annual Hawaii International Conference on System Sciences, p. 113 (2005). DOI 10.1109/HICSS.2005.299

51. Dorries, K., White, J., Kauer, J.: Rapid classical conditioning of odor response in a physiological model for olfactory research, the tiger salamander. Chemical Senses **22**, 277–286 (1997)
52. Dorsch, R., Wunderlich, H.: Using mission logic for embedded testing. In: Proceedings of the Conference on Design, Automation and Test in Europe. IEEE Press, piscataway, NJ, USA (2001)
53. Dreyfus, H.: What Computers *Still* Can't Do: A Critique of Artificial Reason, pp. 265–266. MIT Press (1992)
54. Dreyfus, H.L.: Why heideggerian ai failed and how fixing it would require making it more heideggerian. Philosophical Psychology **20**(2), 247–268 (2007)
55. Drosopoulos, S., Wagner, U., Born, J.: Sleep enhances explicit recollection in recognition memory. Learning and Memory **12**, 44–51 (2005)
56. Drummond, M., Bresina, J.: Anytime synthetic projection: Maximizing the probability of goal satisfaction. In: Proc. of AAAI-90. American Association for Artificial Intelligence, Morgan Kaufman (1990)
57. Dubois, D., Berre, D.L., Prade, H., Sabbadin, R.: Using possibilistic logic for modeling qualitative decision: ATMS-based algorithms. Fundamenta Informaticae **37**(1-2), 1–30 (1999). URL citeseer.nj.nec.com/dubois98using.html
58. Duda, R.O., Hart, P.E., Stork, D.G.: Pattern Classification, chap. 3.7. John Wiley and Sons, Inc. (2001)
59. Durkin, T.: What the media couldn't tell you about mars pathfinder. Robot Science and Technology (1998)
60. Eaton, R.L.: Hunting behavior of the cheetah. Journal of Wildlife Management **34**(1), 56–67 (1970)
61. Edelman, G.M.: Synthetic neural modeling and brain-based devices. Biological Theory **1**, 8–9 (2006)
62. Eichenbaum, H.: Declarative memory. In: L.R. Squire, D.L. Schacter (eds.) Neuropsychology of Memory, pp. 351–360. The Guilford Press, New York (2002)
63. Ernst, G.W.: Sufficient conditions for the success of gps. J. ACM **16**, 517–533 (1969)
64. Ernst, G.W., Newell, A.: GPS: A Case Study in Generality and Problem Solving. Academic Press, London, UK (1969)
65. Etzioni, O., Hanks, S., Weld, D., Draper, D., Lesh, N., Williamson, M.: An approach to planning with incomplete information. In: W. Nebel, Bernhard; Rich, Charles; Swartout (ed.) Proceedings of the 3rd International Conference on Principles of Knowledge Representation and Reasoning, pp. 115–125. Morgan Kaufmann publishers Inc.: San Mateo, CA, USA, Cambridge, MA, USA (1992). URL citeseer.ist.psu.edu/article/etzioni92approach.html
66. Ferrer, G.J.: Anytime planning through local plan reuse. Ph.D. thesis, University of Virginia (2002)
67. Fikes, R.E., Nilsson, N.J.: Strips: A new approach to the application of theorem proving to problem solving. Artificial Intelligence **2**, 189–208 (1971)
68. Firby, R.J.: An investigation into reactive planning in complex domains. AAAI-87 pp. 202–206 (1987)
69. Freedman, D.A.: A note on screening regression equations. The American Statistician **37**, 152–155 (1983)
70. Freedman, W.J.: How and why brains create meaning-t from sensory information. International Journal of Bifurcation and Chaos **14**(2), 515–530 (2004)
71. Freeman, W.J.: The physiology of perception. Scientific American **242**, 78 (1991)
72. Freeman, W.J.: How Brains Make Up Their Minds. Columbia University Press, New York (2000)
73. Futuyma, D.J.: Evolution. Sinauer Associates (2005)
74. Gat, E.: Reliable goal-directed reactive control of autonomous mobile robots. Ph.D. thesis, Virginia Polytechnic Institute and State University (1991)
75. Gigerenzer, G., Todd, P.M., the ABC Research Group: Simple Heuristics that Make Us Smart. Oxford University Press (1999)

76. Gilks, W.R., Richardson, S., Spiegelhalter, D.J.: Markov Chain Monte Carlo in Practice, chap. 1. Chapman and Hall/CRC (1996)
77. Ginsberg, M.L., Smith, D.E.: Reasoning about action I: a possible worlds approach. In: F.M. Brown (ed.) The frame problem in artificial intelligence: proc. of 1987 workshop, pp. 233–258. Morgan Kaufmann (1987). URL citeseer.ist.psu.edu/ginsberg87reasoning.html
78. Goldsmith, J., Littman, M.L., Mundhenk, M.: The complexity of plan existence and evaluation in probabilistic domains. In: Proceedings of the Thirteenth Annual Conference on Uncertainty in Artificial Intelligence (UAI–97), pp. 182–189 (1997)
79. Graziano, M.S., Hu, X.T., Gross, C.G.: Coding the location of objects in the dark. Science 277 (1997)
80. Grenning, J.: Extreme programming and embedded systems. online (2004). DOI http://www.objectmentor.com//resources//articles//EmbeddedXp.pdf
81. Griffin, D.R.: Animal Minds. The University of Chicago Press, Chicago and London (2001)
82. Gronlund, S.D., Carlson, C.A., Tower, D.: Episodic memory. In: F.T. Durso (ed.) The Handbook of Applied Cognition, 2 edn. Wiley (2007)
83. Gruber, T.R.: Technical report ksl 93-04: Toward principles for the design of ontologies used for knowledge sharing. Tech. rep., Knowledge Systems Laboratory, Stanford University (1993)
84. Guan, J., Offutt, J., Ammann, P.: An industrial case study of structural testing applied to safety-critical embedded software. In: Proceedings of the 2006 ACM/IEEE International Symposium on Empirical Software Engineering, pp. 272–277. ACM, New York, NY, USA (2006). DOI http://doi.acm.org/10.1145/1159733.1159774
85. Gunderson, J., Gunderson, L.F.: Mom! the vacuum cleaner is chasing the dog again! In: Proceedings of the 4th Workshop on Performance Metrics for Intelligent Systems, p. unknown. Gaithersburg, MD (2003)
86. Gunderson, J.P.: Adaptive goal prioritization by agents in dynamic environments. In: Proceedings of the IEEE Systems, Man, and Cybernetics 2000, pp. 1944–1948 (2000)
87. Gunderson, J.P.: A probability–aware planning and execution system. Ph.D. thesis, University of Virginia, Computer Science (2003)
88. Hammond, K.: Probabilistic functionalism: Egon brunswik's integration of the history, theory, and method of psychology. In: K. Hammond (ed.) The Psychology of Egon Brunswik, pp. 15–80. Holt, Rinehart and Winston (1966)
89. Hammond, K., Hamm, R., Grassia, J., Pearson, T.: Direct comparisons of the efficacy of intuitive and analytical cognition in expert judgment. IEEE Transactions on Systems, Man, and Cybernetics 17(5), 753–770 (1984)
90. Hammond, K.R.: Is it possible to learn by intervening?, chap. 9, pp. 233–255. Oxford University Press (1996)
91. Hammond, K.R., Stewart, T.R., Brehmer, B., Steinmann, D.O.: Social judgment theory. In: M. Kaplan, S. Schwartz (eds.) Human Judgment and Decision Processes, pp. 271–312. Academic Press (1975)
92. Hammond, R.K., R., S.T.: The Essential Brunswik. Oxford University Press (2001)
93. Harnad, S.: The symbol grounding problem. Physica D 42, 335–346 (1990)
94. Harnad, S.: The symbol grounding problem. Physica D 42, 335–346 (1990)
95. Hayes, P.J.: The frame problem and related problems in artificial intelligence. In: B. Webber, N. Nilsson (eds.) Readings in Artificial Intelligence, pp. 223–230. Tioga, Palo Alto, CA (1981)
96. Heisenberg, W.: Nuclear Physics, chap. 2. Molecules and Atoms, p. 30. The Philosophical Library, New York (1953)
97. Herrick, C.: The Brain of the Tiger Salamander. The University of Chicago Press (1948)
98. Hughes, P.M., Luczak, E.C.: The generic spacecraft analyst assistant (gensaa) a tool for automating spacecraft monitoring with expert systems. In: The 1991 Goddard Conference on Space Applications of Artificial Intelligence, pp. 129–139 (1991)
99. Huntsberger, T.: Biologically inspired autonomous rover control. Autonomous Robots 11(3), 341–346 (2001)

100. Ijspeert, A., Crespi, A., Ryczko, D., Cabelguen, J.: From swimming to walking with a sala-mander robot driven by a spinal cord model. Science **315**, 1416–1419 (2007)
101. Inoue, S., Matsuzawa, T.: Working memory of numerals in chimpanzees. Current Biology **17**(23), 1004–1005 (2007)
102. Jaccard, P.: Étude comparative de la distribution florale dans une portion des alpes et des jura. Bulletin del la Société Vaudoise des Sciences Naturelles **37**, 547–579 (1901)
103. Jaeger, R.G.: Dear enemy recognition and the costs of aggression between salamanders. The American Naturalist **117**(6), 962–974 (1981)
104. James, W.: The Principles of Psychology, vol. 1. Henry Holt, New York (1890)
105. Jameson, K.A.: Tetrachromatic color vision. In: The Oxford Companion to Consciousness, pp. ??–?? Oxford University Press (2007)
106. Johannsen, W.: The genotype conception of heredity. The American Naturalist **15**(531), 129–159 (1911)
107. Kaelbling, L.P.: An architecture for intelligent reactive systems. In: M. Georgeff, A. Lansky (eds.) Reasoning about Actions and Plans. Morgan-Kaufman (1987)
108. Kahneman, D., Slovic, P., Tversky, A.: Judgment under uncertainty: Heuristics and biases. Cambridge University Press (1982)
109. Kahneman, D., Tversky, A.: Prospect theory: An analysis of decision under risk. Economet-rica **47**(2), 263–292 (1979)
110. Kay, L.M., Freedman, W.J.: Bidirectional processing in the olfactory-limbic axis during ol-factory behavior. Behavioral Neuroscience **112**(3), 541–553 (1998)
111. Kelly, I., Melhuish, C.: SlugBot: A robot predator. Lecture Notes in Computer Science **2159**, 519–524 (2001). URL citeseer.ist.psu.edu/682961.html
112. Kirkwood, W.: Development of the dorado mapping vehicle for multibeam, subbottom, and sidescan science missions. Journal of Field Robotics **24**(6), 487–495n (2007)
113. Kobayakawa, K., Kobayakawa, R., Matsumoto, H., Oka, Y., Imai, T., Ikawa, M., Okabe, M., Ikeda, T., Itohara, S., Kikusui, T., Mori, K., Sakano, H.: Innate versus learned odour processing in the mouse olfactory bulb. Nature **450**, 503–508 (2007)
114. Koehnemann, H., Lindquist, T.: Towards target-level testing and debugging tools for embed-ded software. In: Proceedings of the Conference on Tri-Ada '93, pp. 288–298. ACM, New York, NY, USA (1993). DOI http://doi.acm.org/10.1145/170657.170742
115. Koenig, S., Simmons, R.: Real-time search in non-deterministic domains. In: Proceedings of the International Joint Conference on Artificial Intelligence (IJCAI), pp. 1660–1667 (1995)
116. Koshland, D.E.: A response regulator model in a simple sensory system. Science **196**, 1055–1063 (1977)
117. Kozma, R., Aghazarian, H., Huntsherger, T., Tunstel, E., Freeman, W.: Computational as-pects of cognition and consciousness in intelligent devices. Computational Intelligence Mag-azine, IEEE **2**, 53–64 (2007)
118. Leitner, A., Ciupa, I., Manuel, B., Fiva, A.: Contract driven development = test driven de-velopment: Writing test cases. In: Proceedings of the 6th Joint Meeting of the European Software Engineering Conference and the 14th ACM SIGSOFT Symposium on the Foun-dations of Software Engineering, pp. 425–434. ACM Press, New York, NY, USA (2007). DOI http://doi.acm.org/10.1145/1287624.1287685
119. Lewis, C.I.: Mind and the World-Order. Scribners, New York (1929)
120. Lieberherr, K.J., Holland, I.: Formulations and Benefits of the Law of Demeter. SIGPLAN Notices **24**(3), 67–78 (1989)
121. Lifschitz, V.: Frames in the space of situations. Artificial Intelligence **46**, 365–376 (1990)
122. Littman, M.L., Dean, T.L., Kaelbling, L.P.: On the complexity of solving markov decision problems. In: Proceedings of Uncertainty in Artificial Intelligence 1995 (1995)
123. Littman, M.L., Goldsmith, J., Mundhenk, M.: The computational complexity of probabalistic planning. Journal of Artificial Intelligence Research **9**, 1–36 (1998)
124. Malthus, T.R.: An Essay on the Principle of Population, 6 edn. J. Johnson (1826)
125. Marcer,   P.:   Nature,   congition   and   quantum   physiscs. http://www.bcs.org.uk/siggroup/cyber/cmg-wid.htm (2002)

126. Marco, D.B., Healey, A.J., McGhee, R.B.: Autonomous underwater vehicles: hybrid control of mission and motion. Autonomous Robots **3**(2–3) (1996)

127. Matuszek, C., Witbrock, M., Kahlert, R., Cabral, J., Schneider, D., Shah, P., Lenat, D.: Searching for common sense: Populating cyc from the web. In: Proceedings of the Twentieth National Conference on Artificial Intelligence. Pittsburgh, Pennsylvania (2005)

128. McCarthy, J., Hayes, P.: Some philosophical problems from the standpoint of artificial intelligence. In: B. Meltzer, D. Michie (eds.) Machine Intelligence 4, pp. 463–502. Edinburgh University Press, Edinburgh, UK (1969). (Also in Webber, B. L. and Nilsson, N. J., editors, *Readings in Artificial Intelligence*, pp. 431–450. Tioga, Palo Alto, USA, 1981)

129. McDermott, D.: Ai, logic and the frame problem. In: The Frame Problem in Artificial Intelligence: Proceedings of the 1987 Workshop, pp. 105–118. Morgan Kaufmann, Lawrence, USA (1987)

130. Miller, G.A.: The magical number seven, plus or minus two: Some limits on our capacity for processing information. Psychological Review **63**, 81–97 (1956)

131. Minsky, M.: A framework for representing knowledge. In: P.H. Winston (ed.) The Psychology of Computer Vision, pp. 211–277. McGraw-Hill, New York, USA (1975)

132. Mitchie, D.: Turing, Alan Mathison, pp. 847–849. MIT Press (1999)

133. Moravec, H.: Mind Children, chap. 2, pp. 51–74. Harvard University Press (1988)

134. Morris, W. (ed.): American Heritage Dictionary of the English Language. American Heritage (1969)

135. Myers, S.D.: Design of an autonomous exterior security robot. In: Conference on Intelligent Robotics in Field, Factory, Service, and Space, vol. 1. NASA (1994)

136. NASA: Mars climate orbiter mishap investigation board phase i report. Tech. rep., National Aeronautics and Space Administration (1999)

137. Nebel, B., Koehler, J.: Plan reuse versus plan generation: A theoretical and empirical analysis. Artificial Intelligence **76**((1-2)), 427–454 (1995). URL citeseer.nj.nec.com/nebel95plan.html

138. von Neumann, J.: The Computer and the Brain. Yale University Press (2000)

139. Newell, A., Simon, H.: Gps, a program that simulates human thought. In: E.A. Feigenbaum, J. Feldman (eds.) Computers and Thought. R. Oldenbourg KG. (1963)

140. Newell, A., Simon, H.A.: Human Problem Solving. Prentice-Hall, Englewood Cliffs, USA (1972)

141. Nishikawa, K.: Emergence of novel functions during brain evolution. Bioscience **47**, 341 354 (1997)

142. NIST: The economic impacts of inadequate infrastructure for software testing. Tech. rep., National Institutes of Standards and Technology, Gaithersburg, MD (2002)

143. Norman, D.A.: Things that make us Smart, chap. 5: The Human Mind. Addison–Wesley Publishing Company (1993)

144. P., G.J., Gunderson, L.F.: Autonomy (what's it good for?). In: Proceedings of the 7th workshop on Performance Metrics for Intelligent Systems. National Institutes of Standards and Technology, Gaithersburg, MD (2007)

145. Pai, M.: Latest tornadoes bring destruction; red cross provides care (2008). DOI http://www.redcross.org/article/0,1072,0_332_7777,00.html

146. Panksepp, J.: Affective Neuroscience : The Foundations Of Human And Animal Emotions. Oxford University Press, New York (1998)

147. Park, D., McGuire, J.M., Majchrzak, A.L., Ziobro, J.M., Eisthen, H.L.: Discrimination of conspecific sex and reproductive condition using chemical cues in axolotls (*Ambystoma mexicanum*). J. Comp Physiol A (2004)

148. Parker, L.E., Draper, J.V.: Robotics applications in maintenance and repair. In: S. Nof (ed.) Handbook of Industrial Robotics, chap. 53. Wiley, New York (1999)

149. Parkin, A.L.: The structure and mechanisms of memory. In: B. Rapp (ed.) The Handbook of Cognitive Neuropychology, chap. 16. Psychology Press (2001)

150. Parr, W.V., Heatherbell, D., White, K.G.: Demystifying wine expertise: Olfactory threshold, perceptual skill and semantic memory in expert and novice wine judges. Chemical Senses **27**, 747–755 (2002)

151. Pearl, J.: Probabilistic Reasoning in Intelligent Systems: Networks of Plausible Inference, Revised 2nd ed. Morgan Kaufman, San Mateo, CA (1988)
152. Pepperberg, I.M., Gordon, J.D.: Number comprehension by a grey parrot (*psittacus eritha-cus*), including a zero-like concept. Journal of Comparative Psychology **119**(2), 197–209 (2005)
153. Peters, J.T., Hammond, K.R., Summers, D.A.: A note on intuitive vs. analytic thinking. Organizational Behavior and Human Performance **12**, 125–131 (1974)
154. Pettre, J., de Heras, P., Maim, J., Yersin, B., Laumond, J.P., Thalmann, D.: Real-time navigating crowds: Scalable simulation and rendering. Computer Animation and Virtual World (CAVW) Journal - CASA 2006 special issue (2006)
155. Phelps, E.A.: Human emotion and memory: interactions of the amygdala and hippocampal complex. Current Opinion in Neurobiology **14**, 198–202 (2004)
156. Pietsch, P.: Scrambled salamander brains: A test of holographic theories of neural program storage. Anatomical Record (1972)
157. Pike, J.: Rq-1 predator medium altitude endurance unmanned aerial vehicle. Tech. rep., Federation of American Scientists (2002)
158. Pitman, J.: Probability, chap. 3, pp. 222–236. Springer–Verlag, New York (1993)
159. Poincaré, H.: The foundations of science: Science and hypothesis, the value of science, science and method. The Science Press, New York (1905)
160. Portas, C.M., Strange, B.A., Friston, K.J., J., D.R., Frith, C.D.: How does the brain sustain a visual percept. Proceedings of the Royal Society of London, B **267**, 845–850 (2000)
161. Pressman, R.S.: Designing the Solution, chap. 4, pp. 95–160. McGraw Hill (1988)
162. Purves, D.: Perception as probability. Brain Research Bulletin **50**, 321–2 (1999)
163. Quillian, M.R.: Semantic memory. In: M.L. Minsky (ed.) Semantic Information Processing, pp. 227–270. MIT Press (1968)
164. R., G.P.: Ecology and Evolution of Darwin's Finches. Princeton University Press, Princeton, NJ (1999)
165. Reynolds Jr., P.F., Natrajan, A., Srinivasan, S.: Consistency maintenance in multiresolution simulations. ACM Transactions on Modeling and Computer Simulation **7**(3), 368–392 (1997)
166. Rich, E., Knight, K.: Artificial Intelligence, 2nd edn., chap. 7. McGraw–Hill (1991)
167. Rich, E., Knight, K.: Artificial Intelligence, 2nd edn. McGraw–Hill, Inc., New York (1991)
168. Riddoch, M.J., Humphreys, G.W.: Object recognition. In: B. Rapp (ed.) The Handbook of Cognitive Neuropsychology, pp. 45–74 (2001)
169. Ridley, M.: Evolution and Classification: the reformation of cladism. Longman Group, Essex (1986)
170. Riseborough, P.: Automatic take-off and landing control for small uavs. In: The Proceedings of the 5th Asian Control Conference., pp. 754–762 (2004)
171. Rosenbaum, R.S., Stuss, D.T., Levine, B., Tulving, E.: Theory of mind is independent of episodic memory. Science **318**, 1257 (2007)
172. Roth, G.: Neural mechanisms of prey recognition: An example in amphibians. In: Predator-Prey Relationships: Perspectives and Approaches from the Study of Lower Vertebrates. The University of Chicago Press (1986)
173. Rumelhart, D.E., Lindsay, P.H., Norman, D.A.: A process model for long-term memory. In: E. Tulving, W. Donaldson (eds.) Organization of Memory, chap. 6, pp. 197–246. Academic Press (1972)
174. Ryan, J.P., Chavez, F.P., Bellingham, J.G.: Physical-biological coupling in monterey bay, california: topographic influences on phytoplankton ecology. Marine Ecology Progress Series **287**, 23–32 (2005)
175. Sacerdoti, E.D.: The non-linear nature of plans. In: IJCAI-75 (1975)
176. Schacter, D.L.: Amnesia observed: Remembering and forgetting in a natural environment. Journal of Abnormal Psychology **92**(2), 236–242 (1983)
177. Schacter, D.L.: Implicit memory: History and current status. Journal of Experimental Psychology **13**(3), 501–518 (1987)

178. Schacter, D.L.: Searching for Memory: The Brain, the Mind, and the Past. Basic Books, New York (1996)
179. Scherer, W.T., Rotman, F.: Combinatorial optimization techniques for spacecraft scheduling automation. Annals of Operations Research **50**(1), 525–556 (1994)
180. Schooler, J.W., Engstler-Schooler, T.Y.: Verbal overshadowing of visual memories: Some things are better left unsaid. Cognitive Psychology **22**, 36–71 (1990)
181. Schraft, R.D., Schmierer, G.: Service Robots. A. K. Peters (2000)
182. Schulenburg, E., Elkmann, N., Fritzsche, M., Girstl, A., Stiene, S., Teutsch, C.: Lisa: A robot assistant for life sciences. In: KI 2007: Advances in Artificial Intelligence. Springer Berlin / Heidelberg (2007)
183. Sharma, J., Dragoi, V., Tenenbaum, J.B., Miller, E.K., Sur, M.: V1 neurons signal acquisition of an internal representation of stimulus location. Science **300** (2003)
184. Shaw, K.T., Gifford, R.: Residents' and burglars' assessment of burglary risk form defensible spaces. Journal of Environmental Psychology **14**, 177–194 (1994)
185. Shumyatsky, G.P., Malleret, G., Shin, R.M., Takizawa, S., Tully, K., Tsvetkov, E., Zakharenko, S.S., Joseph, J., Vronskaya, S., Yin, D.Q., Schubart, U.K., Kandel, E.R., Bolshakov, V.Y.: Stathmin, a gene enriched in the amygdala, controls both learned and innate fear. Cell **123**, 697–709 (2005)
186. Simmons, R., Goodwin, R., Haigh, K.Z., Koenig, S., O'Sullivan, J.: A layered architecture for office delivery robots. In: W.L. Johnson (ed.) Proceedings of First International Conference on Autonomous Agents, pp. 245–252. ACM Press, New York, NY, Marina del Rey, CA (1997)
187. Simone, L.: If I Only Changed the Software, Why is the Phone on Fire? Elsevier, Burlington, MA, USA (2007)
188. Singh, A.K.: Field Theory, chap. 14, pp. 390–410. Motilal Banarsidass Publishers, Delhi, India (1991)
189. Solms, M., Turnbull, O.: The Brain and the Inner World. Oteh Press, New York (2002)
190. Stewart, T.R.: Judgment analysis: Procedures. In: B. Brehmer, C.R.B. Joyce (eds.) Human Judgment: The SJT View, pp. 41–74. Elsevier Science Publishers, B.V, Amsterdam, The Netherlands (1988)
191. Stickgold, R., Hobson, J.A., Fosc, R., Fosse, M.: Sleep, learning, and dreams: Off-line memory reprocessing. Science **294**, 1052–1057 (2001)
192. Streidter, G.F.: Principles of Brain Evolution. Sinauer Associates, Inc, Sunderland, MA (2005)
193. Tate, A., Hendler, J., Drummond, M.: A review of ai planning techniques. In: J. Allen, J. Hendler, A. Tate (eds.) Readings in Planning, pp. 26–49. Kaufmann, San Mateo, CA (1990)
194. Thomason, R.H., Horty, J.F.: Nondeterministic action and dominance: foundations for planning and qualitative decision. In: TARK '96: Proceedings of the 6th conference on Theoretical aspects of rationality and knowledge, pp. 229–250. Morgan Kaufmann Publishers Inc., San Francisco, CA, USA (1996)
195. Thrun, S.B.: Efficient exploration in reinforcement learning. Tech. Rep. CMU-CS-92-102, Carnegie Mellon University, Pittsburgh, Pennsylvania (1992). URL citeseer.ist.psu.edu/article/thrun92efficient.html
196. Tolman, E.C., Brunswik, E.: The organism and the causal texture of the environment. Psychological Review **43**, 43–77 (1935)
197. Treisman, A.M., Kanwisher, N.G.: Perceiving visually presented objects: Recognition, awareness and modularity". Current Opinions in Neurobiology **8**(2), 218–226 (1998)
198. Tse, T.H., Lau, F.C.M., Chan, W.K., Liu, P.C.K., Luk, C.K.F.: Testing object-oriented industrial software without precise oracles or results. Communications of the ACM **50**(8), 78–85 (2007)
199. Tsuda, T., Kato, D., Ishikawa, A., Inoue, S.: Automatic tracking sensor camera system. In: M.A. Hunt (ed.) Machine Vision Applications in Industrial Inspection IX. SPIE–The International Society for Optical Engineering (2001)
200. Tulving, E.: Episodic and semantic memory. In: E. Tulving, W. Donaldson (eds.) Organization of Memory, pp. 381–403. Academic Press (1972)

201. Tulving, E.: How many memory systems are there? American Psychologist **40**, 385–398 (1985)
202. Vere, S.: Planning in time: Windows and durations for activities and goals. IEEE Trans. on Pattern Analysis and Machine Intelligence **5**(3), 246–267 (1983)
203. Walker, I., Hoover, A., Liu, Y.: Handling unpredicted motion in industrial robot workcells using sensor networks. Industrial Robot: An International Journal **33**, 56–59(4) (2006). DOI doi:10.1108/01439910610638234. URL http://www.ingentaconnect.com/content/mcb/049/2006/00000033/00000001/art00007
204. Walter, W.G.: A machine that learns. Scientific American pp. 60–63 (1951)
205. Werblin, F., Roska, B.: The movies in our eyes. Scientific American pp. 72–79 (2007). DOI http://192.192.169.81/sa/pdf.file/en/e063/e063p032.pdf
206. Whorf, B.L.: Science and linguistics. Technology Review **42**(6), 229–231, 247–248 (1940)
207. Wilde, O.: The Picture of Dorian Gray. Lippincott's (1890)
208. Zadeh, L.A.: Fuzzy logic and approximate reasoning. Synthese **30**, 407–428 (1975)
209. Zilberstein, S.: Resource-bounded sensing and planning in autonomous systems. Autonomous Robots **3**, 31–48 (1996)

Index

Reification Engine, 125

abbreviations, list of, xv
acronyms, list of, xv
amnesia, 26
analysis
  cladistic, 18
anthropomorphizing, 95
assumption
  closed world, 91
assumptions
  simplifying, 10
Atkinson, R., 26
Attention
  definition of, 187
attention, 93, 137
  mechanism, 91

brains
  and quantum effects, 81
Brooks, R., 13
Brunswik
  Egon, 7, 68
Brunswik, E., 25

closed-world assumption, 33
cognition, 121
coherence, 12
concept, 108
correspondence, 103, 154
Current World State, 68, 79

Darwin, C., 17
deliberation, 22
  human, 121
  machine, 122
Deliberative System

definition of, 187
Dennett, Daniel, 58
distal
  definition of, 187
distributions
  Poisson, 110

Embedded Systems
  testing, 159
emotion
  fear, 29
  panic, 30
  rage, 30
  seeking, 30
emotional state, 96
emotive tags, 29, 96
engram
  defintion of, 187
enteroception
  definition of, 188
Extreme Programming, 157

Feature
  definition of, 188
Freeman, W., 22

Genotype
  definition of, 188

Harnad
  Steven, 67
Heisenburg, W., 15
heuristic
  definition of, 188

Information processing, 121
internal state, 126

Jena, 104
JUnit, 160

Malthus, T., 17
mapping
  bidirectional, 66
Markov Chain Monte Carlo (MCMC)
  definition of, 188
MCMC simulation, 135
memory
  engram, 26
  episodic, 27, 87, 92, 93
  explicit, 27
  implicit, 26
  persistent, 87
  procedural, 26, 109
  semantic, 28, 33, 125
  transient, 88
  working, 26
Mental Model, 77
  persistence of, 77
mind
  theory of, 93

neurotransmitter
  broadband, 92
neurotransmitters
  broadband, 96

object constancy, 81, 180
objects
  semantically tagged, 77
ontological relationship
  example of, 104
ontology, 104, 125
  definition of, 188
  Jena, 104
  OWL, 104
  persistent nodes, 116
  rough, 122
  transient nodes, 116
OODA loop, 42
OWL, 104

pattern recognition, 66
PerCept
  data-derived, 71
  library of, 68
Perception/Action, 40
PerCepts, 116
Phenotype
  definition of, 188
plan
  failure of, 134

planner, 122
planning
  and execution, 32, 122
  brute force, 129
Plato
  Ideal, 70
POC
  definition of, 188
preafference, 22
  definition of, 188
prey recognition, 5
Probability of Occurrence
  definition of, 188
Programming
  Extreme, 157
proprioception
  definition of, 188
proximal
  definition of, 189

reactive system, 46
reactive systems, 121
reasoning, 137
recognition, 21
  definition of, 189
  implementation of, 81
  pattern, 66
reflex, 46
reification, 18, 22
  definition of, 189
representation
  internal state, 92
robot
  Basil, 69
  delivery, 43
  industrial, 44
  mobile, 42
  Rosie, 39
  teleoperated, 44, 65
  Xavier, 43
rough ontology, 122
  definition of, 189

salience
  in memory, 94
Schacter, D., 26
semantics, 72
sensor
  smart, 76
Shiffrin, R., 26
state
  emotional, 96
symbol
  sense, 125

symbol grounding, 66
symbols, list of, xv
systems
    reactive, 13

tags
    emotive, 29, 96
Testing
    dynamic, 167
    embedded systems, 159
    failing to, 158
    static, 165
    use of mock objects, 160
testing
    bench, 160

thing constancy, 81
traits
    conservation of, 18
transient
    objects, 116
Tulving, E., 27

unmanned aerial vehicle, 47
unspecified
    definition of, 189

WorldSet
    definition of, 189
WorldState
    definition of, 189

symbol grounding, 46
symbols, literal, 45
syntax
    real, 43

tags
    emotive, 28, 36
testing
    dynamic, 102
    embedded systems, 139
    fuzzy sets, 156
    haiku, 105
    area of mock-up test, 160
issues
    haiku, 150

thing, coherency, 51
time
    Construction of, 14
    transport
    hypertext, 116
Turing, F., 27

unmanned kernel vehicle, 37
    suspended
    definition of, 189

WorldSet
    definition of, 189
WorldState
    definition of, 189